UNFINISHED BUSINESS: DEMOCRACY IN NAMIBIA

EDITED BY BRYAN M. SIMS AND MONICA KOEP

idasa

AN AFRICAN DEMOCRACY INSTITUTE

2012

EMBASSY OF DENMARK

Idasa wishes to thank the Embassy of Denmark for its funding of this project.

Published by Idasa, 357 Visagie Street, Pretoria 0001

© Idasa 2012

ISBN 978-1-920409-79-1

First published 2012

Editing by Hilda Hermann

Design, layout and production by Bronwen Müller

Cover by Mandy Darling, magentamedia

CONTENTS PAGE

FOREWORD

Idasa developed the Democracy Index to assess the depth of democracy in South Africa. The initial list of 150 questions, designed by Robert Mattes and Richard Calland, was honed to 100 in 2005 and used for Idasa's most recent South Africa Democracy Index in 2010. The research relies on expert analysis to answer questions that interrogate how closely, in practice, democracy meets the broad ideal of self-representative government. More specifically, to what extent can citizens control elected officials and government appointees who make decisions about public affairs; and, how equal are citizens to one another in this accountability process? The Index assesses a country through five focus areas: participation, elections, accountability, political rights and human dignity.

Idasa is expanding the Index into Southern Africa in an effort to broaden the capacity of individuals and organisations monitoring and supporting democratic governance efforts in the region. As the tool is tested in different countries, it will be enhanced and nationalised. The hope is that citizens of any country can use the Index to assess and debate the state of its democracy. The purpose of the scores is to assist citizens in making their own judgements, based on the information made available, to stimulate national debate and to provide democracy promoters with a tool for identifying issues and needs that can be addressed by education, advocacy, training, institution building and policy revision. This is the inaugural Index for Namibia and is intended to set a benchmark for democracy to be measured against.

All of the authors selected to contribute, as well as one of the co-editors, are based in Namibia and/or are Namibian. Together, their expertise is grounded in years devoted to activism, civil society, academia and government. Authors were asked to provide a numerical score for each question and a narrative justifying their score. The group convened twice to ensure both a common understanding of the Index and peer review of the assessment process. The second meeting took the form of a validation workshop at which other members of civil society, academia and government were invited to comment on the analysis. While authors were requested to consult other indices and to reflect the opinions of an expert reference group, ultimately this is an individual expert assessment. As such, each set of Democracy Index results stands on its own and is not suitable for statistical comparison across years or cross-country comparative ranking.

It is through its use by Namibians that the Idasa Democracy Index can enhance research capacity, assist representative groups to lobby for greater democratic depth and quality, and spark participatory engagement between governments and citizens. Idasa is grateful to its in-country partners for their willingness to try out the tool, their commitment to the process and the ongoing work on democracy that they do.

KARIN ALEXANDER, Team Leader: Measuring and Monitoring Democracy, Idasa

Acronyms and Abbreviations

ACC	Anti-Corruption Commission
ACDEG	African Charter on Democracy, Elections and Governance
ALP	African Legislatures Project
ANC	African National Congress
APRM	African Peer Review Mechanism
ART	antiretroviral therapy
BIG	Basic Income Grant
CAN	CBNRM Association of Namibia
CAT	Convention against Torture
CBNRM	community-based natural resource management
CBO	community-based organisation
CEDAW	Committee on the Elimination of Discrimination Against Women
CERC	Central Election Results Centre
CERD	Committee on the Elimination of Racial Discrimination
CFDS	Comprehensive Food Distribution Scheme
CoD	Congress of Democrats
CSO	civil society organisation
DCP	Development Capital Portfolio
DELK	Evangelical Lutheran Church (Deutsche)
DPN	Democratic Party of Namibia
DTA	Democratic Turnhalle Alliance
ECN	Electoral Commission of Namibia
EEC	Employment Equity Commission
EISA	Electoral Institute for Sustainable Democracy in Africa
ETSIP	Education and Training Sector Improvement Programme
FFF	Forum for the Future
GDP	gross domestic product
GIPF	Government Institution Pension Fund
ICCPR	International Covenant on Civil and Political Rights
ICESCR	International Covenant on Economic, Social and Cultural Rights
IMF	International Monetary Fund
IPPR	Institute for Public Policy Research
ISS	Institute for Security Studies
ITUC	International Trade Union Confederation
KAS Foundation	Konrad Adenauer Stiftung Foundation
LAC	Legal Assistance Centre
LGBT	lesbian, gay, bisexual and transgender
LRDC	Law Reform and Development Commission
MAG	Monitor Action Group
MDG	Millennium Development Goals
MISA	Media Institute of Southern Africa
MP	Member of Parliament

MUN	Mineworkers Union of Namibia
NANGOF	Namibia Non-Governmental Organisations Forum
NBC	Namibian Broadcasting Corporation
NDP	National Development Plan
NED	National Endowment for Democracy
NGC	Namibia Grape Company
NGO	non-governmental organisation
NHE	National Housing Enterprise
NHIES	Namibia Household Income and Expenditure Survey
NID	Namibia Institute for Democracy
NSHR	National Society for Human Rights
NTA	National Training Authority
NUDO	National Unity Democratic Organisation
NUNW	National Union of Namibian Workers
OHCHR	Office of the High Commissioner for Human Rights
OPG	Office of the Prosecutor General
PDNA	post-disaster needs assessment
PEMMO	Principles for Election Management, Monitoring and Observation
PEPFAR	US President's Emergency Plan for Aids Relief
PLAN	People's Liberation Army of Namibia
PPP	Public Private Partnerships
RDP	Rally for Democracy and Progress
SACU	Southern African Customs Union
SADC	Southern African Development Community
SADC–CNGO	Southern African Development Community–Council of Non-Governmental Organisations
SAWIP	South Africa-Washington Internship Program
SITO	States in Transition Observatory
SMS	short message service
SPYL	SWAPO Party Youth League
SWANU	South West Africa National Union
SWAPO	South West Africa People's Organisation
TIPEEG	Targeted Intervention Programme for Employment and Economic Growth
TUCNA	Trade Union Congress of Namibia
UDF	United Democratic Front
UDHR	Universal Declaration of Human Rights
UDP	United Democratic Party
UN	United Nations
UNDP	United Nations Development Programme
UNHCR	United Nations High Commissioner for Refugees
UNITA	União Nacional para a Independência Total de Angola
UNSCR	United Nations Security Council Resolution
USAID	United States Agency for International Development
WFP	World Food Programme

INTRODUCTION

By Monica Koep and Bryan M. Sims

2011 marked a series of political watershed moments within Africa. Following nearly five decades of civil war, the nation of South Sudan was born. Popular uprisings in North Africa led to the demise of autocratic regimes that had ruled for decades in Egypt, Libya and Tunisia, while inspiring similar protests throughout the Middle East. Significant elections took place in Côte d'Ivoire, Liberia, Niger and Zambia. The International Criminal Court moved ever closer towards prosecuting those responsible for Kenya's 2007 post-electoral violence. It is within this wider context of reinvigorated momentum for democratisation that we must endeavour to assess the state of democracy, as well as the extent to which all stakeholders contribute to its wellbeing or its erosion in any given country.

In a range of regional and international comparative indices, Namibia is consistently ranked among the most democratic societies in Africa and is acknowledged for its achievements since an internationally-supervised settlement secured its independence in 1990. Over the past 21 years, as Namibia has undergone various stages of democratic transition and consolidation, its key institutions have generally functioned well and maintained the rule of law. As a result, Namibians possess a deep trust in their Constitution and political arrangement.

However, while it may be stated that Namibia is among Africa's few stable constitutional democracies, there is a need to reflect on the quality of not only its democracy, but also its state of development, and to assess the ability of the Namibian government to meet the economic expectations and fulfil the social aspirations of all Namibians. As the mean score of 5.51 suggests, and as the authors will demonstrate further, Namibia's democracy is insufficient as it does not adequately ensure that the needs of Namibians – whether socio-economic or political – are met. While there has undoubtedly been significant progress since 1990, Namibian democracy is developing slowly, particularly in terms of its ability to impact on poverty reduction and inequality. Without seeking to address the issues that the authors in this Index reveal, the long-term viability of Namibia's democracy remains uncertain.

Although the 2008 Afrobarometer survey noted positive trends in democratic values – for example, more Namibians rejected military, one-party and one-man rule – overall, Namibian's patience with democracy has fallen sharply. In 2003, 31% of Namibians were ready to try another form of government, whereas this view rose to 53% in 2008. Therefore, we must ask ourselves why Namibia, a country that overcame the shackles of both colonialism and apartheid, possesses representative and democratic institutions, is rich in resources and is continuously demonstrating a respectable level of economic performance, is struggling to develop and take forward the values and beliefs that defined the struggle that led to independence.

While the country has achieved a new rights-oriented political dispensation, a mixture of political, social and economic stresses – such as intolerance, racial tensions and gender inequality, as well as those related to poverty, education, health and unemployment – are threatening to further weaken the quality of Namibia's democracy and testing the commitment of Namibians to democratic systems, institutions and processes.

Participation among Namibians in governance and civic life is low. Despite civil society's critical role in the liberation struggle and negotiations that led to the international settlement, civil society today has a much smaller presence. There is a lack of linkages between most Namibians and civil society, particularly in rural areas where two-thirds of Namibians live. Distance, poor infrastructure and a lack of means to participate hinder political and social integration.

Wealth and access to resources, particularly land, remain concentrated among a few; political patronage is weakening demand for democracy; and there has been little redress of an ethnically-based, one-party dominant political system that is increasingly sewing division among people. If the Rally for Democracy and Progress (RDP) is able to consolidate and strengthen its platform, it will truly test not only the South West Africa People's Organisation's (SWAPO) commitment to democracy, but Namibians as well. However, in the short term, the majority of Namibians are less concerned with protecting rights and more preoccupied with securing basic means for their survival.

WHY MEASURE DEMOCRACY IN NAMIBIA?

In reviewing the state of Namibian democracy, Idasa recognises that the country has created the formal framework for a sustainable democracy. Namibia's rights-based Constitution enshrined, among other things, multi-party democracy, human rights and equality. However, for democracy to be truly consolidated in Namibia, democracy must be complemented by sustainable development fuelled by significant economic growth and provided through the effective delivery of services by government.

This Index embarks on a detailed consideration of Namibia's democracy through the use of Idasa's Democracy Index, comprising 100 questions, which interrogates how closely, in practise, Namibian-lived democracy meets the broadly defined ideal of popular self-government. The purpose is to assess the state of Namibia's democracy in terms of the constitutional framework that defined the country's transition to democracy. Additionally, the current state of democracy in Namibia is assessed against a set of contextualised indicators to encourage debate around issues that emerge from this process.

The authors were asked to score each question between 1 and 10 using the following guide: 1–4 means inadequate or falling short of the democratic ideal; 5 stable but insufficient; 6 stable and adequate; 7 improving; and 8–10 excellent and as close to the democratic ideal as possible. Authors were requested to weigh their scores, differentiating between procedural forms of democracy and substantive access to rights, treating the latter as more significant. Average scores at the end of each section, and of the complete Index itself, establish a benchmark for democracy to be qualitatively measured against in the future.

BACKGROUND TO NAMIBIA

In May 1884, the German flag was hoisted at Lüderitz Bay in what thereafter became known as German South-West Africa, with the inland borders being delineated by the Anglo–German Agreement of 1890.

Subsequent colonial expropriation of land and cattle between 1884 and 1907 led to bitter conflicts between the colonial administration and the Herero and Nama peoples, resulting in acts of genocide against large parts of those population groups during prolonged waves of anti-colonial resistance.

German colonialism ended with that country's defeat at the end of World War I. In terms of the Treaty of Versailles, Namibia was placed under protection by the League of Nations as a C mandate. This mandate was subsequently delegated by the British government to the government of South Africa to exercise under the supervision of the League of Nations. During its guardianship of Namibia, the South African government imposed the apartheid system on the territory, leading to the termination of the mandate. After the revocation had been upheld by the International Court of Justice in 1971, several General Assembly Resolutions from the United Nations (the successor body to the League of Nations) called upon South Africa to withdraw its control of the country.

In August 1966, faced with South Africa's obduracy and persistent refusal to depart from the territory, and confronted with further institutionalisation and the entrenchment of racial discrimination, SWAPO, together with allied parties, launched an armed struggle aimed at achieving independence for the country.

Military pressure, coupled with widespread support from the international community, led to the adoption in 1978 of United Nations Security Council Resolution 435 (UNSCR 435). This formed the basis for subsequent negotiations during the 1980s on Namibia's right to self-determination. Eventually, military and political developments in the domestic, regional and international arena led to the full implementation of Resolution 435. Namibia's first free and fair elections for a constituent assembly were held in December 1989, under the auspices of the United Nations. The elected representatives drafted the Constitution, in terms of which they re-constituted themselves as the first parliament and elected the leader of SWAPO as the first President of the Republic of Namibia.

Namibia's political transition was unique in that it emerged from an internationally led process that culminated in a negotiated settlement that paved the way for independence on 21 March 1990.

Namibia's Constitution evolved from the 1982 Constitutional Principles agreed upon by the United Nations Security Council. The Constitution provides for the preservation of fundamental human rights and freedoms (Chapter 3), which cannot be amended, insinuating that the government does not have the right to interfere with individual freedoms. Furthermore, the Constitution guarantees a multi-party democracy, the separation of powers among the three branches of government, and includes provisions that allow citizens to seek redress and restitution if their rights are infringed upon, as well as regular elections.

The Constitution is widely acknowledged as one of the most liberal in Africa and provides for robust democratic institutions, processes, adequate checks and balances, and solid protections for basic rights. These include key protections around arrest and trial, political participation (including political parties), property and non-discrimination, while providing for the redress of inequalities resulting from apartheid colonialism and giving special status to women in terms of affirmative action. Article 21 ('Fundamental Freedoms') contains 10 personal rights to speech, belief, religion, assembly, association, movement, residence and work, which have been incorporated in legal and political practice in Namibia. When constitutional issues have been contested, the document has stood the test and the courts have ruled against the ruling party or the executive.

PARTICIPATION

Citizen participation as a concept is a crucial element of law and policy making. It consolidates and entrenches support for democracy, while legitimising and strengthening the institutions that maintain and give expression to it. In Section 1, William Lindeke examines both the manner and extent of participation in Namibia following 21 years of democracy. He contends that, despite a prolonged period of apartheid colonialism that imposed a rigid ethnic character on Namibian society, Namibians recognise the legitimacy of the State to a high extent – with the exception of the Caprivi secessionists in 1999 – with the majority of institutions, including parliament, the army, local and regional governments, police, courts, the ruling party and traditional leaders, receiving more than 60% on trust levels. Also, Namibians are among the leaders in Africa with regards to political participation, as evidenced by high voter turnout, engagement with political representatives and activity within civic organisations.

Analysing the four previous rounds of Afrobarometer surveys conducted in the country over the course of the last 13 years, Lindeke notes that Namibians are among the most satisfied populations in terms of the perceptions people hold about its democracy. However, he identifies a number of risks that, if not addressed, could significantly depreciate the state and quality of Namibian democracy, including executive dominance within a one-party dominant political system, as well as SWAPO's slow and incomplete transition from being a liberation movement to becoming a transparent, democratic and fully-functioning electoral party.

Yet, according to Lindeke, while Namibia had initially been an outlier in terms of being characterised by a concurrent strong supply of democracy and a relatively weak demand for democracy (in comparison to other countries surveyed under the Afroba-rometer), the country has been tending towards the mean and showing signs of a maturing democracy. Namibians are internalising democratic values beyond the stated preferences of their leaders, many of whom are often perceived as venerated liberators, and democratic institutions are becoming entrenched. But, despite the rising demand for democracy, there are some worrying trends. There has been a decline in support for elections among Namibians and only a small percentage believed that voters should demand vertical accountability from elected officials.

Lindeke concludes that, while basic freedoms are highly valued and identified closely with democracy, Namibians seem to be more deferential toward their leaders than citizens as in most liberal democracies. Namibians tend to delegate responsibility to their elected representatives and trust them to act in their best interests and to do what is right for the nation. However, governing elites seem once again to be centred on hegemony through the centralisation of power and control over government. Never-theless, he believes that 'Namibia's experience thus far shows promise of a better future' as within emerging democracies, such as Namibia, citizen participation is a process that demands time and continuous learning.

ELECTIONS

In Section 2, Theunis Keulder examines Namibia's electoral system and its associated institutions. Keulder found that while Namibia has regularly held free and fair elections since independence, with relatively high levels of participation, weaknesses in electoral legislation and institutions, particularly the Electoral Commission of Namibia (ECN), as well as political intolerance have compromised the electoral processes and, at times, have led to incidents and levels of violence that are incommensurate with consolidating democracies.

He argues that, while the formal mechanisms of an electoral system are in place, short-comings in operational procedures – for example, inaccurate voters' rolls, outdated procedures incorporated into electoral legislation, and the lack of organisational and institutional capacity – have contributed to a growing apathy towards public affairs, particularly among younger Namibians, and a growing lack of confidence in the elec-toral system among the population as a whole.

The right to form and join political parties, to be elected to public office and to partici-pate in the conduct of public affairs is allowed in terms of the law. However, in the run-up to the 2009 National and Presidential elections, human rights monitors and the media reported several incidents involving political violence and intolerance with increasing regularity. Additionally, particular regions are considered 'no-go areas' for certain political parties, as intimidation and violence are used to prevent members of the opposition from campaigning in some constituencies.

It is within this context that the accusations of fraud concerning the 2009 elections and unresolved legal challenge launched by nine opposition political parties under the leadership of the RDP must be considered. While the judiciary is considered independent, these recent developments have shaken confidence in Namibia's electoral institutions and have raised serious concerns about both SWAPO's co-option of these institutions and its campaigning methods.

Keulder concludes that, while the current electoral regime was able to meet Namibia's immediate needs following independence, Namibia today is faced with 'outdated' legislation and weakened institutions, and requires extensive electoral law reform for 'the long-term political health of the country and its democratic prospects'.

ACCOUNTABILITY

Lesley Blaauw seeks to ascertain the answers to three principal questions: to what extent are the institutions that have been established to monitor performance able to do so; to what extent is the principle of the separation of powers adhered to; and how successful are political institutions and mechanisms in effecting these principles, as well as what mechanisms are in place to deal with possible transgressions in Namibia? Primarily, he examines executive accountability, legislative oversight and judicial independence.

In his analysis, Blaauw makes two arguments. First, he states that, at a formal level, the constitutional, legislative and regulatory frameworks in Namibia do not lend themselves to underpinning the separation of powers necessary for democratic consolidation and nurturing a culture of accountability. Specifically, the institutional structures and the political dominance of the executive over the legislature functions as a primary obstacle to ensuring accountability from the executive to parliament. Second, in practice, legislative functions do not to reside with the legislature but rather with the executive.

While recognising a lack of accountability from those in elected office, Blaauw concludes that the examples elected leaders have set have permeated Namibian society. Ethnic and political affiliations seem to have become more important than the integrity of the institutions established to ensure vertical accountability.

In this regard, the integrity of the judiciary in the eyes of ordinary citizens, and the way in which it seems to guard against parochial influences, speaks to the strength of an institution that is intent on retaining its independence, regardless of political pressure.

POLITICAL FREEDOM

Phil ya Nangoloh recognises that the Namibian Constitution provides a valuable framework for entrenching political and civil rights. In the penultimate section, he evaluates the state of political and civil rights in Namibia against the Bill of Rights within Chapter Three of the Constitution, as well as core international and regional human rights treaties. While looking forward, Ya Nangoloh posits that a major obstacle to the country's further consolidation of democracy has been government's inability, or refusal, to acknowledge significant violations of human rights during the liberation struggle, as well as the role government played in its borderlands with Angola during that country's civil war.

In examining the gap between the principles and values contained in the constitutional and legislative frameworks and the lived realities of ordinary citizens, he argues that the formal structures associated with political and civil rights are not always accessible to the majority of Namibians. Poverty compromises the ability of Namibians to obtain the means to exercise their rights and government has not designed policies or implemented programmes that seek to adjust these economic and social imbalances. Furthermore, media partiality and journalistic integrity in Namibia vary significantly. At times, the media comes under severe government scrutiny for stories that cast officials in poor light.

For these reasons, Ya Nangoloh believes that Namibian democracy faces significant challenges in fully implementing political and civil rights. He lists the lack of credible opposition parties and the centralisation of power in the hands of one political party as major threats and contributors to the erosion of the rights that were fought for during the liberation struggle.

HUMAN DIGNITY

In the final section, Toni Hancox and Ricardo Mukonda of the Legal Assistance Centre reiterate that the relationship between democracy and development is a mutually reinforcing one, since sustaining democracy is reliant on sustainable human development.

Yet, despite having a constitution that was recognised by the world for enshrining fundamental human rights and freedoms, Namibia remains one of the most unequal societies in the world, with the wealthiest 10% earning 128 times more than the poorest 10% of the population. As the authors demonstrate, the government's social welfare policies are failing to reverse the ever-widening gap between rich and poor.

Hancox and Mukonda posit that one major obstacle to holding government accountable for ensuring human dignity, is that the Namibian Bill of Rights does not recognise the majority of socio-economic rights as being justiciable. Instead, except for the rights to culture and education, social, economic and cultural rights are enumerated in Chapter 11 of the Constitution, referred to as the Principles of State Policy. As these rights are not entrenched within the Bill of Rights, this implies that, in the Namibian context, all human rights are not regarded as being indivisible, interdependent, interrelated and of equal importance for human dignity.

Poverty is more concentrated in rural areas and certain regions are also more adversely affected. Almost one in two citizens in rural areas is poor, in comparison to 17% of the urban population. While social welfare policies have made some inroads in addressing poverty and unemployment, there seems to be little political will within the executive and legislature to further expand the reach and depth of these schemes, such as the Basic Income Grant, or to work with civil society in the implementation of pro-poor policies.

The authors argue that equity in access to healthcare is hindered by two major factors: accessibility and affordability. The distances to health facilities, particularly in rural areas, continue to negatively impact the ability of individual citizens to obtain the required services. However, government has focused great resources on HIV/Aids. Specifically regarding the provision of antiretroviral therapy since its introduction in 2003, when coverage was only 3%, Namibia now provides antiretroviral treatment to approximately 90% of those in need.

The authors conclude that the only way to enforce socio-economic rights would be to invoke Article 144 of the Namibian Constitution, which provides that international agreements binding upon Namibia shall form part of the law of Namibia.

THE STATE OF NAMIBIAN DEMOCRACY

IDASA'S DEMOCRACY INDEX

The authors were asked to score each question between 1 and 10 using the following guide:

1–4   inadequate or falling short of the democratic ideal

5   stable but insufficient

6   stable and adequate

7   improving

8–10   excellent and as close to the democratic ideal as possible

SECTION 1: PARTICIPATION AND DEMOCRACY

NATIONHOOD

1.	To what extent do leaders and legal citizens agree on the identity of the nation established by the territorial and legal state?	8
2.	To what extent do political leaders agree that democracy is the only appropriate form of making collective decisions for their nation?	7
3.	To what extent do political leaders and citizens resort to violence or illegal activity to settle political disputes?	8
4.	Do the majority of citizens agree that democracy is the only appropriate form of making collective decisions for their nation?	7

PARTICIPATION AND INVOLVEMENT

5.	To what extent do citizens participate in political life? Are citizens willing to participate in elections and become involved in other ways to influence government and hold it accountable?	5
6.	To what extent do citizens feel prepared and competent to take part in political life?	5
7.	To what extent do citizens feel that participation in political life can give them some ability to influence collective decisions?	5
8.	To what extent do citizens feel that the impact of their participation will be equal to other citizens?	5

GOVERNMENT LEGITIMACY

9.	To what extent do citizens feel that the government in general, and the present government in particular, has the right to make binding collective decisions?	8

CITIZENSHIP OBLIGATIONS AND DUTIES

10.	To what extent do citizens meet their legal obligations?	6

TOLERANCE

11.	To what extent do citizens tolerate ideas, peoples and practices with which they disagree?	8

SECTION 1 SCORE: 6.5

SECTION 2: ELECTIONS AND DEMOCRACY

ELECTIONS

12.	Is appointment to legislative and executive office determined by popular election?	9
13.	To what extent are elections for government based on universal suffrage and secrecy of the ballot?	6
14.	Do all citizens believe that their vote is secret?	6
15.	To what extent do citizens believe that their electoral system reflects the will of the people? How much does the electoral system impact on representivity?	5

EQUAL VOTES		
16.	Do the votes of all electors carry equal weight?	**7**
17.	To what extent do citizens believe that they have equal influence?	**7**
OPEN COMPETITION		
18.	Is there equal opportunity for all groups who wish to organise and stand for office? Does social grouping make a difference?	**6**
19.	Are all political parties able to campaign free of threat?	**5**
20.	Are all citizens free to form opinions, voice them, persuade others and vote, as they like, free of threat?	**6**
21.	How effective a range of choice does the electoral and party system allow the voters? Is there an open competition of ideas and policies?	**6**
ELECTION RULES		
22.	To what extent are voter registration procedures independent of control by government or individual political parties?	**6**
23.	To what extent are election procedures independent of control by government or individual political parties?	**5**
24.	To what extent are the advantages of incumbency regulated to prevent abuse in the conduct and contesting of elections?	**3**
25.	To what extent are voters able to register and to what extent have they registered to vote?	**7**
26.	Are election procedures free from abuse? And to what extent do citizens see election procedures as free from abuse?	**5**
VOTER INFORMATION		
27.	How much information is conveyed to voters by the official election information system?	**3**
28.	How much information about political parties and candidates is conveyed by the news media? And how fairly is this done?	**7**
29.	How much access do political parties have to the media and how equitable is this?	**6**
30.	To what extent do the campaigns of political parties reach all sections of society?	**6**
31.	Do voters know enough about all political parties to be able to make an informed choice?	**5**
ELECTORAL PARTICIPATION		
32.	How extensively do citizens participate in elections?	**7**
33.	How are citizens able to influence the electoral process in ways other than the vote?	**7**
PROGRESS AND DEMOCRACY		
34.	To what extent is the management and control of the elections delegated to an independent body?	**6**
35.	Are there mechanisms for the review of the electoral system and are these open to citizen participation?	**8**

ELECTORAL OUTCOMES		
36.	Are the announced election results congruent with how the electorate actually cast their ballots?	8
37.	Do citizens believe that their vote makes a difference?	8
38.	Do security forces, the government and political parties accept the election results?	6
39.	Do citizens accept the election results?	7
40.	How closely does the composition of the legislatures and the selection of government reflect the election outcome?	8
41.	How far do the legislatures reflect the social composition of the electorate? To what extent are women represented in parliament?	4
FUNDING ELECTIONS		
42.	To what extent are private donations to political parties permitted and are they subject to regulation (such as transparency and limits), in order to prevent them from having a disproportionate impact on voter choice and electoral outcome?	3
43.	Is campaign finance – both income and expenditure – regulated? Are political parties regulated by accepted procedures and non-partisan bodies? How extensive is the independent oversight of election expenditure?	1
44.	Is there public financing of political parties?	5

SECTION 2 SCORE: 6

SECTION 3: ACCOUNTABILITY AND DEMOCRACY

EXECUTIVE ACCOUNTABILITY, LEGISLATIVE OVERSIGHT AND JUDICIAL INDEPENDENCE		
45.	How far is the executive subject to the rule of law and transparent rules of government in the use of its powers? To what extent are all public officials subject to the rule of law and to transparent rules in the performance of their functions?	5
46.	How extensive and effective are the legislature's powers to scrutinise the executive, hold it to account, initiate and scrutinise as well as amend legislation between elections? Is the legislature able to hold the executive to account for the implementation of legislation and policy?	5
47.	To what extent has legislative and executive power been devolved and what impact has this had on popular control?	4
48.	How independent are the judiciary and the courts from the executive and from all kinds of interference?	5
PUBLIC PARTICIPATION AND ACCOUNTABILITY		
49.	How open, accessible, extensive and systematic are the procedures/mechanisms for public consultation and participation on legislation and policy making? How equal is the access which interest groups/citizens have to influence the law-making process?	4

50.	How open, accessible, extensive and systematic are the procedures/mechanisms for public consultation and participation on executive policy? And how equal is the access which citizens have to influence executive policy?	4
51.	How far does government cooperate with relevant partners, associations and communities in forming and carrying out policies and how far are people able to participate in these processes?	4
LAW-MAKING AND THE BUDGET PROCESS		
52.	How extensive are the powers of legislative bodies, and how effective are they at legislating?	4
53.	How rigorous are the procedures for parliamentary approval, supervision of and input into the budget and public expenditure?	4
54.	How much say does the public have in the development of the budget? How well do parliamentary procedures allow the public to participate in decisions relating to resource allocation?	3
ACCESS TO INFORMATION		
55.	How independent and accessible is public information about government policies and actions and their effects? How comprehensive and effective is legislation in giving citizens the right of access to government information?	5
ACCESSIBILITY AND INDEPENDENCE		
56.	How accessible are elected representatives to members of the public? What impact does the electoral and party system have on the way in which MPs represent people?	5
57.	How far are MPs protected from undue influence by outside interests? Are potential conflicts of interest regulated?	4
58.	How effective is the separation of public office, elected and unelected, from party advantage and the personal, business and family interests of office holders?	3
59.	How effective and open to scrutiny is the control exercised by the legislature and the executive over civil servants?	5
60.	How far is the influence of powerful corporations and business interests over public policy kept in check, and how free are they from involvement in corruption?	5
61.	To what extent is the public service protected from corrupt practices? To what extent are public officials protected from undue influence by outside interests? Are potential conflicts of interest regulated?	4
62.	Are public servants who blow the whistle on corruption encouraged and protected? Are citizens who blow the whistle on corruption protected?	7
63.	To what extent can the government carry out its responsibilities in accordance with the wishes of the citizens free of interference or constraint from political or economic forces outside of Namibia?	4
64.	How far is the government able to influence or control those things that are most important to the lives of its people, and how well is it organised, informed and resourced to do so?	4
SECTION 3 SCORE: 4		

SECTION 4: POLITICAL FREEDOM AND DEMOCRACY

CIVIL AND POLITICAL RIGHTS

65.	How free are all people from intimidation and fear, physical violation against their person, arbitrary arrest and detention?	5
66.	To what extent are people able to protect themselves against discriminatory treatment by the State?	4
67.	To what extent are people able to use the legal system to protect their person and property against the State?	6
68.	How effective is the protection of the freedoms of expression, information and assembly for all persons irrespective of their social grouping?	4

FREEDOM OF ASSOCIATION AND PARTICIPATION

69.	How secure is the freedom for all to practise their own religion, language and culture?	6
70.	To what extent do people feel free to associate with others in order to influence government? To what extent does government action encourage or discourage people to associate with others in order to influence government?	5
71.	To what extent do people organise themselves into associations in order to influence government and to what extent are the associations of civil society independent of government?	5
72.	How far do women participate in political and public life at all levels?	7
73.	How free from harassment and intimidation are individuals and groups working to protect human rights?	4

POLITICAL PARTIES

74.	How freely are political parties able to form, recruit members and engage with the public?	4
75.	How free are opposition or non-governing parties to organise within the legislature and outside of it?	5
76.	How fair and effective are the rules governing party discipline in the legislature and within the party?	5
77.	How far are parties effective membership organisations, and how far are members able to influence party policy? Are all individual members privy to sufficient information about their party, including details of private donors?	4
78.	To what extent are political parties able to aggregate the interests of all social groups?	4

MEDIA RIGHTS

79.	To what extent does the legal system ensure that print and electronic media are free to print or say what they want about those in power in both government and the private sector?	6

80.	To what extent are people and organisations able to disseminate their views via print or electronic media?	6
81.	To what extent are the print and electronic media independent from government? How pluralistic is the ownership of print and electronic media?	6
82.	To what extent do citizens have equal access to adequate information, including news and other media?	5

SECTION 4 SCORE: 5

SECTION 5: HUMAN DIGNITY AND DEMOCRACY

SOCIO-ECONOMIC AND CIVIL RIGHTS' PROTECTION

83.	How far are economic and social rights, including equal access to work, guaranteed and enforced for all? Are civil rights of the marginalised and post vulnerable protected in criminal and criminal procedure law?	5
84.	How effectively are the basic necessities of life guaranteed, including (a) Clean, adequate and reasonably accessible water (b) Adequate food (c) Adequate housing and shelter (d) Adequate and unimpeded access to land	4

HEALTH CARE

85.	To what extent is the right to adequate health care protected in all spheres and stages of life? Is treatment available for illnesses such as HIV/Aids? Is access to this treatment equitable and is the health service of reasonable quality?	5

EDUCATION

86.	How extensive and inclusive is the right to education and training, including education in the rights and responsibilities of citizenship?	4

POVERTY

87.	Are vulnerable and marginalised groups such as children, the disabled and women adequately protected from poverty?	5
88.	How much impact on political participation does poverty have? How far are poor people able to participate in the wider Namibian society? To what extent are they excluded?	5
89.	To what extent is the State 'progressively realising' the social, cultural and economic rights in accordance with its constitutional obligations?	4

JOBS, AND RIGHTS IN THE WORKPLACE

90.	Is there equal opportunity for all in the workplace?	5
91.	How far are workers' rights to fair rates of pay, just and safe working conditions and effective representation guaranteed in law and practice?	6
92.	How far are wage levels and social security or other welfare benefits sufficient for people's needs, without discrimination/equally?	5

DELIVERY OF SOCIAL AND ECONOMIC RIGHTS		
93.	Are public goods, for example water provision or local services such as waste collection, equally available to citizens and communities at similar levels of efficiency and competence?	5
94.	To what extent has privatisation had an impact on the adequate provision of public goods and services?	6
95.	To what extent do public-private partnerships or does privatisation facilitate or impede access to socio-economic rights, particularly for the poor?	3
96.	To what extent are private companies accountable for the delivery of socio-economic rights as a result of privatisation or public-private partnerships? To what extent is this accountability overseen by citizens or their representatives?	4
97.	To what extent do citizens feel they are receiving equal access to public resources regardless of their social grouping?	5
CORPORATE GOVERNANCE		
98.	How rigorous and transparent are the rules on corporate governance; and how effectively are corporations regulated in the public interest?	4
99.	To what extent are companies duty-bound to play a role in the realisation of socio-economic rights? And to what extent do they prioritise responsible social investment?	5
100.	Is the private sector meeting its new obligations, such as in relation to equity and empowerment responsibilities?	5
SECTION 5 SCORE: 6		
TOTAL SCORE: 5.5		

SECTION 1

PARTICIPATION AND DEMOCRACY[1]

WILLIAM LINDEKE

Namibia experienced decades of armed struggle and internal popular mobilisation to gain independence in 1990. Besides the early resistance to colonial intrusions and genocide, modern participatory resistance began in the late 1950s. Popular participation was one of the central foundations to Namibia becoming independent. Civil society formations such as trade unions, churches, teacher and student groups, as well as communities, were active in confronting colonial oppression. Political parties, including the South West Africa People's Organisation (SWAPO), the South West Africa National Union (SWANU), and many others, which were not banned by the apartheid colonial regime (as had happened to the African National Congress (ANC) and others in South Africa), were active both within and outside the country. Independence came on the heels of a massive 96% turnout in the United Nations (UN) supervised elections of 1989 (Thornberry 2004).

This popular participation in elections, a characteristic of the nation's birth, has contributed towards Namibia becoming one of Africa's best performing democracies. Peace and stability, recurrent elections, and respect for rights and freedoms are all key features of independent Namibia (Lindeke 2011). The achievement of independence has featured a reorientation of public participation to a large degree, away from a confrontational approach to a more supportive mode of interaction. This is certainly true of most civil society participation. However, labour relations continue to be collectively antagonistic and confrontational, as is discontent with local authorities' service delivery and sometimes with traditional authorities.

Only a few large public clashes have occurred between the public and the national government – mostly over ex-combatants' benefits, illegal shebeen owner's rights, and benefits for 'struggle children'. Even these have been essentially peaceful. Otherwise, for the most part, civic participation follows routine democratic channels, for example, demonstrations and petitions or appeals to agencies of horizontal accountability, such as the Ombudsman's office and the Anti-Corruption Commission (ACC). Namibians also are likely to seek some influential person to intercede than is true for most African democracies (Logan, Fujiwara & Parish 2006). Additional conflicts revolve around succession issues within traditional authorities. At times, hidden political party and factional disputes behind the scenes complicate the participative process.

To a great extent the population trusts the government to do the right thing and gives it strong support. Many of the activists of earlier years now work for government or other public or private agencies and are trying to develop the country from within the ruling party. Many of the strongest institutional voices of the past, such as the churches, students and the unions, remain formally or informally affiliated to SWAPO, and while they may be muted public voices, they often exert influence behind the scenes. Call-in radio, letters to the editor and short message service (SMS) newspaper pages reflect a vibrant interest on the part of the 'attentive community' over the years. Civil society is a vocal, but much smaller, participant articulating its concerns mainly through a diverse media, but also mobilising the public and directly lobbying government and parliament.

This chapter will examine the manner and extent of participation over the past few years, as well as the longer legacy of 21 years of independence. While most of the chapter's content reflects internal evaluations such as the Afrobarometer[2] findings, media reports and expert evaluations, it will start with comparative external evaluations – many of which place Namibia's democratic performance in terms of policy and governance among the best in Africa, alongside those of Botswana, Mauritius and South Africa.

The World Bank's report, *Governance Matters VIII* (Kaufmann, Kraay & Mastruzzi 2009), ranks 212 'entities' (countries) by combining separately compiled measures or indices of other organisations' original research. This respected index indicates Namibia's relatively high ranking on key variables going back to 1996. One important example is the category of 'Voice and accountability', where Namibia ranks fourth among African countries.[3] The score on this measure has consistently been 'positive'.[4] This variable measures '... perceptions of the extent a country's citizens are able to participate in selecting their government, as well as freedom of expression, freedom of association, and a free media' (Kaufmann *et al.* 2009). Although this is heavily weighted toward civil liberties and freedoms, it also measures election-related and parliamentary participation. Namibia ranked high in Africa in terms of several other key governance measures and has scored fairly consistently over time in these rankings. Along with Botswana, Mauritius, South Africa, Tunisia and Cape Verde, Namibia is consistently a leading African performer.

The 2011 Ibrahim Index of African Governance evaluated Namibia's conditions in a similar manner and ranked it sixth overall in Africa, with a score of 69.7 out of 100 in the 2010 data. 'Participation' has also been a strength for Namibia in the recent Ibrahim rankings. In the 2010 report, Namibia ranked second in political participation, ahead of Botswana and Mauritius, but behind South Africa. However, in the 2011 report, Namibia's ranking on several sub-measures declined significantly, possibly due to by-election turmoil, the contested nature of the national elections in November 2009, and the subsequent court challenges.[5] The overall classification of 'participation' slipped to a much lower 14 in the 2010 report and 11 in 2010 data. A 20-point decline was reported from 2006 to 2011. It is not yet clear whether the controversial 2009 election cycle has marked a turning point in Namibian political participation. Nevertheless, a sharp decline in election civility in Namibia was noted by several external agencies, and a severe poisoning of relations between opposition political party leaders and the Electoral Commission occurred.

A closer examination of specific aspects of citizen and elite participation follows.

NATIONHOOD

1. *To what extent do leaders and legal citizens agree on the identity of the nation established by the territorial and legal state?* (8)

The special circumstances of the UN-supervised independence process (UN Security Council Resolution 435) implanted a strong sense that Namibia was special. The long struggle against colonialism and apartheid had forged a high degree of common purpose. Many other well-known forces that influence national identity over ethnic identity are at work in Namibia. Factors such as urbanisation, education, higher income, an armed struggle for independence, and a later independence achievement, among others, have been identified as increasing the predominance of national identity over ethnic identity in African countries (Robinson 2009). He summarises research from the field and suggests that, 'A strong prediction that emerges from this literature is that "modernisation" – increased education, industrialisation, and urbanisation – is positively correlated with national identification' (Robinson 2009:6). These factors are all on the increase in Namibia.

Economic success also supports nationhood by delivering material goods. Namibia has been elevated to an upper-middle income country, despite high levels of unemployment and an extreme income inequality.[6] The common agenda for an economic future found in the long-term development plan, *Vision 2030*, is also shared widely among the populace and almost universally adopted as motivation for common agendas and actions. Additionally, independence saw steady urban growth, a concerted (though disappointing in terms of results) emphasis on education, and expanded modern economic development, which all should contribute to stronger national identity.[7] A stronger national identity provides a common focus for constructive citizen participation.

A large dominant ethnic group also can build support for the larger national project. In many respects the dominance of the Oshivambo-speaking group (50% of the population), and its overwhelming 90% plus voting for the ruling SWAPO party and government, predetermine stronger nationhood values and participation in support of government than might otherwise be the case. SWAPO also receives a majority of the other voters as well. Indeed, both SWAPO supporters and Oshivambo speakers express a slightly stronger preference for democracy than do others (R4/Q30). Long-term hegemony by a single party or ethnic group has a tendency to fossilise people and policies around the dominant positions, thus creating excessive and unhealthy uniformity, while choking off creativity and diversity.

To the contrary, in its long history, apartheid colonialism attempted somewhat successfully to graft a rigid character of ethnic separation onto Namibian society. One important consequence of this structuring has been the common experience of monocultural life for many rural people. Ethnic issues have not disappeared and, indeed, seem to be simultaneously resurging. On the whole, however, over the past 21 years Namibia has managed to avoid repetitive collective violence and destructive dissent around ethnic identities. Public participation in the political process revolves around common institutions and policies, and not around whether one desires to be in or out.

Namibia is not very different from other African countries in terms of these identities. Table 1 shows figures from the 2008 Afrobarometer survey on the issue of national and ethnic identity, broken down by urban and rural differences, and by gender, together with the 2006 totals for trend comparison. The differences are mostly within the 3%

margin of error. Namibian respondents are slightly above the 20-country average with fully 80% of the respondents in 2008 reporting either 'equal or more national identity'.

Table 1: Ethnic or national identity						
	Urban %	Rural %	Male %	Female %	Total % 2008	Total % 2006
I feel only (ethnic group)	7	11	8	11	9	5
I feel more (ethnic group) than Namibian	9	11	10	11	10	10
I feel equally Namibian and (ethnic group)	45	44	46	43	45	40
I feel more Namibian than (ethnic group)	12	10	12	10	11	10
I feel only Namibian	26	23	23	24	24	28
Source: Institute for Public Policy Research (2009) / Q83 Which of the following statements best expresses your feelings?						

This measure of identity has changed slightly since 2006, which might reflect the increase in new ethnic political parties in the lead-in to the 2009 election.[8] Again these are neither large nor dangerous changes and may only reflect the pre-election influence. The 2009 election outcome did see a small increase in the share of votes for the more ethnic-based parties, but this growth was mainly at the expense of the opposition Democratic Turnhalle Alliance (DTA) rather than the ruling party. Nationhood remains the dominant theme in Namibia, which keeps political participation within appropriate constitutional and democratic bounds.

Examining the issue of identity from a generational perspective, one finds that younger respondents have a slight bias of a very few percentage points toward national identity, with older ones being slightly more ethnic, but without any dramatic difference or clear hierarchy of age differences, as most differences remain within the margin of error. This situation around ethnic and national identity is unlikely to change dramatically in the future. Even so, government leaders are somewhat ambivalent about identity, repeatedly beseeching the public to remember their roots on the one hand, while launching a new public 'nationhood' promotion campaign in 2011 on the other.

When the responses are broken down by region, the most 'ethnic' regions are in the east, where Hereros support traditional ethnic parties such as the National Unity Democratic Organisation (NUDO), and in the Omusati area of founding President Sam Nujoma's origin. This is interesting in the sense that supporters of Nujoma's faction of the ruling party (referred to by opposition politicians as the 'Omusati Clique') were accusing their rivals from other regions of being 'tribalist' and of fomenting 'tribalism'. Party and government leaders have warned traditional leaders against becoming involved in party-political activities, but never shy away from including them in big events, and the government provided all recognised traditional leaders with new 4x4 vehicles and a driver just before the election in 2009.

Table 2 shows a breakdown of identity responses by region in the 2008 Afrobarometer survey.

Table 2: Identity by region					
Region	I feel only (ethnic group) %	I feel more (ethnic group) than Namibian %	I feel equally Namibian and (ethnic group) %	I feel more Namibian than (ethnic group) %	I feel only Namibian %
Caprivi	8	12	52	10	19
Erongo	5	8	19	20*	46*
Hardap	4	13	63	2*	17
Karas	2	4	63		31
Kavango	9	13	36	21	22
Khomas	6	10	46	14	23
Kunene	4	17	41	10	29
Ohangwena	6	10	56	7	19
Omaheke	16*	2	64	9*	9*
Omusati	15*	14*	27	11	34
Oshana	14	4	43	6	29
Oshikoto	6	15	47	14	17
Otjozondjupa	22*	11*	56	2*	9*
Total	9	10	45	11 —	24

Source: Institute for Public Policy Research (2009). * 'Outlying' results that deviate from the averages.

When the question of identity is broken down by self-reported ethnic identity group-ings, only a few of the smaller groups are less national in identity than average. Among the larger groups, only Namas have weak national-only responses. However, they make up for it with a larger than average equal identity at 60%. Only marginal, smaller groups with some history of grievance (San, Baster, Mafwe) show majority 'ethnic' responses, indicating again that Namibians have strong national identities in general, with 80% claiming 'equal or national identity'. This is identical to the 20-country Afrobarometer average in 2008.

Robinson (2009) shows similar results in the 2006 Afrobarometer survey of 18 countries depicted in Figure 1, where Namibia has the third highest national identity score, behind Tanzania and South Africa. As far as the general public is concerned, Namibia continues to feature strong national identity. Leaders and ethnic brokers have created some isolated problems. For example, Baster leaders fought to maintain a separate sovereignty in 1990 and were even threatening violence. This issue was negotiated successfully by the then prime minister and has not recurred.

Figure 1: Nationalism in 2006 by country

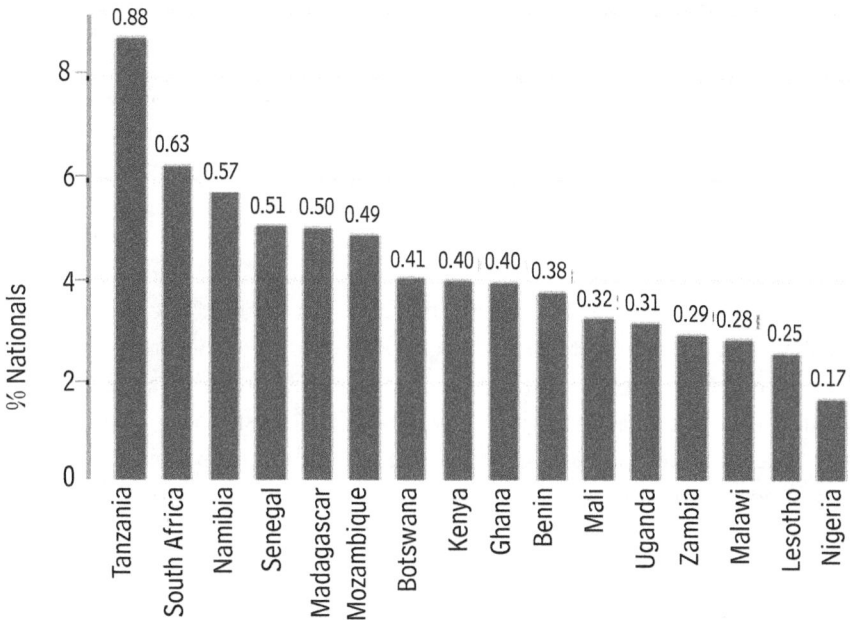

Source: Robinson (2009:14)

The brief Caprivi uprising in 1999 reflected a minority reaction in the region to declining political prospects of elites, who then manipulated ethnic sentiments. The subsequent treason trial is ongoing, over a decade later, but no additional violence has been recorded. At the time of the uprising, the population of Caprivi was responding positively towards the government and the ruling party, as shown in the first Afrobarometer survey just before the outbreak. The respondents in Caprivi had typically positive responses with regard to their preference for democracy, the Constitution reflecting their values, and the fairness of the 1994 election in line with other regions. The Caprivi situation is the only instance of domestic collective violence since independence, and it was instigated from above rather than being fed by popular sentiment, which differed little from those in other parts of the country in terms of their trust and support for the Constitution, government, and democracy (Afrobarometer Working Paper #11).

The subsequent State of Emergency excesses, including allegations of torture, have left people in parts of the region embittered and more volatile in terms of voting patterns than is typical in Namibia.

2.   To what extent do political leaders agree that democracy is the only appropriate form of making collective decisions for their nation?   (7)

Namibia's leaders have accepted democratic standards, at least at the formal procedural levels. Speeches and celebrations highlight respect for human rights, the importance of parliament, and election-related responsibilities. The Constitution is acclaimed and great pride is taken in the international recognition of Namibia's democratic successes. Beyond saying and seeming to do the right things, Namibia's leaders have created and sustained many of the necessary institutions for an effective democratic consolidation (Lindeke 2011). Large public consultations are a regular feature of policy development, from the Land Conference in 1991 to the National Education Conference in 2011. However, many of these public meetings are characterised more by appearance than by substance.

At the same time, SWAPO's transition from a liberation movement into an electoral party has seemed partial at best. Executive dominance within a one-party dominant political system is a widely recognised limitation, featuring the maintenance of party hegemony, promoting ideological and other solidarity with longstanding friends, and, cynics might say, spreading enrichment to preferred beneficiaries. Namibia follows the British tradition of government dominating legislative processes, so opposition parties and the general public are constrained by the super majority of SWAPO. Civil society groups attempt to influence the process through committee hearings, and opposition parties have been active in debates and in the introduction of important motions. Counterbalancing the hegemonic tendencies without undermining the accumulated democratic successes will present a major challenge over the next decade.

Despite the proclamation of democratic values, the incongruity of government support for African dictators (from Nigeria's Sani Abacha to Zimbabwe's Robert Mugabe) has long been criticised, and Namibia has also been slow to act on its democratic values by not ratifying the African Charter on Democracy, Elections and Governance (ACDEG) and by not joining the African Peer Review Mechanism (APRM). The recent tendency towards recentralisation of power and control, together with the perpetuation of secrecy habits honed in the liberation struggle, raises questions about the sincerity of many leaders' proclaimed commitment to democratic values.

Furthermore, the failure to create a sharp boundary between the ruling party and government also reflects some ambiguity of commitments. It seems democracy is only best when it produces the desired result. Threats to ruling party hegemony frequently elicit intemperate language and, in 1999, 2008 and 2009, some confrontational physical behaviour from certain elements within SWAPO. Commitments to the constitutional guarantees for freedom of expression were severely tested under the proclaimed exemption of 'provocative' words from opposition parties and others. Call-in radio shows were taken off the air or smothered, and restrictions were brought into other communication arenas. The decade-long boycott of *The Namibian*, removed mid-2011, further illustrates a persistent duality of values between democracy and control.

Beyond government and the ruling party, some political parties and civic groups lack adequate internal governance and transparency structures, especially with regard to the administration of finances. The lack of accountability around the use of taxpayers' money has long been a complicated problem for political parties. Furthermore, both ruling and opposition members have been notoriously weak on accountability through their failure to supply asset declaration forms to parliament. Other civic bodies (student and HIV/Aids groups among others) have encountered difficulty in accounting to donors in appropriately transparent ways. Although Namibia features frequent circulation of some elites, it also has a culture of perpetual leadership. Term limits seem not to apply to private organisations or political parties.

However, none of these words or deeds has an excessively disruptive impact on the general character of the country's democratic processes. Namibia is a successful democracy and its leaders take pride in that fact. The renowned Bertelsmann Transformation Index of 2011 rated Namibia's democracy higher than its economy or management at 7.8 out of 10, ranking it 28th out of 128 countries. In the opinion of the index, '... all influential actors respect the democratic institutions and do not openly question their legitimacy'. Furthermore, 'there are no significant anti-democratic veto actors' (Bertelsmann Stiftung 2011:12, 28). Both Namibians and external analysts recognise that there is a strong democracy developing here. Nonetheless, there is too much reliance on elite commitments to democracy and not enough on enhancing citizen commitment to actively participating and protecting it.

3. To what extent do political leaders and citizens resort to violence or illegal activity to settle political disputes? (8)

With the major exception of collective violence being the brief uprising of a small group of Caprivi secessionists in 1999, Namibia has been largely free of collective violence since independence. Otherwise, neither leaders nor citizens have resorted to violence or major illegal actions[9] to resolve political issues and no anti-regime violence has been recorded. The closing of the Tsumeb Copper Mine in 1998 came dangerously close to erupting into industrial violence, save for the intervention of the then prime minister, Hage Geingob. While very few cases of politically-driven direct physical confrontation were recorded in the two decades after independence, by contrast, individual violence, especially domestic violence against women and children, is epidemic.

Opposition political parties have frequently claimed that their followers have been intimidated, especially in the northern parts of the country, areas where the ruling party receives more than 90% of the votes, thus heightening peer pressure into intimidating and threatening behaviour. When prompted on the issue, 33% of Afrobarometer respondents in 2008 claimed to have a fear of political violence during election campaigns (2008: Q47). A near majority of 49% of Namibians felt that political party competition leads to violent conflict 'often or always' (2008: Q45a), although the survey was conducted during the period of conflictual by-elections in late 2008 and that may have increased levels of concern. However, when asked in an open-ended question to identify the most important problems facing the country in 2006 and 2008, less than 3% of respondents indicated 'political violence, ethnic tensions or political instability' as one of their three choices in recent years (2008:Q56; 2006:Q63). This figure did not change, despite the increased party conflict around the time of the 2008 survey.

During election periods, and especially when SWAPO disaffiliated parties are a potential hazard to the ruling party's hegemony, hate speech and physical intimidation become more intense. This happened as a result of the Congress of Democrats (CoD) challenge in 1999 and again in 2008 and after, when the Rally for Democracy and Progress (RDP) presented a new breakaway threat and faced increased hostility from ruling party militants. This was centred on a series of by-elections in 2008, when the most intense competition occurred amid conditions of uncertainty.[10] Claims of 'provocation' were echoed among party activists (trying to claim exemptions from constitutional freedoms), and competition over rally locations threatened to get out of hand.

Cooler heads prevailed, as SWAPO stalwart Andimba Toivo ya Toivo issued a public call for tolerance of differences, and then President Pohamba made a New Years' appeal in the same vein. The Election Commission of Namibia was noticeably inactive at the height of party confrontations, while police responses were uneven. As the election results began to show that the threat was not as great to SWAPO domination as had been anticipated, confrontations stopped escalating, and the 2009 election proceeded to its conclusion with only a few isolated but disturbing incidents recorded by the Institute for Public Policy Research's (IPPR's) Election Watch.[11] The 2010 regional and local elections also featured a few violent confrontations, but these were isolated incidences that engaged different participants.

Overall, neither officials, nor opposition leaders nor citizens resort to force to resolve public as opposed to private issues. Similarly, Namibians involved in traditional and labour-related disputes have not resorted to actual force, but rely on petitions, marches and the legal system to resolve their differences, and leaders from government, church and civil society have been active participants in trying to resolve disputes well before they reach conflict levels. However, domestic types of violence involve many complex economic, social and cultural issues, some of which may relate to weak internalisation of equality of rights values in Namibia's early transition from colonial control.

4. Do the majority of citizens agree that democracy is the only appropriate form of making collective decisions for their nation? (7)

The Afrobarometer surveys directly address this question. Namibia had initially been an outlier in terms of the unique relations of a strong supply of democracy with a relatively weak demand for democracy. This was particularly true for the early 2000s. By the end of the decade in Round 4, however, the results were not so atypical, as Namibian results regressed towards the Afrobarometer mean. This means that the demand for democracy had strengthened, as might be expected after a longer satisfactory experience with the system, while the supply of democracy seems to have slipped a little. Nonetheless, Namibia harbours one of the most satisfied populations in terms of the feelings that its people have toward its democracy.

Popular attitudes, like those of political leaders, are somewhat ambivalent and intertwined with ethnic identity and loyalty to the ruling party among Oshivambo speakers, especially in the rural north-central areas. One important measure used in the Afrobarometer surveys is the idea that respondents should reject alternatives to democracy as a gauge of the strength of their commitment to democratic values. Although the majority of Namibians turn down each of the posited alternatives – one-party rule, one-person rule, and military rule – the country ranks as one of the lower rejecters of authoritarian alternatives among the 20 survey countries, above South Africa but below the 20-country average.

Figure 2 shows how Namibian respondents' views have changed over five different survey rounds conducted in the country. In the 2008 survey, the rejection of these non-democratic alternatives recorded the highest levels, suggesting a strengthening of popular commitments to democratic values. Nonetheless, these are still well below those of other African democracies such as Ghana, Botswana and even Zambia.

Another measure of democratic values can be found in the direct preference for democracy as indicated in Figure 3. Again, the demand for democracy by Namibians is rather weak compared to other African democracies, although the trend of preferring democracy seems to be strengthening slightly over the past three surveys, as it has in the overall 20-country survey. This is an encouraging sign that Namibians are internalising democratic values beyond just following their leaders' stated preferences. It seems that people do not, in fact, actually prefer non-democratic alternatives, but that they thought that it mattered little whether there was democracy or not.

Figure 2: Rejecting non-democratic alternatives

2.1 Variable: Reject military rule
Question: There are many ways to govern a country. Would you disapprove or approve of the following alternatives? The army comes in to govern the country.

2.2 Variable: Reject one-party rule
Question: There are many ways to govern a country. Would you disapprove or approve of the following alternatives? Only one political party is allowed to stand for election and hold office.

2.3 Variable: Reject one-person rule
Question: There are many ways to govern a country. Would you disapprove or approve of the following alternatives? Elections and Parliament/National Assembly are abolished so that the President/Prime Minister can decide everything.

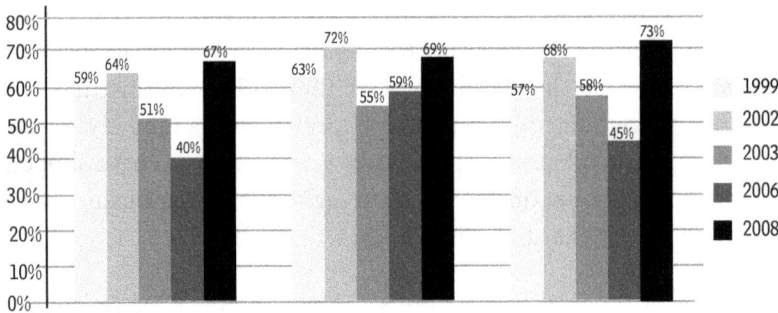

(Percent who disapprove/strongly disapprove of military rule, one-party rule and one-person rule)

Source: Logan (2009)

Figure 3: Preference for democracy

Question: Which of these statements is closest to your own opinion?
A: Democracy is preferable to any other kind of government.
B: In some circumstances, a non-democratic government can be preferable.
C: For someone like me, it doesn't matter what kind of government we have.

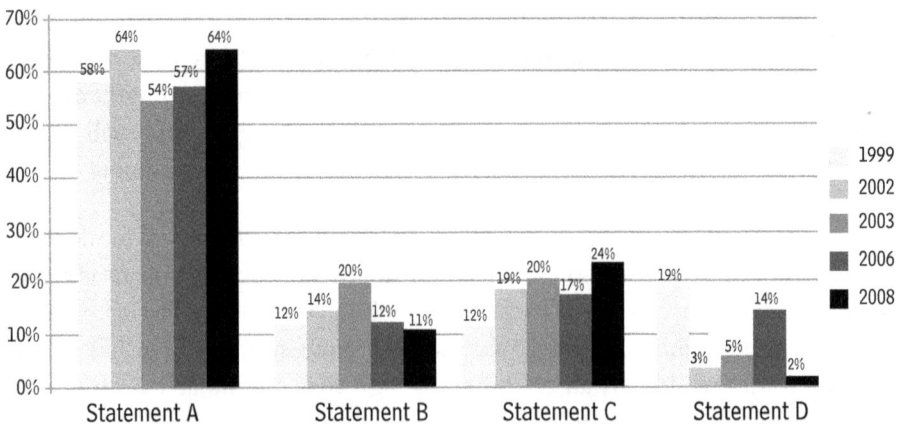

Source: Logan (2009)

A very different result is found in the declining belief in elections, as shown across four surveys depicted in Figure 4. Possibly the difference is found in the greater importance of rights as the central point of democracy among Africans as opposed to elections being the centrepiece. Many African countries, including Namibia, experienced sham elections in the past, so perhaps elections by themselves do not carry the same weight as elsewhere. In 2006, a full 50% of three responses around the 'meaning of democracy' went to civil liberties/personal rights issues and only 15% responses to elections. A majority of 53% were able to provide a response to the English language term 'democracy', while 22% required a translation into a local language. Disturbingly, 25% could not formulate a response and answered 'don't know'. Irrespective, Namibians express less demand for democracy than do citizens of other high-performing African democracies.

Figure 4: Support for elections over time

Question: Which of the following statements is closest to your view? Statement A or Statement B. A: We should choose our leaders in this country through regular, open and honest elections. B: Since elections sometimes produce bad results, we should adopt other methods for choosing this country's leaders.

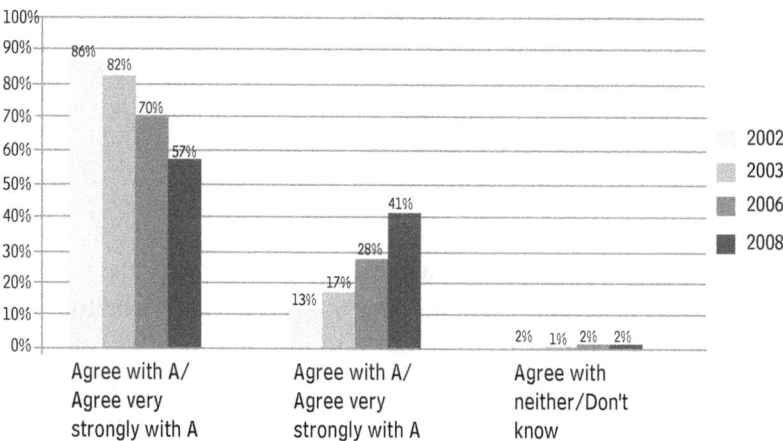

Source: Logan (2009)

Compared to the demand preference for democracy in Figure 3, survey respondents see a solid supply of democracy as depicted in Figure 5. The stark contrast between supply and demand variables a decade ago, which led Christiaan Keulder and Tania Wiese (2005) to characterise Namibia as a 'democracy without democrats', has receded slightly as satisfaction has declined (down 11% from the 2002 peak) and demand, as indicated above, has increased (up 10% from the 2003 low). Namibia is now more typical of Afrobarometer countries, though at present still stronger on supply than on demand for democracy. With 67% of respondents saying they are satisfied or very satisfied with the democracy that Namibia has, Namibia ranks a strong fourth among the 20 survey countries. Namibians have consistently expressed the view that the country is a functioning democracy, with more than 70% agreeing with this over the past decade in most opinion surveys.

Figure 5: How democratic is Namibia?

Question: In your opinion, how much of a democracy is Namibia today?

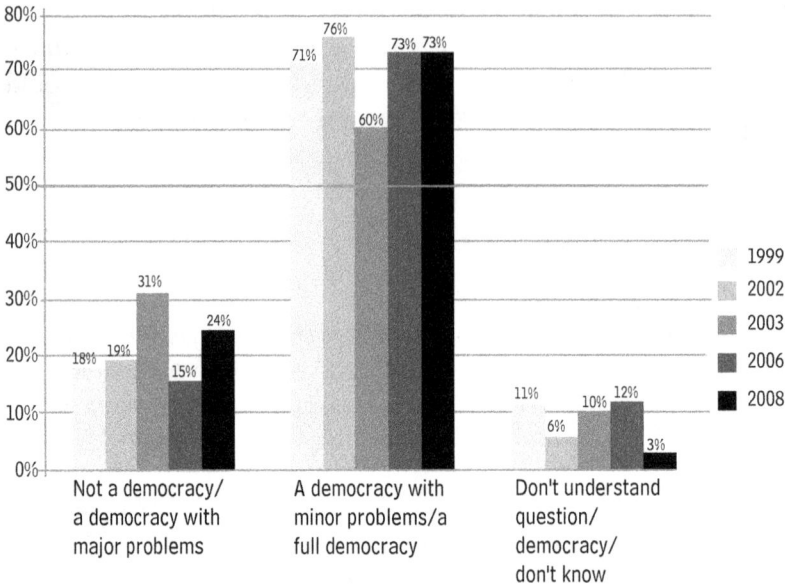

Source: Logan (2009)

Despite the declining value placed on elections as a method for choosing leaders, nearly 80% of Namibians consistently find their elections over the past decade to be free and fair. The next round of the survey will provide a chance to measure the 2009 election process and the performance of the Election Commission of Namibia (which also registers strong popularity, with 63% positive trust up to 2008). Elections are necessary but insufficient criteria for democratic consolidation. The actual casting of votes, the main public activity, has been highly respected as part of the democratic process and has not been at the centre of election controversies to date. Some scholars of democracy have suggested that public confidence in elections is one of the more important contributors to democratic expectations and, therefore, consolidation of democratic preferences. This makes the way in which problems around the 2009 election are resolved all the more important.

One critical insight from the 2006 Afrobarometer survey concerned Namibia's likelihood of remaining democratic in the future. Namibians were more confident about a democratic future than respondents in the Botswana survey, with 63% saying it was 'likely or very likely' to remain so (Q48). Combined with the strong support for the

Constitution 'representing the values and hopes of the people' (69% for Q52a in 2006), these opinions may indicate the presence of important citizen support bulwarks against non-democratic change.

Figure 6: Election rating trends

Question: On the whole, how would you rate the freeness and fairness of the last national eletion? Was it:

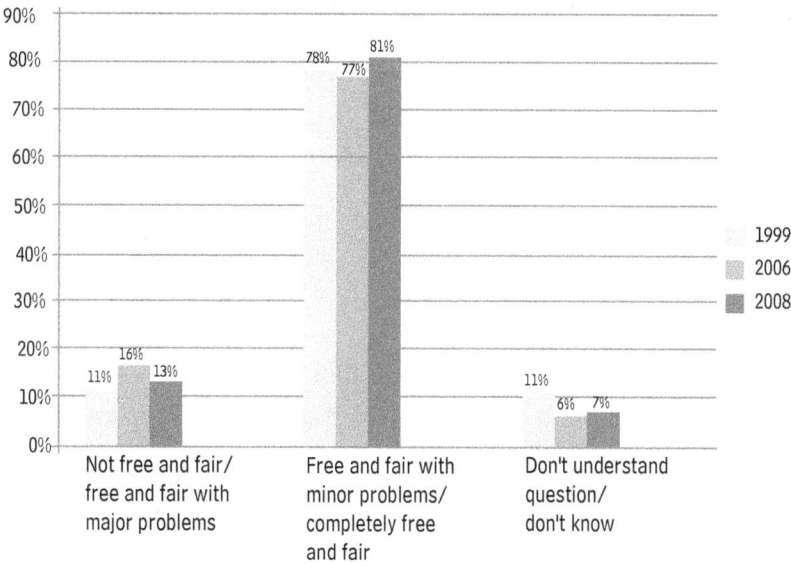

Source: Logan (2009)

PARTICIPATION AND INVOLVEMENT

5. *To what extent do citizens participate in political life? Are citizens willing to participate in elections and become involved in other ways to influence government and hold it accountable?*   (5)

6. *To what extent do citizens feel prepared and competent to take part in political life?*   (5)

7. *To what extent do citizens feel that participation in political life can give them some ability to influence collective decisions?*   (5)

8. *To what extent do citizens feel that the impact of their participation will be equal to other citizens?*   (5)

Election turnouts are often a clear reflection of the level of people's political participation. The polls in Namibia suggest that the population is still engaged in elections, although there is high variability as shown in Table 3. In the 2008 Afrobarometer survey, some 63% of respondents indicated that they had voted in the last election (a reasonable figure, considering mortality rates and those too young to vote in 2004). Voting age turnout at 60–80% for the past two or three elections is relatively high and comparable to African peers such as Ghana, Cape Verde and Mauritius, but higher on average than Botswana (44%) and South Africa (56%). At this most symbolic and change-effecting level, Namibian citizens have been actively involved in political processes. Additionally, the number of spoiled ballots at 1.3% is in line with other well-performing African democracies and suggests that citizens possess the required basic knowledge and competence to participate at this level. Only 5% said they had chosen not to vote.

Some elections seem to elicit stronger turnouts than others. When SWAPO feels threatened or needs a decisive show of support from voters, the party is able to mobilise its structures and achieve its desired results at the polls. Participation within the ruling party is not as visible, but is an important measure of public policy dialogue given the large numbers in the party and its active structures.

Table 3: Election turnout since 1989

1989 CA	1992 LA	1992 RC	1994 NA	1998 LA	1998 RC	1999 NA	2004 LA	2004 NA	2004 RC	2009 NA	2010 LA/RC
97%	82%	81%	76%	34%	40%	61%	44%	85%	55%	69%*	38%

CA = Constituent Assembly; LA = Local Authority; NA = National Assembly; RC = Regional Council.
* Under court review; voters roll and therefore turnout are contested.

Additional measures of the levels of public engagement can be found in the Afrobarometer survey. Namibians are more likely to engage non-governmental leaders or local government personnel in larger numbers, as is true of other Africans. 'Ordinary people are more likely to experience day-to-day interactions with local government entities or with informal, traditional or religious leaders in the community' (Bratton 2010). Table 4 shows the percentages of the 2008 Namibian respondents who said they contacted various types of influential people. As one might expect, interactions with local and accessible contacts are more frequent than those with members of the more distant national government. A majority of 55% of Namibian respondents indicated that they would join with others to make elected local officials listen to a matter of importance. Rural Namibians were also more than twice as likely to know who their regional councillor was as urban respondents. Bratton (2010:20) also finds that the more citizens engage with local leaders between elections, the more positive their perceptions are of those leaders' 'responsiveness'.

Table 4: Citizen contact with influentials during the past year						
Local Authority	Regional Councillor	National Council	National Assembly	Government Official	Religious Leader	Traditional Leader/ Influential Person
17%	21%	5%	3%	20%	30%	23%/22%
Source: Bratton (2010)						

Citizens also actively participate in other sectors of society through organisational membership and leadership activity in voluntary associations, which is highest in the religious sphere. Some 31% of Namibian respondents indicated that they held active or leadership role in religious groups, compared to a 44% average for all Afrobarometer countries. In civic organisations, Namibians were at 12%, while the 20-country average was 24% (Bratton 2010:8). No significant differences were indicated for urban/ rural or for gender in Namibia. A 2010 study by the Namibia Institute for Democracy (NID) (NID 2010) found a complex web of reasons why civil society organisations are not more successful at influencing the policy and law-making processes. Partly, interaction is hindered by the executive dominance of the party and governmental system, and partly by weaknesses in the non–governmental organisations (NGOs) themselves. Some 31% of the Round 4 Afrobarometer respondents in Namibia said that local NGOs were too strong, while 20% felt they were too weak. Finally, around 30% of the Namibian workforce belongs to unions and, therefore, engage in strike activity and occasional union issues off the shop floor.

Other Namibians participate in demonstrations around important issues (13% had done so during the past year), while a majority express the opinion that they would be willing to participate. Additional activities would include participation through the media, especially comments on the SMS page or call–in shows. Many citizens bring issues to the ACC or the Ombudsman's office for official consideration. SWAPO members primarily operate through party structures and, thus, are largely absent from other civil society engagements. Some Namibians are now becoming more active on social media sites on the Internet. For example, the IPPR 'Politics Watch Namibia' Facebook page has over 1 100 'friends' who can follow discussions or participate, while the Election Watch website[12] received thousands of hits during the delayed vote count in 2009. Several other Namibian websites are also active for those on–line, including some 20% of Afrobarometer respondents.

Respondents in 2008 expressed an interest in public affairs (59% 'somewhat or very interested'). This interest level is down from the 2006 survey, when 77% indicated such an interest. The difference seems to be related to changing attitudes of younger, so called 'born free' respondents (IPPR 2009a). The percentage of respondents feeling close to a political party also seemed to decline for the same reason. Nonetheless, most

Namibian respondents to the Afrobarometer survey indicted that they follow public affairs. Some 71% of Namibian respondents said they get news from the radio every day. Additionally, 61% of respondents said they discussed political matters 'occasionally or frequently' and 66% said they 'feel close to a political party'. All of these responses suggest an engaged and active public.

By contrast, several questions elicited responses indicating a passive public that defers responsibilities to leaders. While relatively few (under 10%) ever engage elected leaders at any level of government, local government and non-government leaders are accessed more often. A majority of respondents had not attended a single meeting in the past year. Furthermore, 68% of respondents in the early 2000s felt that 'people are like children' and needed to be governed as if by parents, compared to 32% who felt government was like an employee and voters were like the boss (Afrobarometer Working Paper #34:21). Apart from this, only small percentages felt that voters should be able to demand vertical accountability from elected officials. On this dimension, in 2006, Namibia was the lowest in the 18-country survey, with only 6% of citizens positing that voters should hold the National Assembly accountable.

When asked in 2008 (R4/Q73), 'Who should be responsible for making sure that, once elected ...

- ... National Assembly representatives do their jobs?', only 15% say the voters.
- ... local authority councillors do their jobs?', only 21% say the voters.
- ... the president does his job?', only 27% say the voters.

A slim majority of Afrobarometer respondents think that 'elections ensure that representatives to the National Assembly reflect the views of voters' well or very well (Q72a). However, only 37% thought that 'elections enable voters to remove from office leaders who do not do what the people want' well or very well (Q72b). This reflects the ongoing limits of a party-list system with party ownership of the seats. On the demand side of politics, ordinary Namibians are still not particularly interested in exercising control and would rather play a more passive role in politics. The high trust ascribed to all levels of government allows this hands-off stance to almost conform to the kind of conservative position proposed by British conservative Edmund Burke, with elected officials being viewed as trustees looking out for the interests of voters with whom they never interact. Some political scientists refer to this situation as a delegative democracy.

Namibians are like people in other countries who complain that politicians only pay them any attention during election campaigns. By an overwhelming majority (77%), Namibians said that Members of Parliament 'never or only sometimes ... try to listen to what people like you have to say' (Q54a, b). The party-list electoral system for the National Assembly means that voters have no specific person representing them, and they may thus feel alienated from this body to a greater extent than for other leaders (such as local government, religious, or traditional ones). When asked if it is easy or difficult for an ordinary person to have their voice heard between elections, 59% said 'somewhat or very difficult'.

Some 32% of Namibian respondents reported that they thought 'ordinary people could do something to improve the local authority' to 'some' or a 'great deal' (Q61). At national level, 59% of respondents said it is 'somewhat difficult or very difficult [for an] ordinary person to have his voice heard between elections' (Q74). However, on occasions when people feel aggrieved, they do march and toi-toi to the relevant authorities with their petitions. Namibians expect equal treatment, even if they know that treatment will not be equal. For example, Namibians frequently express concern when some categories of workers receive benefits that do not apply to their category of workers, especially in the public sector. Equally, at local level, complaints against favouritism in government allocations are a regular feature of the SMS pages and call-in radio.

The focus of the liberation struggle was against discrimination in all its forms and in particular in support of 'one person, one vote'. The general expectation is for equal treatment. In 2008, 25% of respondents said that their ethnic group was treated unfairly 'often or always'. When asked how often people are treated unequally, 34% said 'often or always' compared to the 20-country average of 51%. In the open-ended question about major problems, barely 6% offered these problems in their three choices. Again, equality is the norm.

Many Namibians recognise and even favour special treatment such as affirmative action and black economic empowerment. Yet, they also express indignation about favouritism as a form of corruption by officials, and see the unfairness of policies and performance that benefit the few. By a division of 66% to 32% in 2008, Namibians favoured treating everyone equally over elected officials favouring their own community (Q17). Similarly, by 65% to 33%, respondents thought that government policies had favoured the few and not the many (Q11).

GOVERNMENT LEGITIMACY

9. *To what extent do citizens feel that the government in general, and the present government in particular, has the right to make binding collective decisions?* (8)

High levels of legitimacy are essential to ensuring that governments do not govern through bribery or repression. Namibians grant very high legitimacy to their government and their democracy. In 1999, 66% of respondents said that the 'Constitution expresses the values and aspirations of the Namibian people' (Afrobarometer Working Paper #1:32). This response included the highest result of six southern African countries on a combined legitimacy index, as well as on the highest trust in State and political institutions in the sub-region (34). In 2006, the same question received 69% positive responses (only 12% disagreed), with nearly identical answers from rural and urban areas, and from both genders (Q52a). This is a political system that enjoys high trust and legitimacy at institutional and constitutional levels.

Namibian respondents in the Afrobarometer survey placed very substantial 'trust' in governmental officials to do the right thing. The president achieved the second highest ranking out of 20 countries. Nearly all of the institutions measured – including parliament, the army, local and regional governments, police, courts, the ruling party and traditional leaders – received over 60% trust levels (Q49). Government performance also received high marks in the survey; for example, President Hifikepunye Pohamba received an 88% approval rating (Q70). Government performance, over a range of about 15 policy areas, received majority support (Q57), and trust in the ruling party is very high. In this respect, governmental institutions in Namibia have very strong legitimacy across regions, ethnicities, age and other social categories.

In the 2008 survey, several questions asked about the government's right to make collective decisions. The results are shown in Table 5. By very large majorities of 76–82% Namibians agree that the listed agencies have the right to make collective decisions. Given the high levels of trust and performance-related respect for a wide range of political and governmental institutions, Namibians hold the government in high regard. No doubt respondents and citizens carry over positive sentiments from party to government, but even these relative non–partisan authorities score high.

Table 5: Binding authority to make collective decisions			
	Courts Q44a	Police Q44b	Tax department Q44c
Agree	43%	44%	40%
Strongly agree	38%	38%	26%

CITIZENSHIP OBLIGATIONS AND DUTIES

10. To what extent do citizens meet their legal obligations? (6)

Namibians generally express a commitment to using proper procedures and expect the system to eventually produce the desired results. This accounts to some extent for the low experience of bribe-giving (around 5%) over the decade of Afrobarometer surveys. Namibians have been willing to be patient and law abiding when things do not go as they should. They are much more likely to wait, file a complaint through proper channels, or seek the intervention of some important person than to seek the bribery option. Corruption, though, has been identified as a more or less serious problem over the past decade, judging by the frequency of high-profile cases. However, 26–28% of Namibians report paying income tax (39% of urban respondents) and other government fees, while over 80% make a contribution for healthcare or education, and over 60% pay for public utilities (Q64a–e).

Nonetheless, widespread poverty has at times driven people to be less than law abiding. For example, pensioners are often found in arrears on public payments (the city of Windhoek is the latest to forgive millions in such fees). Many people also evade the legal requirements for backyard housing, unlicensed shebeens and other unregistered businesses. Although there are some passive boycotts against paying for public services, and illegal connections to utilities reflect lingering liberation attitudes toward government, most Namibians play by the rules and expect others to do the same. Property crimes and domestic violence, however, remain serious problems since independence, with some horrific cases reported.

Both the police and the courts are accorded high trust levels (2008:Q49) – above 70%. Political challenges to elections, traditional authority succession and land disputes have all resorted to the courts rather than the streets. Asked if ordinary people who break the law go unpunished, 67% said 'never or rarely', while 29% thought 'often or always' (2008:Q45e). Very harsh penalties have been placed on theft of livestock and, in recent years, longer sentences for murder and rape have been introduced into the legal system. However, none of the exceptions to lawfulness seems to be a direct challenge to the State or the system of democratic governance. In general, the rules of the game are effectively managed and citizen compliance with legal obligations, especially in collective action, appears stable and consistent.

Tolerance

11. To what extent do citizens tolerate ideas, peoples and practices with which they disagree?   (8)

Since independence, government leaders and citizens have been engaged in a general process of national reconciliation in order to overcome the negative consequences of past hostilities. Although the official narrative of the liberation struggle has reified certain features of the past that are ritually invoked as ideology, the actual processes of policy development and operational implementation have conformed to a reconciliation process that has included retention of existing government employees, recognition of property rights and other constitutional protections, integration of armed combatants from different sides, and inclusion of diverse participants in national life. This approach has facilitated a generally peaceful and democratic independence experience for all citizens.

However, Namibians express less trust in their fellow citizens than people do in other Afrobarometer countries. In 2008, for example, Namibians were significantly more likely to not trust other Namibians than the 20-country average, and significantly less likely to trust them 'somewhat or a lot'. That level of trust has decreased since Round 3 in 2006, as shown in Table 6. In 2006, 70% of the respondents thought that 'you must be very careful in dealing with people' (Q83). While trust in government institutions is high in Namibia, trust in other people is not.

Some factions within the ruling party have adopted what Andre du Pisani called 'libratory intolerance'. At times there is an attempted closing-down of discussion on issues of national importance once President Nujoma or other senior officials have declared the party's official position. A circling of the wagons then occurs and dissenters are fearful or cautious about taking risks. A similar tendency of deference and unquestioning loyalty can be discerned in critics of the party and government. Some see no evil, while others fail to see any good.

Table 6: Trust other Namibians: How much do you trust other Namibians? (R4/ Q84c) People from other ethnic groups? (R3)				
	2006 Survey	2008 Survey	Namibia mean	AB mean
Not at all	21%	30%	62%	57%
Just a little	37%	32%		
Somewhat	29%	25%	37%	42%
A lot	11%	12%		

In some respects, Namibians show more tolerance toward others in terms of support for political freedoms than their African counterparts. Some 69% of respondents said a person 'should be able to join an organisation whether or not government approves of it', while 74% believe that 'the media should be able to publish any story without fear of being shut down'. Additionally, 78% thought that people 'should be able to speak their minds no matter how unpopular their views' (Q19–21).

Conclusion

By African standards, Namibia is a high-performing democracy. Several international indices that measure democratic governance, especially democratic participation, rate Namibia highly, as shown in this chapter. The country's citizens turn out to vote, and in general it has enjoyed political stability and effective governance since independence in 1990. According to several rounds of Afrobarometer surveys, Namibians express high levels of trust in elected officials and governing institutions. Respondents are very satisfied with the democracy that Namibia has created, and they regard it as a full democracy. They also express confidence in the elections through 2008 as being 'free and fair'. There has been a peaceful transfer of office from the founding president to his preferred successor. Contested election outcomes in 2004 and 2009 were taken to the courts rather than to the streets.

Although the commitment of Namibians to democracy as the 'only game in town' is relatively low, compared to other African democracies, positive responses are on the increase. Namibians, however, do not engage actively in holding government accountable. Although basic freedoms are highly valued and identified closely with democracy, Namibians seem to be more deferential towards their leaders than liberal democratic theory would suggest they should be. They seem to delegate responsibility to leaders and trust them to do the right things. The ruling elites, by contrast, have exercised lawful and democratic practices to a greater extent than demanded by the public. Current priorities of the governing elites seem once again to be centred on hegemony through the centralisation of control over government before the next generation takes over. This seems to come at the expense of greater popular involvement in decision making and governing the country. Democratic values and practices have yet to be deeply and irreversibly ingrained in the body politic, but Namibia's experience thus far shows promise of a better future.

SECTION SCORE: 6.5

REFERENCES

AFRICAN DEVELOPMENT BANK. 2011. *The middle of the pyramid: dynamics of the middle class in Africa* [online]. Available: http://www.afdb.org.

AFROBAROMETER. Briefing papers and working papers, various [online]. Available: http://www.afrobarometer.org.

BERTELSMANN STIFTUNG. 2011. *BTI2010 – Namibia Country Report*. Gütersloh: Bertelsmann Stiftung. Available: http://www.bertelsmann-transformation-index.de/

BRATTON, M. 2010. *Citizen perceptions of local government responsiveness in Sub-Saharan Africa.* Afrobarometer Working Paper #119:2. Available: http://www.afrobarometer.org.

BRATTON, M., LOGAN, C., CHO, W. & BAUER, P. 2004. *Afrobarometer Round 2: compendium of comparative results from a 15-country survey.* Working Paper #34. Cape Town: Idasa. Available: http://www.afrobarometer.org.

DU PISANI, A. & LINDEKE, W.A. 2010. 'Political party life in Namibia: Dominant party with consolidating democracy' in Lawson, K. (series editor) *Political parties and democracy. Volume IV: Political parties and democracy in Africa and Oceania.* Co-editors: Sindjoun, L. & Simms, M. New York: Praeger Publishers/ABC-Clio.

___. 2011. 'Stuck in the sand: Opposition political parties in Namibia' in Solomon, H. (ed.) *Against all odds: Opposition political parties in southern Africa.* Johannesburg: KMM Review Publishing Company.

HOPWOOD, G. 2008. *Guide to Namibian politics.* Windhoek: Namibia Institute for Democracy.

IPPR. 2009a. *Namibia: Political party prospects.* Afrobarometer briefing paper. Available: http://www.ippr.org.na.

___. 2009b. *Summary of results: Round 4 Afrobarometer survey in Namibia.* Windhoek: IPPR. Available: http://www.ippr.org.na.

KAAPAMA, P. 2010. 'Electioneering and parties' platforms in the 2009 Namibian presidential and national elections' in *Perspectives: Political analysis and commentary from southern Africa.* Cape Town: Heinrich Böll Stiftung Southern Africa.

KAUFMANN, D., KRAAY, A. & MASTRUZZI, M. 2009. *Governance matters VIII: Aggregate and individual governance indicators, 1996-2007.* Policy research working paper #4978. Washington, DC: World Bank Development Research Group.

KEULDER, C. 2006. *Afrobarometer survey findings: Summary of results, survey in Namibia.* Cape Town: Idasa. Available: http://www.afrobarometer.org.

KEULDER, C & WIESE, T. 2005. *Democracy without democrats? Results from the 2003 Afrobarometer survey in Namibia.* Working Paper #47. Cape Town: Idasa. Available: http://www.afrobarometer.org.

LINDEKE, W.A. 2011. 'High level performance in an African democracy: Stock taking in Namibia after twenty-one years'. Dakar: Codesria Conference paper publication forthcoming.

LOGAN, C. 2009. *Popular attitudes toward democracy in Namibia: A summary of Afrobarometer indicators, 1999-2008* [online]. Available: http://www.afrobarometer.org.

LOGAN, C., FUJIWARA, T. & PARISH, V. 2006. *Citizens and the State: New results from Afrobarometer Round 3.* Working Paper #61:39 [online]. Available: http://www.afrobarometer.org.

MELBER, H. 2010. 'Namibia's elections 2009: Democracy without democrats?' in *Perspectives: Political analysis and commentary from southern Africa.* Cape Town: Heinrich Böll Stiftung Southern Africa.

MO IBRAHIM FOUNDATION. 2011. *Ibrahim Index of African Governance* [online]. Available: *http:// www.moibrahimfoundation.org*.

NID. 2010. 'The influence of non-governmental organizations on the parliamentary law-making process in Namibia' (draft). Windhoek: NID.

ROBINSON, A.L. 2009. *National versus ethnic identity in Africa: State, group, and individual level correlates of national identification*. Afrobarometer Working Paper #112 [online]. Available: http://www. afrobarometer.org.

THORNBERRY, C. 2004. *A nation is born: The inside story of Namibia's independence*. Windhoek: Gamsberg Macmillan Publishers.

ENDNOTES

1   The author wishes to express gratitude to colleagues Professor Andre du Pisani, Graham Hopwood, and Fredrico Links for their ongoing dialogue on Namibian democracy, and to the roundtable and other colleagues involved in this project.

2   The Afrobarometer is produced collaboratively by social scientists from 20 African countries. Coordination is provided by the Centre for Democratic Development (CDD-Ghana), the Institute for Empirical Research in Political Economy (IREEP-Benin) and Idasa (South Africa). Support services are provided by Michigan State University and the University of Cape Town. For more information, see: http://www.afrobarometer.org. Fieldwork for this survey was conducted by an experienced professional team from Survey Warehouse in Windhoek, coordinated by the IPPR as national partner. Face-to-face interviews were conducted in five languages with a nationally representative, probability sample of 1 200 respondents across all 13 regions in November 2008 (and earlier surveys). Selection proportionate to population size based on the most recent (2005) census estimate ensures that every eligible adult has an equal and known chance of being selected. The final sample size of 1 200 supports estimates to the national population of all adults that is accurate to within a margin of error of plus/minus three percentage points at a confidence level of 95%.

3   This index point uses 13 different input sources to measure this performance out of the 35 separate data sources for the whole index.

4   This measure has a 2008 rating of +0.57 (giving a range of +0.44 to +0.70), which is quite high among African countries. The scale for this index ranges from -2.5 to +2.5, with only a handful of African countries achieving a positive rating.

5   The 'free and fair election' category had already declined from a previous third ranking trend to 11, over the past two years. The category of 'free and fair executive elections' was more volatile over time, but dropped from a 9 to a 15 ranking by 2008/9. The category 'electoral self-determination' also dropped from a number 1 ranking to number 13 in 2007/8 and 26 in 2008/9. The overall decline was 20 points from 2006 to 2011, suggesting an impact from election problems.

6   The African Development Bank (2011) has indicated that Namibia has one of Africa's growing 'middle class' experiences, which '... is also essential for the growth of democracy' (p. 2). Namibia ranks seventh by their most inclusive measure with 47.6% counted as middle class and the sixth highest gross national income in Africa at US$6 260. By a more restrictive measure, Namibia ranks in the middle among African countries (p. 5). Namibia also has the highest marginal middle-income group who might be more vulnerable to economic swings (p. 18).

7   Namibia has spent upward of 20% of its budget on education since independence. Self-reported literacy is above 80%, but comparative regional examination results place Namibia lower than its peers. Both the Education and Training Sector Improvement Programme (ETSIP) initiative and the national Education Consultative Conference of 2011 highlight the shortcomings that remain in this policy sector despite the admirable spending levels.

8   The respondents indicated a reduction of about 4% in national identification only, an increase in equal identities of 5% and an increase of about 4% in ethnic only. One of the factors that can influence short-term ethnic loyalty is the approach of an election. This might help explain a slight surge in ethnic identity in the Afrobarometer from Round 3 in 2006 and Round 4 in November 2008 (just a year after and before national elections respectively).

9   For example, no political parties have been outlawed, nor any journalists arrested or deported. No spontaneous violence has occurred during the voting process as happened in Zambia in 2011. Perhaps the closest Namibia comes to this is in the declared 'no-go areas' claimed especially by the ruling party supporters. Again these are relatively isolated, if troubling, incidences. The suspected abuse of the intelligence service for party-political purposes is another possible abuse.

10 This took place during the Round 4 Afrobarometer fieldwork and may have influenced some responses, but similar results were also recorded in Round 3 in 2006.

11 Fewer than 20 incidents were reported over the 13-month period. See http://www.electionwatch.org.na.

12 See http://www.electionwatch.org.na.

Section 2

Elections and Democracy

Theunis Keulder

At independence in March 1990, Namibia embarked on a path of peaceful, stable democratic transformation, based on credible and legitimate elections. Over the last 21 years, Namibia has managed a total of 11 elections for the various representative bodies at national and sub-national level, including presidential elections. Voter turnout for national and presidential elections has declined from a 97% turnout for the Constituent Assembly elections leading up to Namibian independence in 1989, to a 69% voter turnout in the last elections held in 2009.[1]

Voter turnout has one major consequence for Namibia's party system. In the absence of a legal threshold, the quota serves as the effective threshold beyond which parties are guaranteed seats and, the lower the threshold, the easier it is for small parties to gain seats (Keulder 2004).

Figure 1: Voter turnout in national and presidential elections since 1989

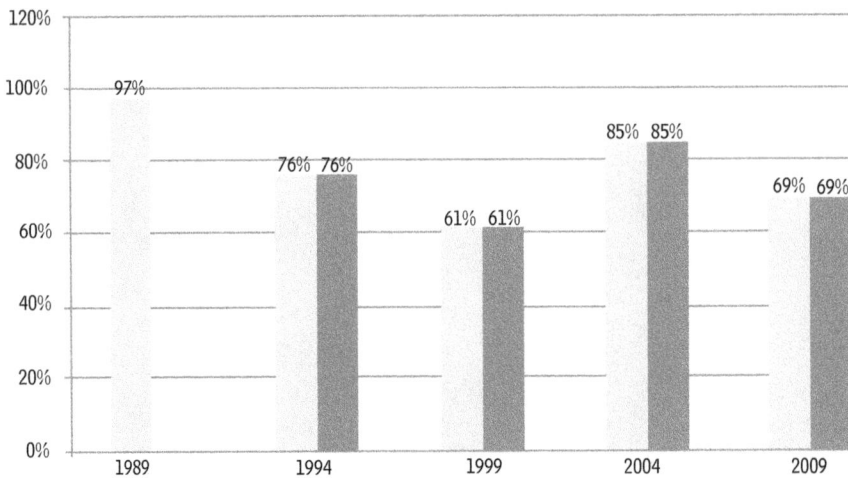

Due to its popularity as liberator of the country, the South West Africa People's Organisation (SWAPO) obtained a majority in the 1989 elections preceding indepen-dence for the Constituent Assembly. However, having achieved less than two-thirds of the vote (57.3%), the party had to settle on a negotiated constitution with opposition parties. With the coming into force of the Constitution of the Republic of Namibia on 21 March 1990, the principle of a multiparty participatory democracy was established through Article 17(1) under Chapter 3 of the Namibian Constitution (Republic of Namibia 1990), which states: 'All citizens shall have the right to participate in peaceful political activity intended to influence the composition and policies of Government. All citizens shall have the right to form and join political parties and ... participate in the conduct of public affairs, whether directly or through freely chosen representatives.'

Subsequently, SWAPO obtained (and has retained) a two-thirds majority in parlia-ment in the 1994 elections, effectively setting Namibia on course as an entrenched one-party-dominated democracy (Links 2010). The resultant steady erosion of effec-tive multipartyism has been exacerbated by the weakening of the opposition and the fragmentation of opposition political parties into ethnic or cultural group-based political organisations.

The formation of a breakaway opposition political party from within SWAPO in 2006, the Rally for Democracy and Progress (RDP), led to a political landscape character-ised by political intolerance and even sporadic violence ahead of the November 2009 National Assembly and presidential elections. Despite such hurdles, the RDP obtained sufficient votes to emerge as the new official opposition within the National Assembly.

A legal challenge as to the validity of the 2009 elections, based on alleged widespread electoral fraud by the Electoral Commission of Namibia (ECN) in favour of the ruling party, was launched by nine opposition political parties under the leadership of the RDP. While there have been a number of interim rulings, to date the case has not yet been finally resolved.

ELECTIONS

12. Is appointment to legislative and executive office determined by popular election? (9)

13. To what extent are elections for government based on universal suffrage and secrecy of the ballot? (6)

14. Do all citizens believe that their vote is secret? (6)

In terms of its Constitution, Namibia is a multiparty democracy with a three-tier governing structure. An executive president is elected by direct, universal and equal suffrage for a five-year term of office, being allowed to serve a maximum of two terms (with the exception of the first president who was – by way of a constitutional amendment – allowed to serve a third term). The legislature comprises two tiers: the National Assembly that consists of 78 seats, 72 of these being contested by proportional representation every five years, with the president directly appointing the other six. The seats are distributed by dividing the total votes by the number of elected seats. The total number of votes obtained by each party is then divided by the quota to give them a preliminary share of the seats. Any seats left over are allocated according to the highest remainder method.

The second tier is that of the National Council, comprising 26 seats, with two members elected per region by and from within the popularly elected regional councils. Elections for regional councils are held every five years through the first-past-the-post system, concurrent with elections for local authorities, which are conducted by proportional representation.

Elections in Namibia are mandated in the Constitution and regulated through the Electoral Act (1992) as amended, the Regional Councils Act (1992) as amended, and the Local Authorities Act (1992) as amended.

Namibia has ratified various binding international treaties and standards making provision for popular elections conducted by universal suffrage and the secrecy of the ballot. The Namibian Constitution provides for such agreements to be binding in terms of Namibian law. For example, Article 25 of the International Covenant on Civil and

Political Rights (ICCPR) (1966), ratified by Namibia, defines the term 'elections' as providing the right and opportunity '[t]o vote and to be elected at genuine periodic elections which shall be by universal and equal suffrage and shall be held by secret ballot, guaranteeing the free expression of the will of the electors'. On 10 May 2007, Namibia signed, but has not yet ratified, the African Charter on Democracy, Elections and Governance (ACDEG), thus moving toward further committing the country to universal suffrage: 'State parties shall recognise popular participation through universal suffrage as the inalienable right of the people' (Chapter 4, Article 4).

Universal suffrage is strongly dependent upon the accuracy and credibility of the voters' list. Ideally, the creation of a voters' list must be a public and transparent exercise. The rules must be established early in the election cycle, allowing for a voter to lodge a complaint against the preliminary voters' list in time, and the process must be finished in good time prior to the election date. The right to vote should not be established on the election day. Including eligible people only on the list is not the only concern; avoiding replication is equally important. Maintaining the list in such a way as to exclude duplicates, and to make sure that deceased people are deleted, is a time-consuming and cumbersome task for election authorities in most countries. In Namibia, the upkeep of the voters' list by the Electoral Commission of Namibia (ECN) has been a reason for much criticism in recent elections, with the Director of Elections admitting before the 2009 general and presidential elections that the ECN did not have an accurate and reliable voters' roll. This is evidenced by the fact that, in the weeks prior to these elections, at least four versions of the voters' roll were released to political parties, the last one on the afternoon before the elections, with the number of voters varying from just over 820 000 to 1.3 million, depending on the version accessed (IPPR Election Watch n.d.f). The state of the voters' roll was one of the central issues prompting a number of political parties to approach the High Court in order to have the relevant election results set aside.

One of the arguments by the ECN for why it is so difficult to service the voters' roll on a continuous basis is that it does not regularly receive updates on the death register from the Ministry of Home Affairs. In 2004, when the ECN received a large donation of computers for staff to compile an electronic database of the voters' roll, it was proposed that the Ministry of Home Affairs might be electronically linked to the ECN and make such information available. This has not happened, however, and the problem remains unresolved.

Secrecy of the vote means that each voter should have the opportunity to cast his or her vote in private without any interference from others. This entails making an informed choice (genuine elections) between parties and candidates, marking the ballot in secrecy and casting it into the ballot box. This process has been established in international law, is supported by election practice and is regarded as a crucial norm of customary international law. The Electoral Act (1992) requires the ECN to safeguard and take active measures to ensure that all votes are cast in total secrecy and are not visible to anyone. While provision is made in the Electoral Act (Article 84(1)) to assist blind and illiterate voters, and voters with a disability that may prevent them from casting their vote on their own, such help is to be provided by polling officers rather than by a person of the voter's choice. Theoretically, this may compromise the secrecy of a blind or illiterate voter's ballot.

Secrecy of the vote also means that the identity of voters cannot be traced and revealed after polling, whether through direct or indirect methods. This tenet was compromised during the 2009 National and Presidential elections, when votes cast in advance at Namibian missions abroad were counted and the results made known before the elections took place. Due to the low number of voters at some missions abroad, it became relatively easy to link those persons to particular votes. For example, advance polling results in 2009 in New York showed that SWAPO had received 24 out of 49 votes, while the RDP had received 22 and other parties three. These results led to calls by the SWAPO Youth League for the recall of Namibia's Ambassador to the United Nations in New York, who was accused of being a 'hibernator' (a pejorative term used to describe government officials not supportive of SWAPO).

The 2008 Afrobarometer survey found that 38% of respondents did not believe that their vote was totally secret, when asked about how likely it was that powerful people would be able to find out how persons had voted (IPPR 2009a), with 29% of respondents stating it was 'somewhat likely' and 9% that it was 'very likely'. This result may also have been the result of some party-political mobilisers telling unsophisticated voters that they could, through 'machines in the sky', see whom they had voted for. This finding may be exacerbated in subsequent opinion surveys of this nature due to, amongst others, the introduction shortly after 2009 polling of so-called verification centres in each constituency where results of all the polling stations in that area were to be verified. This is a clear violation of Section 25(5) of the Electoral Amendment Act of 2009, which states that the only place where re-counting of votes is authorised is at the polling station itself. No recounting of ballots was to be allowed at the verification centres.

The verification centres were established under a shroud of secrecy, with observers and party agents having no prior knowledge of their establishment. Enquiries to certain presiding officers about their location were met with reluctance to disclose their whereabouts. It emerged that one of the polling stations in each constituency was designated as a verification centre under the authority of the relevant returning officer for that constituency. However, while at no stage are ballot boxes and ballots to be handled without the presence of party agents, security personnel and observers in terms of the law, this provision was clearly violated at many centres.[2]

15. *To what extent do citizens believe that their electoral system reflects the will of the people? How much does the electoral system impact on representivity?* (5)

National elections and elections for local authorities are conducted using the system of proportional representation, whereby party representation is proportional to its share of the vote. Candidates are generally not elected to party lists through primary elections within parties. A party's listed candidates are selected by the party with little input from the public; hence the accountability of an elected leader to a specific constituency is compromised. Apart from this, the process of selecting candidates within political parties is just as important, perhaps even more crucial, for ensuring inclusivity than the type of electoral system employed at national level (Molokomme 2000). Ideally, political parties should use internal vetting procedures for selecting candidates seeking political office, with those not surviving such a process at the party level being ineligible. Such selection procedures within parties should be inclusive, transparent and democratic, which, in the case of Namibian political parties, are most often not.

With regard to gender, the National Assembly is not representative of Namibian society, despite having signed and ratified the Africa Union Protocol on the Rights of Women in Africa and the SADC Protocol on Gender and Development. Both mandate the achievement of 50/50 gender balance by 2015. At independence in 1990, the proportion of women in the National Assembly was 8%. Currently, 24% of members of the National Assembly, and 27% of members of the National Council are women. SWAPO has 20.8% women's representation and the RDP 12.5%. The Democratic Turnhalle Alliance, United Democratic Front, National Unity Democratic Organisation, All People's Party, Republican Party, Congress of Democrats and the South West Africa National Union have no women in parliament.

Fifteen of the women in parliament are from SWAPO, with five being cabinet ministers and four deputies. Only two women MPs represent opposition parties. The deputy speaker is a woman and cabinet representation of women stands at 22.7%.

As the Local Authorities Act of 1992 requires that a minimum of 30% of candidates on every party list for local elections must be women, gender representativeness at this level is generally higher with 45% of local authority councillors being women.

Regional council members in Namibia are elected by plurality in single-member constituency elections, a system that has generally led to a severe under-representation of women in southern Africa (Tonchi & Shifotoka 2005). Political parties have been accused of not nominating more women as candidates for regional elections, where the first-past-the-post electoral system is used, out of fear that voters would prefer to vote for male candidates. In 1998, only 6% of regional councillors were women. In 2004 this figure rose to 12.2%, while in 2009, the figure rose to 18%.

Nonetheless, according to the 2008 Afrobarometer survey, when asked to what extent elections ensure that representatives to the National Assembly reflect the views of voters, 53% of respondents indicated that MP's reflect the views of voters 'well' or 'very well'.

EQUAL VOTES

16. Do the votes of all electors carry equal weight?   (7)

17. To what extent do citizens believe that they have equal influence?   (7)

In Namibian terms, equal suffrage means 'one person, one ballot', requiring that the weight of the vote should be the same, independent of where in the country the voter cast his or her vote. The contribution by each voter towards a seat in an elected body should be the same, no matter where the vote is cast.

In the elections for the National Assembly, as well as the presidential election, the size of the constituencies does not matter, as the whole country is regarded as one single constituency and the members, as well as the president, are elected through a party-list system. This is also the case during local authority elections, when all voters in a local authority area belong to one electoral entity.

It is only for elections to the regional council, when the first–past–the–post system is used, that the size of the constituencies plays an important role.

Namibia is divided into 13 regions, which are delineated geographically[3] by a Delimitation Commission. This body is constituted on a temporary basis and exists only for the period of its mandate; upon completion of its task, it is dissolved. In Namibia, the Delimitation Commission may be appointed by the president at intervals of not less than six and not more than 12 years. Currently, each region in Namibia is divided into between six and 12 constituencies, depending on the number of registered voters, in order to ensure that the number of eligible voters residing in the various constituencies falling in the same region is as equal as is reasonably practicable.[4]

In a number of areas, however, there is an imbalance between the numbers of voters per constituency, which in turn has caused an imbalance in the weight of votes from different parts of the country. While there is no substantial evidence to support the accusation, one common criticism voiced is that the Delimitation Commission intentionally created borders that disadvantaged some parties.

Nevertheless, citizens appear to be generally positive about the influence of their votes.

The 2006 Afrobarometer survey found that 77% of respondents felt that the previous election of 2004 had been 'free and fair'. In the 2008 survey this had risen to over 80% (IPPR Election Watch n.d.a).

OPEN COMPETITION

18. Is there equal opportunity for all groups who wish to organise and stand for office? Does social grouping make a difference?   (6)

19. Are all political parties able to campaign free of threat?   (5)

20. Are all citizens free to form opinions, voice them, persuade others and vote, as they like, free of threat?   (6)

The Namibian Constitution protects the freedom of political activity in Article 17, which includes the right to peaceful political activity intended to influence the composition of government, the right to form and join political parties, to be elected to public office and to participate in the conduct of public affairs. The 2008 Afrobarometer survey found that 88% of respondents felt that they were 'somewhat free' or 'completely free' to join any political organisation, while two-thirds of respondents agreed that Namibians should be able to join any organisation, whether or not the government approved of it. Some 91% indicated that they were free to choose who to vote for without being pressured. Fundamental freedoms to give credence to these rights are enshrined in Article 21 of the Constitution, which also includes the freedom of speech. It is mainly through the private print media that citizens are able to voice their opinions freely. A dedicated page of the local daily, *The Namibian*, serves as a platform through which readers' opinions as communicated per SMS. The Namibian Broadcasting Corporation (NBC), the country's public broadcaster, announced in August 2011 that it would reintroduce call-in programmes that enabled listeners to air their views on the issues of the day on the 10 different language services. These shows had been abolished in the run-up to the 2009 national and presidential elections, after complaints regarding abuse by callers had been received.

All political parties have signed an electoral Code of Conduct that provides for the free participation of parties, candidates and citizens in the political processes. It also forbids intimidation and incitement to violence. However, in the run-up to the 2009 national and presidential elections, human rights monitors and the media reported several incidents involving political violence and intolerance with increasing regularity. For example, local human rights organisation NamRights reported that, on at least two occasions, former President Sam Nujoma had reportedly threatened foreigners, Europeans, whites, Jews, Germans and certain churches, as well as opposition parties. According to media reports, Nujoma threatened that 'those who do not [co-operate with us] can pack and go or they will face bullets in their heads' (NamRights 2009). Nujoma's words contravene the electoral Code of Conduct for political parties, as well as the Racial Discrimination Prohibition Act of 1991 and the Namibian Constitution. While the Code of Conduct for political parties' states that: 'Speakers at political rallies may not use language which incites violence in any form against any other person or group of persons', in effect, it is nothing but a 'gentlemen's agreement', because it is not part of the Electoral Act. Apart from this, no action has ever been taken against politicians or members of political parties who violate the Code of Conduct.

Certain regions were effectively declared 'no-go areas' for some parties and violence was used to prevent members of the opposition campaigning in such areas, in contravention of Chapter 3 of the Namibian Constitution, which provides for protection of fundamental rights and freedoms, including political activity.

21. How effective a range of choice does the electoral and party system allow the voters? Is there an open competition of ideas and policies? (6)

Free and fair elections, based on free competition between different political parties, lay the foundation for democratic rule. If the voting electorate is not satisfied with the ruling party/ies' governance, it must be able to change rulers through the electoral process, using its vote in open and free elections.

Namibia has not had an alternation of power between political parties since independence. The former liberation movement SWAPO has not only uninterruptedly ruled Namibia, but also has been able to increasingly dominate and control the parliamentary decision-making process, while opposition parties are weakened by internal quarrelling, splintering, re-establishment and reshuffling (Hunter 2005), and offer few policy alternatives to the governing party. However, political commentators generally agree that policy issues are not usually the deciding factor during election campaigns; rather, factors such as personality and ethnicity influence voting. Furthermore, in Namibia, co-opting communities, particularly by drawing traditional leaders into patronage systems, has been a relatively effective method of attracting voters (Maletzky 2004). In fact, in the run-up to the 2009 elections, only eight of the 14 registered parties had published their election manifestos one month before the election, with some containing only few details and generalised promises around various issues.

Election rules

22. *To what extent are voter registration procedures independent of control by government or individual political parties? (6)*

23. *To what extent are election procedures independent of control by government or individual political parties? (5)*

24. *To what extent are the advantages of incumbency regulated to prevent abuse in the conduct and contesting of elections? (3)*

The ECN is, by way of the Electoral Act (24 of 1992) as amended, empowered to (1) supervise and control the registration of voters for the purpose of any election; (2) supervise the preparing, publication and maintenance of a national voters' register and local authority voters' register; (3) supervise and control the registration of political parties; and (4) supervise and control the conduct of elections.

None of the 2009 election observation missions pointed out any substantive irregularities relating to the registration of voters, with the exception of the National Society for Human Rights (now NamRights) who alleged that some Angolans along the Namibia-Angola border had been registered in order to bolster the support base of the ruling party in that area. However, the organisation provided no evidence to substantiate this claim. NamRights also alleged multiple registrations of ruling-party supporters – a claim that was dismissed by the ECN. Such cases, according to the ECN, were related to instances where people had lost their voter registration cards and were thus merely being issued with duplicates as provided for by the law.

However, the seemingly ineffective and inaccurate non-maintenance of the voters' roll by the ECN eventually led to three different versions being made available before the 2009 elections. It contained names of some very prominent persons who had passed away. According to analysts it was difficult to judge whether this had been due to sheer incompetence, or if this 'incompetence' was part of the system. It is striking, however, how long this problem has been allowed to drag on, despite numerous previous initiatives to correct it. This seems to suggest that the ECN has no sense of urgency in addressing the situation.[5]

In this regard, a problematic practice remains the registration of voters who possess no valid identification document. In such cases, a voter may be listed if a registered voter confirms the identity and nationality of the voter to be registered by way of a sworn statement. Implemented shortly after independence to accommodate voters who had not yet received identity documents, this practice has been continued 21 years after independence. It has been criticised widely because of the possibilities it provides to register non-eligible voters and because one-third of all voters are still registered by way of sworn statements.

The issue of incumbency advantage is a grey area in many democracies (IPPR Election Watch n.d.) and, in Namibia, there are no specific laws regulating party use of State resources. The distinction between ruling party, government and State becomes blurred with statements made by political leaders to the effect that SWAPO is the government. Claims that the ruling party is misusing State resources for political party gain are common and opposition parties complain that they are effectively competing against the State when they participate in elections.

Certainly the ruling party has resources at its disposal and is able to use these to its advantage – for example, in the run-up to the 2009 elections, when 4x4 vehicles were given to traditional leaders. A discerning electorate would know that it is the taxpayers of this country, rather than SWAPO, who footed this bill.

Control over the State media contributes to the incumbency advantage. An analysis of television news coverage of the NBC by the Institute for Public Policy Research (IPPR) shortly before the 2009 elections found that, over a period of three weeks, SWAPO received 82%, 83% and 70% share of news coverage. The analysis also found that it became increasingly difficult to distinguish between some government events and SWAPO rallies: 'There were two events covered on television news in the week under review which appeared to concern the launch of government projects, but speakers wore SWAPO colours and in one instance urged the public attending the event to vote for SWAPO' (IPPR 2009b).

The presidential office provides certain advantages and privileges to the incumbent presidential candidate that its challengers are unable to match, such as official transport to visit constituencies, often under the guise of government business. Apart from this, allegations by members of the public were levelled at certain regional governors who were said to have convened meetings during official working hours under the pretext of voter education, but who were, in effect, demonstrating to residents how to vote for the ruling party.

The issue of public funding of political parties, from which the incumbent party draws the most benefit, is unregulated and will be elaborated upon later in this chapter.

25. *To what extent are voters able to register and to what extent have they*
    registered to vote?   *(7)*

26. *Are election procedures free from abuse? And to what extent do citizens*
    see election procedures as free from abuse?   *(5)*

The basic principle at the core of a voters' register is 'one person, one ballot'. It lists all
eligible voters in a country and is a crucial element in ensuring and maintaining electoral credibility, integrity and legitimacy (IPPR Election Watch n.d.e). By maintaining
a reliable and accurate voters' register, the electoral management body recognises and
respects citizens who are eligible to vote. The voters' register is also a database of all
people who have voted in previous elections and can be used to monitor voting trends
and track citizen participation, as well as reflect public confidence in electoral processes.

In Namibia, the responsibility for compiling and maintaining the voters' roll lies with
the ECN. The Electoral Act (1992) of Namibia makes provision for three types of
voter registration:

- General Voter Registration, which has to take place 'at intervals of not more
  than 10 years' (Section 15). The last general voters' registration was in 2003;
- Supplementary Voter Registration, which takes place during a limited period
  before any proclaimed election or by-election (Section 28); and
- Continuous Voter Registration, for which the Act provides detailed stipulations
  (Section 28A).

For presidential, national assembly and regional council elections, an applicant is
required to register as a voter in the constituency in which he or she resides, and for
local authority elections in the local authority area in which he or she has resided for
more than 12 consecutive months, subject to Article 111(3) of the Namibian Constitution.

Voter registration and voting processes are voluntary. However, employers and persons
in charge of or accommodating any registered voter, are compelled by law to enable
such voter to cast his or her vote in any election for which that voter is registered
(Section 20 of the Electoral Amendment Act, No. 7of 2009).

An applicant aspiring to be registered as a voter must be a Namibian citizen, be 18 years
of age, be able to identify him/herself and must provide proof of having been resident in
the local authority area where he or she applies to be registered as a voter.

In the absence of an identity document, the prospective voter may register by having
two other registered voters, who know the applicant, confirm the applicant's identity
under oath. Presently, about one-third of voters are registered through this method,

raising suspicions about the possibility of abuse in registering non-eligible voters. While the Ministry of Home Affairs is responsible for issuing identity cards to all Namibians, the system is problematic and less than satisfactory.

The voters' roll has become the target of much criticism over the last 10 years, with the ECN being challenged on a number of occasions about its accuracy. An inaccurate voters' register makes it far more likely that some voters might possess more than one voter's card and increases the likelihood of fraud and vote rigging. Apart from minimising voter deception, an accurate voters' register increases citizens' confidence in the credibility of the electoral process and confers legitimacy on it.

In the run-up to the 2009 elections there were at least four different versions of the voters' roll. One, issued to the parties two days before the election, contained the names of 822 344 voters. If this one had been correct, then the eventual turn out of some 810,000 votes was extremely, if not impossibly high. However, the ECN maintains that the official voters' roll was the one published in the *Government Gazette* on 9 November 2009. That register contained the names of 1 181 803 voters (IPPR Election Watch n.d.g). This caused confusion and brought the voters' roll into disrepute. The question arises as to whether this was a deliberate attempt to make it difficult for parties and observers to track down vote rigging, or whether it was due to incompetence on the part of the ECN?

While concerns about the extremely high number of voters registered during the supplementary registration period were explained away by the ECN as having included duplicate voter cards, the sudden removal of many thousands of names after the publication of the preliminary voters' roll, as well as the absence of a number of voters who registered during continuous voter registration, went unanswered.

Many voters with valid registration cards did not appear on the voters' roll, while others, who had reportedly died months and even years before, were still present. In fact, the checking and updating has been so ineffective that the opposition parties were able to claim that 92 000 dead people and 58 000 duplicate names appeared on the voters' register released just before the 2009 election. If true, this would demonstrate that the voters' register was, indeed, highly inaccurate.

VOTER INFORMATION

27. *How much information is conveyed to voters by the official election information system?* (3)

Voter education in Namibia is generally carried out by non-governmental organisations (NGOs), the media, political parties and the ECN. However, the joint Namibia

Non-Governmental Organisations Forum (NANGOF) Trust and the Southern African Development Community–Council of Non-Governmental Organisations (SADC–CNGO) observer mission of the 2009 Presidential and National Elections specifically accused the ECN of not providing critical information to voters, but rather entertaining the nation with radio jingles about their own freeness and fairness. The election dates were announced very late (4 September 2009) by the ECN and not by the Head of State, as required by Section 50(1)(b) of the Electoral Act, No. 24 of 1992 as amended. In fact, the lawful announcement of the election dates by the president was only gazetted on 30 September 2009.

Urgently needed information on the elections, for example what constituted a spoilt ballot, the function of the Central Election Results Centre (CERC), the counting and verification process of ballots, tendered voting, and the ECN structures at constituency level, was not forthcoming.[6]

While the Electoral Amendment Act (2009) makes provision for the registration of organisations and persons conducting voter education to be registered with the ECN, requests by the Namibia Institute for Democracy (NID) to be registered as such have been unsuccessful. The ECN indicated that no practical provisions were in place yet for such registration.

28. *How much information about political parties and candidates is conveyed by the news media? And how fairly is this done?* (7)

29. *How much access do political parties have to the media and how equitable is this?* (6)

30. *To what extent do the campaigns of political parties reach all sections of society?* (6)

One key argument for having a free and vibrant media in a democracy states that citizens have a right to be informed about matters impacting on their daily lives. The media remains one of the most frequently used tools to educate ordinary citizens about political matters and choices. In young democracies, the media is also considered a tool for educating the citizenry about their polity; what is consists of, what its functions are and what its impact is. It is through the media that citizens learn about new institutions, policies and legislation (Keulder 2006).

The Namibian Electoral Act makes no provisions for the availability of free media time to parties participating in an election. Media coverage of elections in Namibia has been severely criticised for being event- and personality-driven and for not focusing on the issues affecting the electorate. Coverage of Namibian election campaigns often revolves around politicians making speeches at rallies and party functions, while very little reportage is provided on pressing social issues such as poverty, unemployment, HIV/Aids, and the promises made to alleviate them over the years by the same politicians.

This 'shallow' coverage is regarded by politicians as a means to elevate themselves in public consciousness, knowing that whatever they say will be published or broadcast with little interrogation of their credentials and fitness to hold public office (IPPR Election Watch n.d.d).

It is especially the State-owned media and the public broadcaster, the NBC, that are often the target of criticism and accusations of bias in favour of the majority party. Whereas registered parties enjoyed free airtime in the run-up to previous elections, this was abolished prior to the 2009 national and presidential elections, due to the inability to agree on a formula for determining airtime allocations. According to an IPPR survey of television coverage of the 2009 elections, it had become difficult to distinguish between some government events and rallies of the ruling party (IPPR 2009b).

Radio seems to be used most often to obtain information, with 71% of respondents of the 2008 Afrobarometer survey indicating that they listen to the news every day. In addition, while survey results indicate that 80% of respondents never use the Internet and 71% never use a computer, social media as a source of political information may still be largely untapped as access to social media through mobile phones has been made more accessible since 2008. Some 64% of respondents in the 2008 Afrobarometer survey indicated that they use mobile phones every day. Although some political parties with the odd Facebook profile have attempted to distribute information through these channels, they have not been used to maximum potential and remain the exception.

31. Do voters know enough about all political parties to be able to make an informed choice? (5)

Of the 14 political parties registered to contest the 2009 national elections, only eight had published their election manifestos one month ahead of the election date. The manifestos contained few concrete policy-related details and consisted mainly of generalised promises, with no information as to how policies would be funded. This leaves such documents open to the allegation that they are not much more than a rather unrealistic wish list, rather than a properly researched set of policy alternatives. Another problem with such manifestos is that they are often not accessible to large parts of the population, seeing that they are not distributed widely, they are only in English, and they are not available on websites (if the party has a website) (IPPR Election Watch 2009).

ELECTORAL PARTICIPATION

32. How extensively do citizens participate in elections?   *(7)*

*33. How are citizens able to influence the electoral process in ways other
   than the vote?*   *(7)*

In Namibia, elections have become a part of the political routine. Voter turnout in
national and presidential elections has traditionally been high since independence, with
participation in elections for regional and local authorities generally being lower.

Table 1: Summary of voter turnout at elections since 1989		
Year	Election	Turnout
1989	Constituent Assembly	97%
1992	Local Authority	82%
1992	Regional Council	81%
1994	National Assembly	76%
1994	Presidential	76%
1998	Local Authority	34%
1998	Regional Council	40%
1999	National Assembly	61%
1999	Presidential	61%
2003	Local Authority	44%
2004	National Assembly	85%
2004	Presidential	85%
2004	Regional Council	55%
2009	National Assembly	69%[7]
2009	Presidential	69%
2010	Local and Regional	38%

The low turnout in the 2010 elections has been attributed to voter fatigue and the fact
that the legal case in which the result of the 2009 national elections was disputed, has
not been adjudicated. However, lower voter turnout could also indicate growing apathy
about politics in Namibia, particularly among younger sections of the population. The
2008 Afrobarometer survey of 1 200 Namibians with a margin of error of 3%, found
that 33% of the 18–24 age group interviewed said they were 'not at all' interested in
public affairs. Of all respondents interviewed, 59% said they were either somewhat

or very interested. The remaining 41% said they were not at all interested or not very interested in public affairs (IPPR Election Watch n.d.c). A summary of Afrobarometer indicators from five surveys between 1999 and 2008 concluded: 'Commitment to elections as the best means for selecting leaders declined by nearly 30 per cent between 2002 and 2008' (IPPR 2009a).

Both governance and the law-making process in Namibia have an institutional dimension that creates space for involvement by its citizens. The Constitution provides for public participation and calls for the facilitation of such a process. This is enshrined in Chapter 11 on Principles of State Policy, Chapter 7 on the National Assembly, Chapter 8 on the National Council and Chapter 12 on Regional and Local Government. It is a process that extends beyond granting the right to vote, and advocates the adoption of strategies and practices that would make public participation and consultation an ongoing feature of the policy-making and legislative processes.

These constitutional provisions seek to ensure that such processes are transparent, effective and accountable to the people of Namibia. Government has acknowledged the critical role of civil society in the development and reconstruction of the country. As a result, a policy of partnership in development has been pursued and civil society organisations have been invited to participate as partners in the formulation and implementation of national policies and programmes. Public hearings by parliament, as well as consultations organised by government Ministries and Constituency Development Committees, are some of the avenues available to civil society.

Given these opportunities for public participation, the levels of engagement should be high. However, despite the efforts of the government in establishing these channels of interaction with civil society, they are generally not being fully utilised; since independence, civil society's input into national development policies and legislation has been negligible. While some civil society actors may not have the relevant knowledge about such means of interaction with government, overall, civil society has demonstrated organisational and operational weaknesses, making it difficult for them to provide meaningful input into proposed policies and laws.

It should be noted, however, that the level of participation of organised civic interest groups has also been influenced by other factors, including the prevailing political culture. Therefore, any analysis of the obstacles to such engagement would be incomplete without an assessment of the limitations of government mechanisms in facilitating public involvement, as well as historical and cultural factors.

The speed and complexity of the legislative and policy-making process, compounded by the transformative nature of Namibia in terms of policies and legislation that seek to correct the inequalities of the past, would mean that there should be a high volume of legislation and policies to be considered. Such speedy law-making processes may result in a short cycle that would mitigate against public participation. In practice, however, there is little opportunity for public participation since the number of bills presented to parliament is comparatively low compared to other countries and is, in fact, declining, even though a number of Acts dating from the pre-independence period, which may contain unconstitutional provisions, remain on the statute books. When public hearings are held, they are primarily conducted in urban areas rather than in rural communities. Generally, short notice of public hearings gives the public very little time to prepare substantive submissions to appropriate committees and structures. Publicity around hearings is often poor and assumes the presence of a highly literate population, whereas, in fact, people are often confused by the complexity of the process, technical jargon and the volume of information. Policy usually originates in government ministries where experts draw up the relevant legislation to address policy issues and problems that a particular Ministry encounters. While in theory it is possible for the public to participate at this level, in practice the complexity and technical nature of the processes diminishes the likelihood of such involvement.

The issue of language also poses a challenge for public participation. Although the public is allowed to attend parliamentary proceedings, as well as meetings of regional councils and local authorities, legislative and policy information is often only available in English. This makes the entire process inaccessible in many ways, as those who do not have English skills are disadvantaged. The better organised and resourced groups in society dominate the process, thus reinforcing inequality.

This uneven distribution of capacity is a major hindrance to meaningful public participation in the legislative and policy-making process as both courses of action are highly dependent on an understanding of the rules that guide them and the opportunities for intervention that exist. In general, communities in Namibia have an inadequate comprehension of their roles as citizens and this affects their capacity to proactively engage with those responsible for law and policy making. While parliamentarians and ministerial officials benefit from the services of legal advisors in the development of policy and legislation, the public is not afforded the same privilege and relevant information is not evenly available.

Critical comments by members of the public on government social policies and their implementation have, at times, been handled in an intimidating manner by politicians, undermining some aspects of civil and political contextual freedoms, and leading to a growing culture of self-censorship by members of the public. Much of this has resulted in Namibia's history as a highly divided society in terms of race and ethnicity, a civil society fragmented along a rural-urban divide, and uneven experiences, resources and capacity around engaging on issues of governance and public policy.

In addition, citizens often do not fully understand the structure and functions of committees in parliament and Constituency Development Committees at a local level, or how to use them to make inputs into the legislative and policy-making process. The rules of engagement and the means to participate are not explicit, there is no standardised procedure for civil society organisations to approach committees in order to raise issues of concern, and committees seem to lack adequate links with communities to receive submissions related to ministerial implementation of legislation and the performance of officials. Where a proposition is made by those who are clear about the rules of the process, feedback is limited and this discourages future participation, while inculcating disillusionment and apathy within civil society.

Consequently, in practice, citizens' engagement with elected leaders on policy matters is generally low. The 2008 Afrobarometer survey established that 96% of respondents stated they had not contacted a member of the National Assembly in the previous year, while 94% of respondents had not been in touch with a National Council member. Some 83% of respondents had had no contact with a local councillor, while 7% had not been in touch with a regional councillor (IPPR Election Watch n.d.b).

PROGRESS AND DEMOCRACY

34. *To what extent is the management and control of the elections delegated to an independent body?* (6)

The ECN was established through an Act of Parliament in order to conduct elections in Namibia. The activities of the ECN are governed by the Electoral Act (No. 24 of 1992) as amended, which gives the Commission the exclusive right to direct, supervise and control in a fair and impartial manner any elections under the Act, including elections for the National Assembly, presidential, regional and local authorities. This body is empowered to: (1) supervise and control the registration of voters for the purpose of any election; (2) supervise the preparing, publication and to maintain a national voters' register and local authority voters' register; (3) supervise and control the registration of political parties; and (4) supervise and control the conduct of elections.

The ECN consists of five members appointed by the president after an application and interview process that is open to the public. After public hearings, a selection committee submits a list of at least eight candidates to the president, from which five commissioners are appointed. Although the term of office is five years, reappointment is possible provided the same procedures are followed at the end of their term of office. The Chair of the Commission is elected from among the five members.

On paper, the present commission selection process appears sound and transparent.

However, in the final instance, the president alone selects the five members and questions about loyalty and possible bias may arise. The involvement of the public in the selection process is relatively limited.

To manage the day-to-day work, a Directorate of Elections has been established. It functions as the secretarial agency of the Commission and is 'responsible for the administrative and clerical work involved in the performance of the functions of the Commission'.[8] The president appoints the director of elections. The director is the executive officer and the permanent secretary of the Commission, making him or her an ex officio member of the ECN without voting rights. He or she works under the authority of and reports to the Commission. Currently, the ECN reports to the speaker of the National Assembly and to the president, not to a member of the Cabinet. This has some obvious disadvantages as the ECN does not report to an assigned minister who would be responsible for the Commission's budget and defending it in the National Assembly.

While the final selection of election commissioners and the appointment of the director of elections by the president raises serious doubts regarding the independence of this election management body to conduct voter registration and election processes among political commentators, a total of 63% of respondents in the 2008 Afrobarometer survey indicated that they trust the ECN 'somewhat' or 'a lot'.

35. Are there mechanisms for the review of the electoral system and are these open to citizen participation? (8)

The Namibian Constitution provides an enabling legal foundation and favourable conditions for free and fair political activity. However, the Electoral Act (No. 24 of 1992) as amended contains numerous weaknesses and omissions, which need to be addressed as a matter of urgency in order to close gaps for possible abuse, chaos and confusion. The extremely late tabling of the Electoral Amendment Act (No. 7 of 2009), only three months before the last set of elections, did not allow for meaningful input from stakeholders.

There is general consensus that the Namibian Electoral Act of 1992, which has subsequently been amended nine times, is outdated and needs to be replaced. Concerns about election practices in Namibia are found in the following areas:
- compilation and maintenance of the voters' roll;
- registration by sworn statements (affidavits);
- the tendered ballot system (a voter voting outside his or her constituency);
- administrative and logistical deficiencies in the organisation of the elections;
- polling and counting procedures;

- the current verification procedure of ballots;
- independence and management capacity of the ECN;
- political finance; and
- absence of an independent election tribunal/court.

A review of the electoral legislative framework would provide an enabling environment for civil society to play an important role in supporting the law reform process. NID, one of the most established NGOs working on democracy and governance issues in Namibia, has initiated an electoral law reform process in partnership with the Law Reform and Development Commission (LRDC), a division of the Ministry of Justice. A series of public hearings, meetings and workshops with electoral stakeholders is to be held to obtain input into new electoral legislation. It is envisaged that this joint initiative will result in a draft electoral bill to be handed over to government during 2012.

ELECTORAL OUTCOMES

36. *Are the announced election results congruent with how the electorate actually cast their ballots?* (8)

37. *Do citizens believe that their vote makes a difference?* (8)

38. *Do security forces, the government and political parties accept the election results?* (6)

39. *Do citizens accept the election results?* (7)

Although the 2004 elections were pronounced free and fair by SADC–Parliamentary Forum observers, a number of incidents and alleged irregularities were registered by opposition parties and the ECN was taken to court. A recount was ordered and conducted, with the initial result ultimately being upheld by the courts. The opposition parties did not file an appeal, citing financial constraints. Simultaneously, the 2008 Afrobarometer survey found that 81% of respondents perceived the 2004 elections to have been completely free and fair, or free and fair with minor problems.

The 2009 national and presidential elections again caused controversy; observers and opposition parties claimed that the conduct of the elections fell short of international standards of transparency, freedom and fairness, as well as those outlined in the Principles for Election Management, Monitoring and Observation (PEMMO) in the SADC. Problems cited included the performance of the ECN; the late introduction of amendments to the Electoral Act; problems with the voters' roll; and short-notice changes to the system of counting and verifying of ballots, exacerbated by the large number of tendered ballots. The late announcement of the results, and disregard of some provisions contained in election legislation, point to institutional and systematic deficiencies that need to be addressed lest future elections are conducted in the same manner.

Subsequently, nine opposition parties[9] filed an urgent application in the Windhoek High Court to challenge the election results. The opposition's attempt to have the High Court order a new ballot or at least a recount of the November presidential and National Assembly votes was dismissed on a technicality, but referred back to the High Court on appeal to the Supreme Court.

The case was, however, again dismissed in the High Court in February 2011, with the ruling that affidavits and evidence supplied by the complainants in the case were insufficient to prove that the integrity of the elections was destroyed through fraud. However, the High Court expressed its concern regarding the ability of the ECN and its director to organise elections. The opposition parties again appealed the verdict based on the fact that additional submissions by the complainants were disregarded by the High Court. The Supreme Court heard the appeal during October 2011 but judgement was reserved.

40. How closely does the composition of the legislatures and the selection of government reflect the election outcome? (8)

41. How far do the legislatures reflect the social composition of the electorate? To what extent are women represented in parliament? (4)

The composition of the legislature reflects the election outcome relatively closely due to the system of proportional representation used in national elections. To what extent candidates on party lists reflect the social demographics of the electorate is, however, up to the political parties, as the public has relatively little control over the placement of candidates on party lists.

The Namibian Constitution (1992, Article 10) provides for formal equality before the law for men and women. Although the Constitution does not mandate quotas to ensure the adequate representation of women in elective bodies, it has created a framework that recognises the marginalisation and discrimination women have experienced, and allows for measures that redress these substantive inequalities.

As a result, the Local Authorities Act (No. 23 of 1992) mandates that 50% of candidates on lists submitted by political parties for local government elections, which are conducted on a proportional representation basis, be women (Tonchi & Shifotoka 2005). Apart from this legal requirement, the advancement of women's representation is dependent on the adoption and implementation of voluntary quotas by the political parties.

The general lack of obligation is borne out by the relatively slow progress that has been made with regard to women's representation in parliament over the years. In the 1989 Constituent Assembly, elected by proportional representation prior to the adoption of quotas by political parties, women formed only 6.9% of the body. In 1999, the proportion of women elected to the National Assembly rose to 25% and remained at this level after the 2004 election, before declining to 22.2% after the 2009 election. Namibia compares poorly with Mozambique (35.6% in 2004) and South Africa (43% in 2009), where proportional representation and voluntary quotas by dominant ruling parties have been combined.

One of the reasons for this state of affairs lies in the attitude of the parties towards the inclusion of women on proportional representation lists where quotas are not mandatory. As the Electoral Institute for Sustainable Democracy in Africa (EISA) observation mission report on the 2004 elections remarked: 'The mission regrets the fact that although the parties had more than 30 per cent women candidates in their lists, women were placed too low on the lists, which resulted in Namibia failing to achieve the minimum 30 per cent target after the elections' (EISA 2010).

In an effort to remedy the situation, there have been various initiatives by civil society to advocate for an increase in the proportion of women in governing structures at all levels in Namibia. Sister Namibia launched a national 50/50 campaign for women's political empowerment and leadership in 1999 based on the *Namibian Women's Manifesto*, developed in partnership with other organisations, and ran the campaign up to the 2004 elections at all three levels of government. The campaign also called for so-called 'zebra style' party lists, alternating male and female candidates. These efforts have, however, met with resistance from all parties.

FUNDING ELECTIONS

42. *To what extent are private donations to political parties permitted and are they subject to regulation (such as transparency and limits), in order to prevent them from having a disproportionate impact on voter choice and electoral outcome?*   *(3)*

43. *Is campaign finance – both income and expenditure – regulated? Are political parties regulated by accepted procedures and non-partisan*

bodies? How extensive is the independent oversight of election expenditure? (1)

44. Is there public financing of political parties? (5)

Political party finance is addressed in the Electoral Act (No. 24 of 1992), but the Act merely deals with the issue of foreign funding of political parties and states that any such funding must be publicly disclosed. While the Act does not outline the methods for this admission, it makes provision for a fine not exceeding N$12 000 or imprisonment for a period not exceeding three years, or both, in the event of a political party being found guilty of non-disclosure. There are no statutory provisions dealing with private domestic donations to parties.

Since 1997, following a Cabinet decision from the previous year, public funds have been distributed annually to political parties represented in the National Assembly through an allocation formula based on the proportion of votes each party received in the most recent National Assembly elections. The total amount of money distributed is set at 0.2% of government revenues. As a result, about N$200 million of government revenue has been disbursed to political parties over the last decade (Links 2010). The funds are intended to help the parties run their legislative offices, and for general political and organisational work. The support is supposed to help ensure the survival of multiparty democracy and to prevent an over-reliance on foreign aid (Boer 2004).

Political parties are not obliged by law to keep or produce any complete and comprehensive audited financial accounts, or to disclose any such accounts to any authority or agency of the State that is tasked with monitoring and regulating political party finances in Namibia. Consequently, none of the country's political parties have ever released such financial records, not even to their own memberships, since independence. Although sporadic calls have been made from various quarters, including the Auditor-General, to bring political party finances within the regulatory ambit of the Office of the Auditor-General, the body that audits all agencies and departments receiving money from the State revenue fund, there have been no moves to change the situation.

While reluctance to change also exists in parties that argue for transparency and accountability when it comes to government expenditure, but are less than accountable concerning their own use of public funds, the issue has been taken up by civil society. A joint study by the IPPR and NID has recommended strengthening the legislative framework to make political party finance in Namibia more visible and accountable, by including laws to specifically deal with the issue of monitoring and regulating such processes, as well as addressing other governance issues within political parties. Stakeholders have been requested to provide inputs on the issue as part of the electoral law reform project being conducted jointly by the LRDC and NID.

CONCLUSION

While Namibia has just completed an election cycle, with national and presidential elections in 2009 and elections for regional and local authorities in 2010, criticism of the implementation of the 2009 elections and the resultant ongoing legal proceedings suggest that the system is flawed and in need of urgent and deep review and reform. The overall score of 5.9 suggests that, as far as elections and democracy is concerned, the situation in Namibia is stable but unsatisfactory.

Although most formal components of a functioning electoral system are in place, there are substantial deficiencies. These are mainly due to shortcomings in the operational procedures implemented by the ECN, as well as outdated procedures incorporated in electoral legislation and a lack of organisational and institutional capacity. The potential fall in trust engendered by these failings seems to contribute to a growing apathy towards public affairs, especially among younger voters, and a growing lack of confidence in the electoral system by the citizenry.

Some 21 years after independence, many components and characteristics of the electoral system and its implementation, which may have been relevant and practical shortly after independence, are presently proving to be outdated or redundant. If the unintended consequences of policy and legislative choices made two decades ago are not addressed, the long-term political health of the country and its democratic prospects might well be compromised.

The need for a comprehensive overhaul of the electoral system in Namibia is underpinned by the fact that current electoral legislation has not kept up with international best practices, a fact that is presently being addressed through efforts at the SADC level, where a best-practice model containing standard characteristics that should be part of any electoral system in the region is being designed.

In Namibia, there is general recognition of the need for extensive electoral law reform. In this regard, NID has embarked on a joint electoral law reform programme, in partnership with the LRDC. A planned series of countrywide consultative workshops with stakeholders will provide the basis for drafting recommendations for electoral law reform, for interacting on these with government, and the subsequent drafting of an electoral bill to be presented to government for tabling in parliament.

Namibia needs to demonstrate that it is not only going through the motions as far as democracy is concerned, but also that the system is substantially responsive to its citizens. The proposed collaborative electoral law reform process is an important first step towards meeting this objective.

SECTION SCORE: 6

REFERENCES

AFROBAROMETER. Briefing papers and working papers, various [online]. Available: http://www. afrobarometer.org.

BOER, M. 2004. *The life of the party: The hidden role of money in Namibian politics*, IPPR Briefing Paper No. 33, September 2004. Windhoek: IPPR.

EISA. 2010. *Election Observer Mission Report No. 34*. Electoral Institute for Sustainable Democracy in Africa (EISA).

HUNTER, J. 2005. *Spot the difference: Namibia's political parties compared*. Windhoek: NID.

IPPR. 2009a. *Summary of results: Round 4 Afrobarometer survey in Namibia*. Windhoek: IPPR. Available: http://www.ippr.org.na.

___ 2009b. TV broadcasting coverage of the 2009 elections: Week 3. 24 November 2009.

IPPR ELECTION WATCH. n.d.a *Faith in democracy deepens* [online]. Available: http://www. electionwatch.org.na/node/19.

___ n.d.b *In power but not in touch?* [online]. Available: http://www.electionwatch.org.na/node/72.

___ n.d.c *Engaged or apathetic?* [online]. Available: http://www.electionwatch.org.na/node/101.

___ n.d.d *Who gets to speak?* [online]. Available: http://www.electionwatch.org.na/node/107.

___ n.d.e *One person, one ballot* [online]. Available: http://www.electionwatch.org.na/node/164.

___ n.d.f *The tendered vote controversy, again* [online]. Available: http://www.electionwatch.org.na/ node/368.

___ n.d.g *The issues at stake* [online]. Available: http://www.electionwatch.org.na/node/372.

___ 2009. *How to produce and effective manifesto* [online]. Available: http://www.electionwatch.org.na.

KEULDER, C. 2004. 'Namibia's dominant party system' in *Election Talk*. Electoral Institute for Sustainable Democracy in Africa (EISA).

___ 2006. Media usage and political knowledge in Namibia: A research experiment among students. Windhoek: IPPR.

LINKS, F. 2010. Transparency in political finance in Namibia. Windhoek: NID/IPPR

MALETZKY, C. 2004. 'Opposition accused of laziness, no imagination' in *The Namibian*, 15 November 2004.

MOLOKOMME, A. 2000. Building inclusiveness in SADC's democratic systems: The case of women's representation in leadership positions. Electoral Institute for Sustainable Democracy in Africa (EISA).

NAMRIGHTS. 2009. *Conflicting messages fan election violence* (press release) [online]. Available: http://www.nshr.org.na/index.php?module=News&func=display&sid=1127.

REPUBLIC OF NAMIBIA. 1990. *The Constitution of Namibia*. Windhoek: The Government of Namibia.

___ 1992. *The Electoral Act of 1992*. Windhoek: The Government of Namibia.

TONCHI, V.L. & SHIFOTOKA, A.N. 2005. 'Gender equality' in *Parties and political development in Namibia* (EISA Research Report 26). Electoral Institute for Sustainable Democracy in Africa (EISA).

ENDNOTES

1   According to the Electoral Commission of Namibia, 798 964 Namibians voted within the country and 1 050 voted at Namibian foreign missions, but the figures are being disputed, particularly because one of the many voters' rolls issued suggests close to 100% turnout. The main complaint from the opposition parties and some observers is that the voters' register was unreliable (the ECN had issued three sets of different numbers at different points in time). Initially the ECN had stated that there were 1 000 163 registered voters, after that the figure changed to 1 163 000, and eventually ended up at 1 300 500.

2   Preliminary statement by the Joint NANGOF Trust and SADC-CNGO Observer Mission (JOM) in respect of the 2009 Namibian presidential and National Assembly elections.

3   Article 102(2) of the Namibian Constitution: 'The delineation of the boundaries of the regions and Local Authorities ... shall be geographical only, without any reference to the race, colour or ethnic origin of the inhabitants of such areas.'

4   Proclamation 12 of 1990, making provision for the establishment of the first Delimitation Commission and the duties thereof.

5   'Namibia's SWAPO: Forfeiting the 'moral high ground'. Henning Melber speaks to Khadija Sharife [online]. Available: http://pambazuka.org/en/category/features/70775.

6   Preliminary statement by the Joint NANGOF Trust and SADC-CNGO Observer Mission (JOM) in respect of the 2009 Namibian presidential and National Assembly elections.

7   It is difficult to assess voter turnout due to the unreliability of the voters' register. Initially, the voters' register published by the ECN contained 1 000 163 names, then it changed to 1 163 000, and ended up at 1 300 500. Eventually, 811 143 votes were cast in the 2009 National Assembly elections, compared to 829 269 in the previous poll of 2004, which represents a decline of 2.2%.

8   Electoral Act (No. 24 of 1992) S11(1)(a). This provision should be read in conjunction with S4(1) of the Act which requires the Electoral Commission 'to direct, supervise and control in a fair and impartial manner, any election under this Act'.

9   All People's Party (APP); the Congress of Democrats (CoD); the Democratic Party of Namibia (DPN); the Democratic Turnhalle Alliance (DTA); the Namibia Democratic Movement for Change (NDMC); the National Unity Democratic Organisation (NUDO); the Rally for Democracy and Progress (RDP); the Republican Party (RP); and the United Democratic Front (UDF).

SECTION 3

ACCOUNTABILITY AND DEMOCRACY

LESLEY BLAAUW

The discourse around the 'new institutionalism' suggests that political democracy is contingent not only on socio-economic and informal conditions, but also on the design of political institutions (Koelbe 1995:231-243). It contends that accountability and democracy interlock where these institutions are geared towards the purposive initiatives of goal-oriented actors. In this context, accountable democratic governance necessitates the 'development of a system of interlocking political institutions and sets of widely shared political values' (Neiryinck & Southall 2003:3-10). In the case of governments, institutional effectiveness refers to the ability of such a government to fulfil its functions and responsibilities as stated in the Constitution, among other instruments, Therefore, from a governmental perspective, effectiveness is contingent upon the checks and balances within government institutions. More specifically, the existence of institutional effectiveness is related to the way different elected and appointed agencies are perceived to have performed or are performing their duties. Accountability and democracy are intimately related because different institutions check and are answerable to each other.

Political accountability in this context refers to 'a relationship between two sets of persons or (more often) organisations, in which the former agree to keep the latter informed, to offer them explanations for decisions made, and to submit to any predetermined sanctions that they may impose' (Schmitter 2004:47-60). This suggests a generic conceptualisation of political accountability premised on a symbiotic relationship between political office bearers and citizens, characterised by mutual responsibilities and potential sanctions. Political accountability plays a critical role in the prevention and redress of the abuse of political power, and needs to be institutionalised for it to be effective. Thus, the proposition here is that 'political accountability must be institutionalised if it is to work effectively. This means that it has to be embedded in a mutually understood and pre-established set of rules' (Ibid.:48). The establishment of institutions tasked with holding political office bearers accountable provides the framework for government to set the rules, and for ordinary citizens to exercise checks and oversight and place institutional limitations on the exercise of power by those elected to political office.

The above presupposes that accountability and democracy are mutually reinforcing, since both play crucial roles in the prevention and redress of the abuse of political power. Accountability in the aforementioned context also performs a dual function. Andrea Schedler posits that 'the notion of political accountability carries two basic connotations: answerability, the obligation of public officials to inform about and to explain what they are doing; and enforcement, the capacity of accounting agencies to impose sanctions on power-holders who have violated their public duties and responsibilities' (Schedler 1999:13-28). The establishment of institutions responsible for ensuring compliance with predetermined rules refer to a particular element of accountability: horizontal accountability. Horizontal accountability refers to 'the existence of State agencies that are legally enabled and empowered, and willing and able, to take actions that span from routine oversight to the imposition of criminal sanctions or impeachment in relation to actions or omission by other agents or agencies of the State that may be qualified as unlawful' (O'Donnel 1999:29-51).

The primary objective of this chapter on Namibian democracy is to ascertain to what extent the institutions established to monitor performance have fulfilled their mandate. In particular, we need to ascertain to what extent the principle of separation of powers is vigorously adhered to. Furthermore, this section sets out to determine how successful political institutions are in effecting these principles, what mechanisms are in place to deal with possible transgressions, and how citizens perceive the responsiveness of government to any demands for accountability. Towards this end, the chapter will look at executive accountability, legislative oversight and judicial independence. Public participation in, amongst others, the budgeting process and access to information viewed as central to measuring government accountability in Namibia, will also be reviewed. Lastly, a number of topics, such as the independence to formulate economic policy and the accessibility of Members of Parliament (MPs) to ordinary citizens will form part of this analysis.

EXECUTIVE ACCOUNTABILITY, LEGISLATIVE OVERSIGHT AND JUDICIAL INDEPENDENCE

45. *How far is the executive subject to the rule of law and transparent rules of government in the use of its powers? To what extent are all public officials subject to the rule of law and to transparent rules in the performance of their functions?*   *(5)*

The Constitution of Namibia in Article 1(3) provides for the separation of powers among the executive, the legislature and the judiciary (Republic of Namibia 1990). This suggests that, in theory, the proper functioning of each branch of government demands the consent of the other to give effect to the notion of checks and balances based on the separation of equal powers. The Constitution also sets out the particular functions to be performed by each of these branches, and the manner in which these roles are circumscribed through adherence to the rule of law.

The executive is tasked with the primary function of performing the daily tasks and activities of the State on behalf of its citizens. Article 27(2) of the Constitution makes allowance for an executive presidency, with the president acting as both head of state and head of government. The extensive powers of the president are prescribed in Article 32.[1] As they are wide-ranging, André du Pisani and William Lindeke have concluded that Namibia essentially has a presidential system of government (Du Pisani & Lindeke 2009a). This reinforces the perception that, while the powers of each branch of government are clearly demarcated in the Constitution, evidence suggests that the executive is the dominant branch of government. Apart from this, the president is required by the Constitution to choose the prime minister and other members of Cabinet from the highest legislative body in Namibia, the National Assembly, as well as appoint six non-voting MPs. The political consequences of the above result in the executive, in particular the presidency, having significant influence over the legislative branch of government. The fact that 60% of members of the executive are derived from the legislature suggests a 'further limiting parliamentary control and diluting the division of powers' (Bertelsmann Stiftung 2010). In addition to the extensive powers that the presidency enjoys, it also commands a great deal of deferential respect from the general populace. For instance, consecutive Afrobarometer surveys indicate the high levels of trust that citizens have in the president: 81% in 2008 and 80% in 2006 (Little & Logan 2009). In the words of Gerhard Erasmus: '… the office of the president is generally held in high esteem and may, ironically, even be "above politics" in the eyes of many' (Erasmus 2010). In part, this may be explained by the leading roles that both the founding president and the present incumbent played in Namibia's long liberation struggle. It was this unquestioned status, coupled with the control that the presidency has over other branches of government, that led to the amendment of the Constitution to enable former President Nujoma to run for a third term of office in 2004. This initiative had been preceded by an extraordinary Congress of the South West African People's Organisation (SWAPO), during which the party's constitution was changed to allow him to serve an additional term in office.

While the above suggests that the legislature might not have sufficient powers to hold the executive answerable, the former may, indeed, invoke constitutional principles to ensure such accountability. For example:

> Parliament possesses some notable controls over the executive. Members of the Cabinet are required to attend meetings of the National Assembly and to be available for the purpose of any queries and debates on the legitimacy, wisdom and effectiveness of government policies. It also has the power to receive reports on the activities of the executive … and to require any senior official … to appear before any of its committees to account for and explain his or her acts and programmes. In addition, the president is obliged to report on government policies during the annual budget debate, and to be available to respond to questions … on the budget and other issues of national concern … Cabinet ministers are individually, as well as collectively, responsible to Parliament … (Good 1997)

Other mechanisms at the disposal of the legislature to check the executive are the constitutional provisions that entitle the National Assembly to monitor executive excesses in general and presidential preponderance in particular. For example, according to Article 32 of the Constitution, the legislature can debate and advise the president on any matter which he or she is authorised to deal with by the Constitution. In addition to the aforementioned, 'the president of the Republic of Namibia is elected by direct universal suffrage, and requires not merely a simple majority, but 50 per cent or more of the votes cast. In addition … executive power in Namibia is vested in the president and the Cabinet, and the former is obliged to act in consultation with the latter' (Ibid.).

While the role of the Auditor-General, who is appointed by the president on the recommendation of the Public Service Commission and approved by the National Assembly, is to report around issues of unauthorised expenditure to parliament on an annual basis and to point out areas in need of improvement, the Office of the Auditor-General has little power to rectify and enforce issues contained in the annual reports. Apart from this, the ability of the legislature to effectively hold the executive accountable is undermined by the party list system, in terms of which members of the National Assembly are elected. Monica Koep asserts that '… in Namibia, the separation of powers is compromised as, in practice, legislative power has been subsumed by executive power. This is due to an electoral system in which most MPs are primarily accountable to their parties rather than the electorate, and the facts that the ruling party holds an overwhelming majority in parliament and that a high proportion of the ruling party's MPs serve in the executive' (Koep 2010).

46. *How extensive and effective are the legislature's power to scrutinise the executive, hold it to account, initiate and scrutinise as well as amend legislation between elections? Is the legislature able to hold the executive to account for the implementation of legislation and policy?* (5)

Namibia has a bicameral system of parliament, consisting of a National Assembly, which has sovereign legislative power, subject to the Constitution, and a National Council, which in terms of Articles 63(1) and 74(1)(a) of the Constitution, is a house of review. The National Assembly has a maximum number of 72 voting members, elected by general, direct and secret ballot according to a proportional representation party list system. Their tenure of office is a maximum of five years. The president may appoint up to six additional non-voting MPs. Apart from its representative and oversight roles, the primary function of the National Assembly is law making.

The National Council is the second chamber and comprises 26 elected members, two from each of Namibia's 13 geographic regions. While the National Council has no legislative power of its own, it may, however, advise the National Assembly by proposing laws and reviewing legislation. If the National Council objects to the principle of any bill, the National Assembly must reconsider the bill, which will then lapse, unless two-thirds of the members of the National Assembly agree to it. Both the Speaker of the Assembly and the chairman of the Council are required to be non-partisan in controlling the deliberations of the members of their chambers.

Efforts have been made to increase the effectiveness of the legislature to scrutinise the executive. André du Pisani and William Lindeke point out that:

> … provisions have been made, following reform proposals in 1996, to make the committees of parliament stronger and more active. A major limitation of the committees is the small number of opposition and backbench members, which stretches their duties thinly across several committees. Combined with a small and minimally skilled staff, these committees have not added quality to the legislative process as had been hoped. The most important committee is that of Public Accounts, which is chaired by an opposition party member (thus far a very skilled and respected one). This committee review reports from the auditor general on spending by various government ministries, parastatals, and lower level governments.

Their hearings are frequently covered by both the electronic and print media and feature more professional and non-partisan performances. It only has powers to make recommendations, however. (Du Pisani & Lindeke 2009a)

Although parliamentary committees have the constitutional powers to request officials from a government office, Ministry, or agency to appear before it, in order to account for their activities, these means are not always effectively employed. In terms of procedure, the committees may invite the Permanent Secretary or Minister to explain the activities of a particular Ministry, agency or State-owned enterprise, and launch an enquiry based on concerns raised by stakeholders and the public about such entities. The verdict on legislative oversight seems to be that 'although some MPS play a constructive and critical role in the legislative process, the role of legislature as an equal branch of Parliament and oversight organ vis-à-vis the executive is not always fully utilised. As a result, executive-legislative relations became tangled' (Koep 2010). Examples of such executive overreach include the decision to send troops to the Democratic Republic of Congo without the full approval of the legislature, and the reluctance of the founding and current presidents to release the findings of various Commissions of Inquiry.

Therefore, given the dominance of the executive over the legislature, it remains doubtful whether the legislature is able to competently fulfil its oversight function and be accountable to ordinary citizens. The fact that members of the executive are also MPs, and that the executive is appointed by the president, compromises their role as legislators. Moreover, the weaknesses of the fragmented opposition parties, both in terms of numbers and capacity, contributes towards the lack of effectiveness of the legislature to hold the executive accountable. Simply put, the de jure constitutional powers of the legislature are not optimised by parliamentarians.

47. To what extent has the legislative and executive power been devolved and what impact has this had on popular control? (4)

The Namibian Constitution states that Namibia is a unitary state. Article 1 of the Constitution defines the country as a sovereign, secular, democratic republic. State authority, we are reminded, is vested in the people, who 'shall exercise their sovereignty through the democratic institutions of the State' (Articles 1, 2). From this reading, the practice of democracy is underpinned by the supremacy of the Constitution, judicial review and enforceable human rights (Erasmus 2010). However, the Namibian Constitution also makes provision for the devolution of power to lower tiers of governance.

Namibia is divided into 13 regional and 107 local units, which are governed by elected local councils. Local authorities range from those which are independent and autonomous, to those which are fully dependent on the central government. The Constitution does not refer to the degree of autonomy for local authorities, nor to any powers to be allocated to and exercised by such bodies (Tötemeyer 2010:108–145). In addition, the National Council 'has no formal law-making function, while its powers of review are limited and can be overruled by the National Assembly' (NID 2010). The Constitution further stipulates that:

> ... *every organ of regional and local government shall have a council as the principal governing body, freely elected in accordance with the Constitution and subsequent Acts of Parliament. Such body will then be entrusted with executive and administrative powers to carry out all lawful resolutions and policies of such council, subject to the Constitution and any other relevant laws.* (Ibid.)

Regional and local authorities fall under the authority of the Ministry of Regional and Local Government and Housing, and, as such, remain responsible to that Ministry for all their actions. Although the legislative framework for decentralisation has been laid, ministries have been reluctant to allow any meaningful process of decentralisation to take root. This not only creates an accountability deficit in respect of real checks and the real power relations within and between institutions, but also contributes towards a lack of accountability by legislators to the general public.

The devolution of authority to lower tiers of government has faced a number of challenges that include a lack of designated funds, as well as regional, economic and social discrepancies. In addition, these lower tiers of governance face a scarcity of trained and well-equipped officials at sub-national governmental level, a lack of necessary infrastructure and other imperfections (Tötemeyer 2010:108–145). As a result, very little real power or accountability has been devolved to the lower tiers of government. In fact, the devolution of accountability was regarded as an administrative rather than a political decision (Geingob 2010). Despite these obstacles, local governing structures in Namibia are perceived to be playing an important grassroots transmission role, by serving as a State-society connecting agency on behalf of Namibia's predominantly rural areas (Forrest 1998). This view is reflected in recent Afrobarometer survey results, which reveal that more than half (55%) of the interviewees see local government as playing the role referred to above (Little & Logan 2009). Nevertheless, it would seem that regional and local government, as well as traditional authorities, are regarded as political tools to strengthen the hold of central government over the Namibian body politic, rather than as a means by which central government shares political decision-making and authority. In fact, the decision by the president in 2010 to appoint regional governors and special advisors serves to strengthen the perception that government controls sub-national structures and continues to hold centralised power in Namibia.

48. How independent are the judiciary and the courts from the executive and from all kinds of interference?   *(5)*

In Namibia, the judiciary as the repository of judicial power consists of a Supreme Court, a High Court and Lower Courts. In terms of the Constitution, High Court has the power to interpret the Constitution and adjudicate on matters between individuals, and between individuals and the State. The judiciary is empowered to review the constitutionality of executive acts and the legislature. Article 78(1) vests judicial powers in the courts of Namibia, whose independence is guaranteed constitutionally under Article 78(2), subject only to the Constitution and the law. This independence is further affirmed under Article 78(3) which declares that 'no member of the cabinet or the legislature or any other person shall interfere with judges or judicial officers in the exercise of their functions, and all organs of the State shall accord such assistance as the courts may require to protect their independence, dignity and effectiveness, subject to the terms of this Constitution or any other law' (Republic of Namibia 1990).

In general, respect for the functions of the judiciary is borne out in a recent study by Peter Von Doepp. He concluded that judges in both the Supreme and High Courts have, on a number of occasions, ruled against government on cases considered to be politically sensitive.[2] The appointment of judges to chair Commissions of Inquiry to investigate, among others, the abuse of political office and allegations of corruption (Bertelsmann Stiftung 2010), points to the high regard that the judiciary enjoys in Namibia. While the outcomes of these investigations and inquiries were usually accepted by political office bearers in the past, three recent rulings by the courts have led to the public articulation of frustration by politicians. The first of such cases ruled against the Ministry of Labour and Social Welfare and in favour of Africa Personnel Services in 2009 (Du Pisani 2010). This case had been brought before the court to prevent Africa Personnel Services, a labour hire company, from continuing this practice. The second ruling concerned the recount of election results in the same year (Blaauw 2010:128-140) – a case which had been brought before the court by a number of opposition parties. Thirdly, more recent pronouncements made by the Minister of Trade and Industry, Hage Geingob, that the judiciary is not a 'holy cow', following a ruling in favour of Walmart, points to the fact that the notion of the legal supremacy of the courts faces serious challenges (Vries 2011). This type of remark may be particularly detrimental and prejudicial to foreign judges on whom the country presently relies. A shortage of funding has also become a serious concern for the judiciary, as it has led to a backlog of cases, which, in turn, casts serious doubts on the effectiveness of the judiciary and the strength of the rule of law.

In addition, legislative changes to broaden the pool from which judicial candidates are recommended by the Judicial Service Commission and made by the president, have increased the likelihood of appointments that are not necessarily based primarily on merit, indicating that the government, even though it accepts the notion of judicial independence in principle, and adheres to court rulings, uses whatever direct and indirect means it has available to exercise its rights to exert influence over the judiciary. Despite these challenges, ordinary citizens still have faith in the judiciary to uphold the rule of law. The 2008 Afrobarometer survey results reveal that 74% of those interviewed trust this institution to fulfil its functions and duties effectively (Little & Logan 2009).

PUBLIC PARTICIPATION AND ACCOUNTABILITY

49. *How open, accessible, extensive and systematic are the procedures/ mechanisms for public consultation and participation on legislation and policy-making? How equal is the access which interest groups/citizens have to influence the law-making process?* (4)

50. *How open, accessible, extensive and systematic are the procedures/ mechanisms for public consultation and participation on executive policy? And how equal is the access which citizens have to influence executive policy?* (4)

51. *How far does government cooperate with relevant partners, associations and communities in forming and carrying out policies and how far are people able to participate in these processes?* (4)

Article 25(1) of the Namibian Constitution guarantees the right of ordinary citizens to not only participate in political activity, but also to hold those accountable that seek to infringe on this right, meaning in Henning Melber's words that 'the Namibian Constitution enshrined a concept that seeks to integrate and secure fundamental freedoms – also for those not represented in the echelons of political power – and keeps them protected from any abusive interference by those elected' (Melber 2010). Citizens' participation in the legislative process is provided through parliamentary committees that offer greater accountability by making the policy and administrative functions of government more transparent. Participation in standing committees ensures that MPs are directly involved in providing oversight of the policy-making process, are engaged in forums for investigations into matters of public importance, provides them with the opportunity to enhance their knowledge of such issues, and enables parliament to make inputs on policy decisions, thereby enhancing the democratic process. Through public hearings, conducted by committees, citizens have the opportunity to feed into this process. However, as there is no automatic referral of bills to committees, and, therefore, no automatic scrutiny and opening up to public input through such hearings, this participatory mechanism is not optimised.

When civil society has attempted to make submissions on issues of public importance or national interest, even when they were broad-based and well-researched, such inputs have not always been taken into account or incorporated into pending legislation. A recent example was the passing of the Statistics Bill by the National Assembly without consultation, and subsequent public hearings by the National Council, whose suggested amendments were disregarded. This casts doubt on parliament's commitment towards a process of consultation that involves all stakeholders.[3] Through regional and local authorities, as well as traditional leaders, citizens also have recourse to sub-national structures. While mention has already been made about the reluctance of central government to devolve real authority to the regional and local structures, traditional authorities in Namibia, arguably, influence a large part of the population. In response to the question about how much trust they have in traditional authorities, approximately 70% indicated that they have a great deal of respect for them (Little & Logan 2009), meaning that they function as significant political institutions, especially in the rural areas.

With regards to the degree of success that people have in communicating their concerns to MPs, the outcome of the 2008 Afrobarometer survey is instructive. On the likelihood of organising communities and lobbying MPs on matters of concern to the public, 53% of respondents were of the opinion that this would not be likely at all, whereas 40% indicated that raising their concerns with MPs would somewhat be likely or 'very likely'. These views found resonance in both urban and rural areas, despite the difference in information and communication between these two areas (NID 2010). There was general scepticism that, even when stakeholder meetings to discuss draft policies were held, the views of ordinary citizens were not accommodated in the final legislation. The African Media Barometer (2009) states that 'people feel that these meetings are fake, that nothing will result from them anyway, because government does not take note of outside input and therefore they are not meaningful'. This perception implies a huge accountability deficit.

In terms of parliamentary procedure, members of the public may attend sittings of the National Assembly and the National Council. Moreover, civil society and individuals are free to make representations at public hearings organised by the standing committees at parliament and others locations throughout the country, the purpose of which is to give ordinary citizens the opportunity to comment on draft legislation and other issues of national importance that might be referred to a committee (Hopwood 2007). In theory, review of legislation in Namibia takes place after wide-ranging consultation with stakeholders. However, in practise the general public is not consulted sufficiently on executive policy, as 'only one of eighteen legislations was reviewed in committees in Namibia on average' (NID 2010:14). Not surprisingly, therefore, when questioned on whether elected officials listen to their concerns, the respondents replied as follows: 45% maintain that they are often listened to, whereas the majority asserts that they are never or only sometimes listened to (Ibid.:10-11). This suggests and reinforces the perception that elected officials are more accountable and loyal to the executive than to ordinary citizens.

Chapter 3 of the Namibian Constitution provides scope for the full participation of ordinary citizens in policy formulation. As such, there is sufficient opportunity for civil society and individuals to compel government to become more accountable in both the policy formulation phase, as well as the execution of these policies. Indeed, there have been some notable cases in which non-governmental organisations (NGOs) have not only participated in policy making, but also were at the forefront of such a process. The Legal Assistance Centre (LAC) has been particularly successful on this front and was instrumental in contributing towards the formulation of the Married Persons Equality Act, the Combating of Rape Bill, regulations for the Combating of Domestic Violence Bill, the Children's Maintenance Act, and the National AIDS Policy (NID 2010:14).

Another area in which government not only cooperates with partners, but also allows ordinary citizens to participate actively in the process of implementing policy relates to the environmental sector. A NID paper points out that, with regard to natural resources and environmental conservation, civil society is an important partner in designing and implementing sustainable development initiatives. In community-based natural resource management (CBNRM) sector, the CBNRM Association of Namibia (CAN), a joint project of the Ministry of Environment and Tourism and CRNRM NGOs, has been set up to mobilise and support conservancies. In the environmental sector, a large number of organisations provide technical advice, legal representation and training to communities (Ibid.:17).

While public participation and accountability remain essential elements in a democracy, and while instances of public participation do occur, the policy and law-making process in Namibia is not generally characterised by a spirit of cooperation and open consultation. Instead, these two processes largely remain the prerogative of the executive.

LAW-MAKING AND THE BUDGET PROCESS

52. How extensive are the powers of legislative bodies, and how effective are they at legislating? (4)

In Article 44, the Constitution states that 'the legislative power of Namibia shall be vested in the National Assembly with the power to pass laws with the assent of the president as provided in this Constitution subject, where applicable, to the powers and functions of the National Council as set out in this Constitution' (Republic of Namibia 1990:29). While this Article suggests that debates about law making and the enactment thereof reside with this body, the dominance of the ruling party means that 'since independence, the cabinet (ministers and deputy ministers) have constituted an absolute majority of the National Assembly, and dominate the chamber in a way that undermines the separation of executive and legislative authorities. This means that laws and policy are made in the secrecy of cabinet meetings, and then defended and passed on the floor of the National Assembly' (Du Pisani & Lindeke 2009a:20). More-over, it also means that 'executive dominance of parliament has been nearly complete, making "separation of powers" and "checks and balances" effectively meaningless' (Du Pisani & Lindeke 2009b:1-22). Apart from this, the relative weakness of the opposition means that, in effect, accountability from the highest legislative organ in Namibia means accountability to the party and president, and not to the people of the country.

The second legislative body in Namibia, the National Council also derives its legislative powers from the Namibian Constitution and serves as a house of review, with the powers to consider bills referred to it by the National Assembly and to report on them (apart from recommending legislation on matters of regional concern). While the National Council has rejected a number of bills referred to it by the National Assembly, it has hitherto not introduced any legislation. André du Pisani and William Lindeke succinctly capture this subordinate role of the National Council by pointing out that 'The National Council has become nearly a one-party rubber stamp since the 2004 elections' (Ibid.:15). The reluctance of MPs to exercise their prerogatives and rights, either due to a lack of appreciation of the need for democratic checks and balances, or a misunderstood sense of loyalty to the party leadership that put them in position, further undermines accountability.

By and large, the ineffectiveness of the National Council in the legislative process has important implications for not only entrenching a system of non-accountability in Namibia, but also has ramifications for the consolidation of democracy and local governance.

53. How rigorous are the procedures for parliamentary approval, supervision of an input into the budget and public expenditure?   (4)

Article 63 of the Namibian Constitution gives the National Assembly the power 'to approve budgets for the effective government and administration of the country'. It furthermore enables parliament 'to provide for revenue and taxation'. In addition to these two provisions, Chapter 16 of the Constitution, which deals with finance, explicitly outlines the role to be played by the National Assembly in the budgetary process. Article 126 states that 'The Minister in charge of the Department of Finance shall, at least once every year and thereafter at such interim stages as may be necessary, present for the consideration of the National Assembly estimates of revenue, expenditure and income for the prospective financial year.' The National Assembly, in turn, 'shall consider such estimates and pass pursuant thereto such appropriation Acts as are in its opinion necessary to meet the financial requirements of the State from time to time' (Republic of Namibia 1990).

Notwithstanding the above, there seems to be a lack of oversight and very little input by parliament on public expenditure in general and the budget in particular.

As stated by Du Pisani and Lindeke (2009a:20), 'the budget debates have never altered a single cent of revenue or expenditure and are more of a political opportunity for opposition parties to raise issues to score political points. Obviously, these budget "debates" last longer in election years.' Recent events reinforced this scepticism, when the introduction of an amendment to the Appropriation Bill for 2011/12 to cater for an increase in the salaries of civil service, led to the conclusion that 'The suddenness with which the amendment was foisted without warning on the legislature and the public underlined the fact that the State's budgeting was firmly controlled by the executive and that outside of Cabinet very few have a say in the final compilation of the budget and prioritisation of expenditure areas' (IPPR 2011a).

While the Standing Committee on Public Accounts, chaired by a member of the opposition, has carried out its mandate with regard to public expenditure in a relatively rigorous and proactive manner over the years, and the Auditor-General of Namibia provides audits on all agencies and departments receiving money from the State revenue fund (Transparency International 2010), thus far, no accounting officer has ever been fired as a result of the mismanagement, misappropriation or overspending of funds.

In general, one might state that parliamentary oversight in terms of the budget and public expenditure is minimal, as the 'National budget is a done deal by the time it reaches parliament and that the legislature effectively plays very little, if any, role in the design of the Appropriation Bill' (Ibid.).

Not surprisingly, the *Open Budget Index 2008* provided the country a score of 47% out of an overall score of 100 for public participation and institutional accountability (International Budget Partnership 2008).

54. *How much say does the public have in the development of the budget? How well do parliamentary procedures allow the public to participate in decisions relating to resource allocation?* (3)

There is no legal stipulation that enables the public to have a direct input into the development of the budget. However, the nature of the Namibian Constitution implies that the social contract that governs relations between the State and civil society demands continuous engagement between these two actors. While the public is generally invited to share their views on any bill before it is passed, the Minister of Finance specifically invites the public, in particular the private sector and academics, to comment on the budget only after it has been tabled. These discussions provide 'a good opportunity for the public and private sector to exchange ideas, identify challenges that remain and raise points of concern' (Schade 2010). In addition to this, the government provides the public with some information on the central government's budget and financial activities during the course of the budget year. However, relevant information and comparative figures are not easily available and it is difficult to track spending, revenue collection and borrowing for any specific year, to plot longer-term trends or to assess budget performance for specific sectors. As mentioned above, the *Open Budget Index 2008* gives Namibia a score of 47% on transparency and, by extension, accountability (International Budget Partnership 2008). To address this shortcoming, the legislature should seek to play a more proactive role in the pre-budget period, should demand regular updates on public expenditure from government ministries, and become more assertive at demanding accountability from the executive.

ACCESS TO INFORMATION

55. *How independent and accessible is public information about govern-ment policies and actions and their effects? How comprehensive and effective is legislation giving citizens the right of access to government information?* (5)

Currently in Namibia, there is no access to information Act or bill. While the Office of the Ombudsman is tasked, in terms of Article 91(a) of the Constitution, to 'investigate complaints concerning alleged or apparent instances of violations of fundamental rights and freedoms' (Blaauw 2009), the African Media Barometer (2009:10) concludes that there is a sense that what the Ombudsman says is not respected by the executive branch of government. In part, this can be explained by the fact that the Ombudsman's functions and its stature is countered by the fact that the office reports to the Ministry of Justice.

Although the Constitution of Namibia guarantees freedom of expression and speech, which includes freedom of the press, under Article 21(1), the same Constitution also circumscribes these rights. For instance, Article 21(2) states:

> *The fundamental freedoms referred to in Sub-Article (1) hereof shall be exercised subject to the law of Namibia, in so far as such law imposes reasonable restrictions on the exercise of the rights and freedoms conferred by the said Sub-Article, which are necessary in a demo-cratic society and are required in the interests of the sovereignty and integrity of Namibia, national security, public order, decency or morality, or in relation to contempt of court, defamation or incitement to an offence.* (Ibid.)

Notwithstanding these provisions, the general public does have access, albeit limited and selective, to information about government policies through certain official websites, private and public radio, and through newspapers, both government-owned and independent of government. In Namibia, the independent media has thus far played a crucial role in keeping the general populace informed about the operations of government.[4] In addition to the privately-owned media outlets, a government-owned newspaper, *New Era*, often features articles that are critical of government, a role that is appreciated by ordinary citizens. On the question of whether the news media should constantly investigate and report on corruption and mistakes made by government, 66% cent of respondents answered in the affirmative. The important role played by the media in Namibia is also highlighted by the African Media Barometer. In 2009 it gave Namibia a 3 out of 5 ranking for its regulatory framework, which actively promotes the freedom of expression, including media freedom.

The national public broadcaster, the Namibian Broadcasting Corporation (NBC), which controls television and radio, generally reports favourably on government policies and decisions. This bias towards the SWAPO-led government is borne out by incidents such as the sacking of the then Director-General of the national broadcaster in February 2009 (Bertelsmann Stiftung 2010) due to his being viewed as sympathetic to the opposition, Rally for Democracy and Progress Party, as well as objections raised by opposition parties with regard to elections-related allocations of air time and pro-SWAPO reporting. For example, in the run-up to the 2009 elections, the National Unity Democratic Organisation (NUDO) branded the NBC, 'SWAPO Broadcasting Corporation' (African Media Barometer 2009:7). Such perceptions are reflected in other quarters, including an Institute for Public Policy Research (IPPR) study in which it was concluded that, in Namibia, 'a culture of openness has yet to take hold within and between the State and broader society' (IPPR 2011b). It seems that government does not regard itself as having to be responsive to the needs of the population or fully accountable to the citizenry.

In fact, it might be stated that what we have in Namibia is a 'continued centralisation of what should be national and public information at senior executive level within government, a state of affairs which often leads to suspicion of manipulating data or of the total blotting out of embarrassing, if not dangerously profligate, incidences of mismanagement and alleged corruption by senior politically appointed officials' (Ibid.). While the government has been responsive to calls for accountability by primarily the independent media, by launching enquiries into allegations of corruption, the finding of these different commissions remain beyond the public domain.[5] While recent interventions by the IPPR, the LAC and NANGOF compelled government to address the issues highlighted by these organisations on the Statistics Bill,[6] in general we may conclude that 'Namibia does not, however, have any right or access to information laws and as such a claim of entitlement to information of any nature cannot be made ...' (IPPR 2011c). This obviously has serious implications for the evolution of a culture of accountability in Namibia.

ACCESSIBILITY AND INDEPENDENCE

56. How accessible are elected representatives to members of the public? What impact does the electoral and party system have on the way in which MPs represent people? (5)

Constitutional provisions dictate that elected officials govern in concert and with the consent of the people. Article 61 of the Constitution states that 'all meetings of the National Assembly shall be held in public and members of the public shall have access to such meetings'. To be sure, '... many MPs take their representative functions seriously through their work in various committees and outreach activities, conducting hearings and meetings in rural areas. Although reports, findings and recommendations are routinely tabled in parliament and forwarded to the relevant ministries, the feedback loop between the executive and the legislative on these suggested actions is not always very efficient' (Koep 2010:7). However, the majority of politicians do not visit their constituencies regularly.

In Namibia, election to the National Assembly takes place in accordance with the proportional representation system. In general, key features of this system weaken the bonds of accountability between elected representatives and citizens. It uses a closed party list on which candidates are selected and ranked by their parties. The electorate does not have a chance to directly elect a particular candidate as the ballot paper consists of parties' names and their symbols rather than a list of those standing for elections. This results in elected candidates owing allegiance primarily to the parties that nominated them, rather than being directly accountable to the electorate, and tends to produce political leaders who are appointed by virtue of their affiliation to their party and not because their followers trust them and put their faith in them. While membership of the National Council is theoretically more representative and accountable, as its members are elected from constituencies in their regions directly by the plurality system[7] and respondents view local councillors as being more responsive than national representatives, the lack of democracy in the country's largest political party – where a few senior leaders dominate decision making, including choosing regional candidates – results in the members of the National Council being no more representative of the electorate than their National Assembly counterparts.

57. How far are MPs protected from undue influence by outside interests? Are potential conflicts of interest regulated? (4)

Constitutional provisions assure ethical government and the avoidance of ministerial corruption and self-aggrandisement. Article 42(1) of the Namibian Constitution states that, during their tenure of office as members of the Cabinet, Ministers may not take up any other paid employment, engage in activities inconsistent with their position as Ministers, or expose themselves to any situation which carries with it the risk of a conflict developing between their interests as Ministers and their private interests – including being a member of a board of directors, owning shares and other activities that might represent such a conflict. The Privileges and Immunities Act (No. 17 of 1996), which deals with the conduct of MPs, reinforces these constitutional safeguards. For instance, S22(1) asserts that 'a member shall not ... take part in any proceedings in which such a member has any interest, whether direct or indirect, which precludes him or her from performing his other functions as a member in a fair, unbiased and proper manner' (IPPR 2011c). The body responsible for oversight in this regard is the Office of the Ombudsman.

The abovementioned provisions are, however, insufficient to force compliance and ensure accountability. This is due to the fact that 'compliance is largely left to the interpretation and discretion of the MPs and members of the executive. Thus it would be difficult, if not impossible, to keep MPs and Ministers under public gaze vis-à-vis potential conflict of interest if little is known about what they actually own and what the nature of their outside interests are' (Ibid.:4). A number of incidences are illustrative of the lack of accountability on the part of MPs. The vice-president of the Democratic Turnhalle Alliance (DTA), failed to recuse himself on two occasions when there was the potential for conflict of interest. In fact, he went so far as to introduce a motion that sought to amend the Liquor Act, to enable him, as a previously disadvantaged Namibian, to obtain additional liquor licenses. On another occasion, in his capacity as a headman, he wanted the National Assembly to consider increasing the remuneration of traditional authorities. Another incident involves the current Minister in the Presidency and Attorney-General, who delivered a proposal from a particular fuel supplier to Cabinet, of which he is a member, with the expectation that the vendor would receive favourable consideration from his colleagues in government and the National Assembly. The absence of a tighter regulatory framework not only allows potential conflict of interest and personal gain to take place, but also adds to the lack of accountability from elected officials to the electorate.

Among the general population, perceptions of corruption in the legislature bear this out. To the question 'How many of the following people do you think are involved in corruption?', respondents stated that they viewed 66% of MPs as party to corrupt practices, and 19% that most/all of them were involved in corruption (Little & Logan 2009). These views of ordinary Namibians are 'illustrative of the fact that the applicable legislative framework – as encapsulated by the Privileges and Immunities Act (No.17 of 1996) and the Namibian Constitution – does not adequately circumscribe the conduct of political office bearers and thus the environment calls for a much more stringent regulatory dispensation' (IPPR 2011c:5). This represents a serious indictment of the accountability of elected officials in Namibia.

58. How effective is the separation of public office, elected and unelected, from party advantage and the personal, business and family interests of office holders? *(3)*

Constitutional provisions and other legislation provide the edifice upon which the distinction between private and personal interests should be based. However, these safeguards have proved insufficient in stemming the perception that connections to political office are often used to advantage certain people. As Bertelsmann Stiftung (2010:11) concludes:

> In Namibia, most political and bureaucratic corruption takes place in a grey zone of activity populated by politicians, holders of high office, parastatals and members of their families. The extractive industries, either through the granting of licenses for mining and fishing or through participations in international companies, offer huge opportunities for enrichment. Serious sanctions, however, are virtually never imposed, even where a commission of enquiry has found spectacular abuse of position. It is a serious weakness that many offenders go unpunished owing to political considerations dictated by ethno-social system of patronage.

Several instances can be cited to demonstrate this state of affairs. For example, with regard to a pilot sanitation project in the five northern regions in 2009/10, reports surfaced that there had been misappropriation of funds involving companies linked to the Omusati region's director of regional planning, a former senior State House employee, as well as a personal assistant to former president Sam Nujoma (IPPR 2011c). In another instance, the acting regional officer of the Caprivi was alleged to have manipulated the regional process so as to award a construction tender to the value of N$20 million to a company in which he and his wife were partners (Ibid.). Two other high-profile cases also highlight the fact that political connections and family ties at times intersect and lead to a conflict of interest. The first involves a public service commissioner who was paid a commission for facilitating the supply of scanners by a Chinese company to the Ministry of Finance. This is ironic in view of the fact that she 'is tasked with monitoring and upholding ethical conduct within the public service' (Ibid.:4). The second relates to the Government Institution Pension Fund (GIPF), where political heavyweights and the permanent secretary in the Ministry of Justice, were alleged to have acted in conflict of interest in dealings between the GIPF's Development Capital Portfolio (DCP) and the controversial Namibia Grape Company (NGC), as it is alleged that these two were instrumental in influencing the DCP decision with regards to the NGC, even though both were members of the board of GIPF (Ibid.).

This lack of accountability and the blurring between public and private interests is also discernable in the way that MPs handle the issue of the mandated disclosure of assets required by both chambers of parliament. While the disclosure of assets is an important component in the fight against corruption and inculcating a culture of accountability, thus far the 'Register of Members' Interests, the National Assembly's asset register, has only been published twice in an independent Namibia – in 2003 and 2009 respectively. In both cases, the listing of assets by senior political figures was incomplete and less than satisfactory. With regard to the National Assembly register, MPs in the Fourth Parliament, from 2005 to 2010, merely detailed what they wished and 13 MPs quite simply ignored the whole process, thereby condemning the asset disclosure exercise to farcical status' (Ibid.:5). The events outlined above not only point to a lack of accountability, but also suggest that the integrity of the governance process is seriously flawed.

59. *How effective and open to scrutiny is the control exercised by the legislature and the executive over civil servants?* (5)

The Constitution enables the legislature to exercise control over both the executive and the public service. In addition, the conduct of civil servants is guided by the Public Service Act (No. 13 of 1995), which states that 'The purpose of the declaration of remunerative work outside employment in the Public Service by staff members is to protect the interests of the Public Service by ensuring that every staff member places the whole of his/her time at the disposal of the government as well as to prevent competition between staff members and persons in the private sector and to prevent a possible conflict of interest' (Republic of Namibia 1995). Furthermore, it regulates the employment, conditions of service, appointments, discipline and discharge of public servants.

To guard against corrupt practices and to ensure accountability, the Act outlines what amounts to corruption. As regards the latter, the Act states that:

- Accepts or demands in respect of the performance of or the failure to perform his or her duties any commission, fee or rewards, pecuniary or otherwise, to which he or she is not entitled by virtue of his or her office, or fails to report forthwith to the Permanent Secretary concerned the offer of any such a commission, fee or reward.
- Uses his/her position or utilises any property of the State to promote or prejudice the interest of any private business or private agency, except in the performance of his/her official duties.
- Uses his/her position to promote or prejudice the interest of any political party.
- Misappropriates or improperly uses any property of the State (Ibid.).

In addition to the above, the Public Service Commission is expected to report to parliament at least once a year. Where the misappropriation of funds is suspected by ministries, the accounting officers are normally called upon to appear before parliamentary standing committees to explain their action. However, while these accountability mechanisms are in place, there are numerous examples of civil servants whose transgressions go undetected, unchallenged and/or unpunished.

In general, the media seem to be the most effective means of naming and shaming public servants and reporting on alleged misdemeanours.

60. How far is the influence of powerful corporations and business interests over public policy kept in check, and how free are they from involvement in corruption? (5)

The funding of political parties in Namibia would be an important prism through which to view the relationships between private corporations and the governing elite. While public funding is provided to political parties, according to a formula based on seats held in parliament, there are no legal mechanisms in place to account for how such funding is used. Neither government nor any other agency holds political parties accountable for their spending (Transparency International 2010). This situation not only promotes non-accountability, but also favours the ruling party. As a result, 'Business, international agencies and governments that wish to remain on government's good side can be influenced or self restrained' (Du Pisani & Lindeke 2009b:1-22). This, coupled with the fact that private businesses are not compelled to disclose any dealings they have with the ruling party and by extension the government, creates fertile ground for unethical behaviour.

Conflict of interest in the private sector is dealt with in the Companies Act (No. 28 of 2004). Disclosure by directors is dealt with in S245 of the same Act. However, while the regulatory framework is in place, this piece of legislation is open to criticism, as an IPPR report (2011c) points out that '... the legislation, in the form of the Companies Act, does not really go far enough, the drafters having erred on the side of broadness ... a little less circumspection and a bit more circumscribing is in order'.

61. To what extent is the public service protected from corrupt practices? To what extent are public officials protected from undue influence by outside interests? Are potential conflicts of interest regulated? (4)

While the overall regulatory framework for guarding against potential conflict of interest that may lead to corrupt practices does exist, 'political rulers have never really considered the issue and thus have never adequately and appropriately legislated for eventualities – such as conflict of interest – that arise as events and the nation go along' (Ibid.). Neither does the Anti-Corruption Act (No. 8 of 2003) make reference to conflict of interest *per se*. Two instances that show up the legislative deficit around this issue occurred recently. In the first instance, a public servant took the public service to court for failure to pay his board member fees as a member of the National Training Authority (NTA). The Labour Commissioner found that the State-Owned Enterprises Governance Act, the Public Service Act and the Vocational Education and Training

Act, were all in conflict and did not properly deal with the payment or non-payment of board fees (Smit, N. 2011), suggesting that, due to different interpretations of essentially the same law, conflict of interest may not be properly regulated. In the second case, the chairperson of the Tender Board failed to recuse himself from a tender board meeting due to the fact that the current provisions of both the State Finance Act and the Public Service Act do not clearly spell out the role of accounting officers, such as permanent secretaries, on such boards (Smit, J. n.d.).

In the absence of clear-cut regulation on possible conflicts of interest, corrupt practices may occur when civil servants take on paid work outside of the public service. An IPPR study (2011c) found that:

> For the period 1 April 2009–31 March 2010, the Public Service Commission recorded a total of 115 cases of remunerative work by civil servants outside the public service. Not surprisingly, the Ministry of Health and Social Services accounts for most cases of civil servants taking up paid work outside the public service. The lucrative nature of operating a private practice entices public health professionals to run private consultancies. For the period 2009/2010, the Ministry of Health and Social Services accounted for 32 per cent of all cases involving public servants engaged in private practice. In a recent case, it was reported that the management of the Katutura State Hospital had deteriorated considerably, thus damaging the levels of service provided to the public, because its medical superintendent, Dr Rheinhardt Gariseb, devoted a disproportionate amount of time and effort to his private practice.

Taking all of the above into consideration, it is thus not surprising that the reputation and standing of the public service is undermined by the perception that people have about its integrity. For instance, the 2008 Afrobarometer survey reveals that approximately half of the 1 200 respondents in Namibia believed that all or most national government officials were corrupt. What is most disturbing about these findings is the perception of high levels of corruption within the law enforcement sector and among tax officials, with some 42% of respondents believing that most or all police officials were corrupt and 38% regarding most or all tax officials as corrupt (Little & Logan 2009).

62. Are public servants who blow the whistle on corruption encouraged and protected? Are citizens who blow the whistle on corruption protected? (7)

While the Anti-Corruption Act does provide some form of protection to informants, this cover derives indirectly from existing laws as there is no dedicated 'whistle blower' legislation (something for which the Anti-Corruption Commission (ACC) has been advocating). In terms of this protection, during an investigation, a witness does not have to identify an informer or give any information about that person that would result in the person being identified. The only exception to this is when it becomes clear that justice cannot be done without revealing the informer's identity or if the informer has lied. In such instances, the court might continue with the proceedings in camera. The court might also prohibit the release of any information that could lead to the public knowing who the informer was. Any informer who assisted the ACC in an investigation is also protected from disciplinary, civil and criminal proceedings (IPPR 2011b).

63. *To what extent can the government carry out its responsibilities in accordance with the wishes of the citizens free of interference or constraint from political or economic forces outside of Namibia?* *(4)*

The Namibian economy is closely linked to South Africa's economy and the Namibian Dollar is pegged to the South African Rand. As a result, economic trends, including inflation, closely follow those in South Africa. Prior to the 2009 global financial crisis, Namibia had experienced steady growth, moderate inflation, limited fiscal debt, a robust mining sector, a fairly developed infrastructure, and a strong legal and regulatory environment. From 1990 to 2008, economic growth averaged 4.5% per year.

However, since the onset of the global economic crisis in 2009, demand for Namibia's commodity exports, mainly diamonds, has not only lowered, but also reduced the transfer payments the country receives due to its membership in the Southern African Customs Union (SACU). Following years of successive growth, the Namibian economy recorded a negative growth of 0.8% in 2009. Following three consecutive years of budget surpluses, the government responded to the sudden economic downturn by running a budget deficit, and fiscal deficits are expected to widen. For the next three years, the International Monetary Fund (IMF) has projected deficits of 8.1%, 7.8% and 3.8% of gross domestic product (GDP) respectively. In 2009 and 2010, public debt stood at 14.9% of GDP, well below the government's target of 25%. Nevertheless, in 2010 the economy has shown signs of a significant rebound due to government investment and rising commodity exports, and economic forecasters are now predicting a growth rate of 4.4% (World Bank 2009).

With a 2009 per capita income of US$4 542.90 the World Bank considers Namibia a middle-income country, with an economy dominated by the primary sector and mining being the major contributor to the economy. The tourism sector, which caters for and targets high-end tourists, has seen steady growth. With unemployment estimated to be around 40%, job creation remains one of the most daunting economic challenges for government. The vexing question of land redistribution remains another economic challenge. Socially, Namibia, like most of southern Africa, continues to be hard hit by the HIV/Aids crisis. It has a prevalence rate of just less than 20% of the adult population (Blaauw & Lestholo 2009). Although Namibia has sustained a noteworthy track record on economic growth and macro-economic stabilisation, and while poverty rates have declined since independence, widespread unemployment and distribution of income and assets remain significant issues. With a Gini coefficient of 0.74,

Namibia is challenged to achieve high rates of growth, create jobs, alleviate poverty, reduce inequality, and raise living standards (World Bank 2009).

Table1: Namibia country indicators (World Bank 2011)	
Total population (millions)	2.2
Population growth (annual %)	1.9
Life expectancy at birth (years)	52
Poverty headcount ratio at $2 a day (purchasing power parity)	62.20
GDP (current US$) (billions)	9.5
GDP growth (annual %)	4.4
GDP per capita (US$)	4 542.90
Inflation	4.5
Foreign direct investment, net inflows (% of GDP)	27.5 (516 million)
Unemployment, total (% of total labour force)	40
Time required to start a business (days)	66
Internet users (%) (2009)	5.87

Overall, the government is making serious efforts to promote industrial and infrastructural development, provide investment incentives to attract foreign capital and enhance the functioning of the free- market economy (through privatisation). While the Vision 2030 long-term planning project exists, goals are still vague in some sectors and consistent implementation is a challenge (Bertelsmann Stiftung 2010). Namibia's linkage to the South African economy, and the fact that it is reliant on exports of primary commodities (approximately 28% of GDP), and international price fluctuations, severely compromises the country's economic independence. Another issue that affects the country's economic autonomy is its reliance on international donors, as Namibia has received large aid flows over the last 21 years, with significant amounts continuing to be directed to education, health (HIV/Aids), water, sanitation and to address rural development.

64. *How far is the government able to influence or control those things that are most important to the lives of its people, and how well is it organised, informed and resourced to do so?*   (4)

The classification of Namibia as a middle-income country belies the profound problems it faces. Among many is the fact that health and education rankings demand huge investments, and while significant allocations by both the government and private sector have resulted in an increase in school enrolment figures, the kind and quality of education provided seems to be inadequate to cater to market needs. Not surprisingly, government has not been able to reverse a spiralling unemployment rate.[8] Moreover,

HIV/Aids remains a daunting medical and social predicament, which not only will significantly reverse the gains made on the education front, but also will continue to prove a huge developmental challenge, along with unemployment, poverty, education, crime and corruption. Additionally, the challenges of effective decentralisation and the implementation of sub-national processes for improved governance, which hitherto remain unfulfilled, add to the perception that service delivery at regional and local level is not up to the required standard. While the budget deficit remains under control, the continued loss of revenue from dwindling receipts from SACU will compel government to intensify its efforts to diversify the economy and increase the collection of revenues from all sources available.

CONCLUSION

Namibia has, by and large, made significant progress in establishing political institutions that are mandated to play a critical role in the consolidation of democracy and the implementation of systems of horizontal accountability. However, at a formal level, the constitutional, legislative and regulatory frameworks do not lend themselves to underpinning the separation of powers so crucial for democratic consolidation and the nurturing of a culture of accountability. In particular, the dominance of the executive over the legislature is one of the major obstacles to ensuring accountability from the executive to parliament. The primary legislative functions seem not to reside with the legislature, as is constitutionally guaranteed, but rather with the executive, as the members of the executive who are appointed by the president are not only loyal to him, but seem to be almost solely responsible for policy and law making. The negligible role that the legislature and the public play in holding office bearers accountable is also discernable in the general law-making and budgeting processes. The absence of a regulatory framework to allow for access to information means that citizens have no means to compel law makers to provide continuous information about public expenditure and other financial matters.

In general, a lack of accountability from office bearers to the citizenry seems to permeate Namibian society, as ethnic and political affiliation is regarded as a more important determinant than the integrity of the institutions that have been established to ensure horizontal accountability. In this regard, the integrity of the judiciary in the eyes of ordinary citizens and in the way it guards against parochial influences, speaks to the strength of an institution that is intent on retaining its independence, regardless of political pressure.

Despite the absence of a culture of accountability, the media, as well as civil society, continue in their efforts to hold elected representatives to account.

SECTION SCORE: 4

REFERENCES

AFRICAN MEDIA BAROMETER. 2009. *Namibia Country Study 2009*. Windhoek: MISA. Available: http://bit.ly/xPgMyF.

AFROBAROMETER. Briefing papers and working papers, various [online]. Available: http://www. afrobarometer.org.

BERTELSMANN STIFTUNG. 2010. *BTI 2010 – Namibia Country Report*. Gütersloh: Bertelsmann Stiftung.

BLAAUW, L. 2009. *Promoting the effectiveness of democracy protection institutions in southern Africa: The case of the Ombudsman in Namibia*, Electoral Institute of Southern Africa Research Report #42. Johannesburg: EISA.

___ 2010. 'A note on the Namibian National Assembly elections of 2009' in *Journal of African Elections*, 9(1):128-140.

BLAAUW, L. & LESTHOLO, S. 2009. 'Namibia' in Kadima, D. & Booysen, S. (eds). *Compendium of elections in southern Africa 1989-2009: 20 years of multiparty democracy*. Johannesburg: EISA.

DU PISANI, A. 2010. 'The paradigm of constitutional democracy: Genesis, implications and limitations' in Bösl, A., Horn, N. & Du Pisani, A. (eds). *Constitutional democracy in Namibia: A critical analysis after two decades*. Windhoek: Macmillan Education Namibia.

DU PISANI, A. & LINDEKE, W. 2009a. 'Namibia' in *Konrad Adenauer Stiftung Democracy Report 2009*. Available: http://www.kas.de/namibia/en/publications/.

___ 2009b. *Political party life in Namibia: Dominant party with democratic consolidation*, IPPR Briefing Paper #44. Windhoek: IPPR.

ERASMUS, G. 2010. 'The Constitution: Its impact on Namibian statehood and politics' in Keulder, C. (ed.). *State, society and democracy: A reader in Namibian politics*. Windhoek: Macmillan Education Namibia.

FORREST, J. 1998. *Namibia's post-apartheid regional institutions: The founding years*. Rochester: University of Rochester Press.

GEINGOB, H. 2010. 'Drafting of Namibia's Constitution' in Bösl, A., Horn, N. & Du Pisani, A. (eds). *Constitutional democracy in Namibia: A critical analysis after two decades*. Windhoek: Macmillan Education Namibia.

GOOD, K. 1997. *Realizing democracy in Botswana, Namibia and South Africa*. Pretoria: Africa Institute.

HOPWOOD, G. 2007. *Guide to Namibian politics*. Windhoek: NID.

INTERNATIONAL BUDGET PARTNERSHIP. 2008. *Open Budget Index 2008*. Washington: IBP

IPPR. 2011a. *The National Budget: The need for a more inclusive approach*, IPPR Democracy Report #3. Windhoek: IPPR.

___ 2011b. *Towards a national integrity system*, IPPR Anti-Corruption Research Programme Paper 1, May 2011.

___ 2011c. *Nothing to disclose*, IPPR Anti-Corruption Research Programme Paper 2, May 2011.

KOELBE, T. 1995. 'The new institutionalism in Political Science and Sociology' in *Comparative Politics*, 27(1):231-243.

KOEP, M. 2010. 'Namibia country report' in *The influence of non-governmental organisations on the parliamentary law-making process in Namibia* (research paper). Windhoek: Namibia Institute for Democracy.

LITTLE, E. & LOGAN, C. 2009. 'The quality of democracy and governance in Africa: New results from Afrobarometer Round 4', *Afrobarometer Working Papers* (Working Paper #108).

MELBER, H., 2010. 'The impact of the Constitution on state- and nation-building' in Bösl, A., Horn, N. & Du Pisani, A. (eds). *Constitutional democracy in Namibia: A critical analysis after two decades*. Windhoek: Macmillan Education Namibia.

NEIRYINCK, K. & SOUTHALL, R. 2003. 'A note on political institutions and democracy in Africa' in *Africa Insight*, 33(2):3-10.

NID. 2010. *The influence of non-governmental organisations on the parliamentary law-making process in Namibia* (research paper). Windhoek: Namibia Institute for Democracy.

O'DONNEL, G. 1999. 'Horizontal accountability in new democracies' in Schedler, A., Diamond, L. & Plattner, M. (eds). *The self-restraining State: Power and accountability in new democracies*. Boulder and London: Lynne Rienner Publishers.

REPUBLIC OF NAMIBIA. 1990. *The Constitution of Namibia*. Windhoek: The Government of Namibia.

___ 1995. *Public Service Commission's Act*. Windhoek: The Government of Namibia.

SCHADE, K. 2010. *National Budget 2010/11: In search of recovery and sustainable growth*, IPPR Briefing Paper #50. Windhoek: IPPR.

SCHEDLER, A. 1999. 'Conceptualizing accountability' in Schedler, A., Diamond, L. & Plattner, M. (eds). *The self-restraining State: Power and accountability in new democracies*. Boulder and London: Lynne Rienner Publishers.

SCHMITTER, P. (2004) 'The ambiguous virtues of accountability' in *Journal of Democracy*, 15(4):47-60.

SMIT, J. (n.d.) 'Tender Board raises questions over Simataa's dual role' in *The Namibian*, 19 April.

SMIT, N. 2011. 'Civil servant wins case against Prime Minister' in *The Namibian*, 14 July.

TÖTEMEYER, G. 2010. 'Decentralisation and State-building at the local level' in Keulder, C. (ed.). *State, society and democracy: A reader in Namibian politics*. Windhoek: Macmillan Education Namibia.

TRANSPARENCY INTERNATIONAL. 2010. *Promoting transparency in political finance in Southern Africa*. Harare: Transparency International Zimbabwe. Available: http://bit.ly/zXLn7T

VON DOEPP, P. 2006. Politics and judicial decision making in Namibia: Separate or connected realms?'. IPPR Briefing Paper #39. Windhoek: IPPR.

VRIES, D. 2011. 'Judiciary not a "holy cow"' in *The Namibian*, 1 July 2011.

WORLD BANK. 2009. *Namibia: Country Brief*. [online]. Available: http://go.worldbank.org/1B6KN88H10.

___ 2011. *The Africa Competitiveness Report 2011* [online]. Available: http://go.worldbank.org/37ODDU30H0.

ENDNOTES

1   Two provisions are of particular importance here: Article 32(2) and Article 32(3)(g). Article 32(2) states that 'in accordance with the responsibility of the executive branch of government to the legislative branch, the president and cabinet shall each year during the consideration of the official budget attend parliament. During such session the president shall address parliament on the state of the nation and on the future policies of the government, shall be available to respond to questions.' Article 32(3)(g) states that the president has the ability to 'establish and dissolve such government departments and ministries as the president may at any time consider to be necessary or expedient for the good government of Namibia'.

2   In 2000, for instance, during the Sikunda and Osire Stars case, the court ruled against government and came under attack from Minister Ekandjo.

3   Personal communication with Graham Hopwood, 20 September 2011.

4   Some of the current leading independent media are:
    • *The AllgemeineZeitung*. This paper, which targets the German-speaking population in Namibia, has been in existence since 1919.
    • *Die Republikein*. This is an Afrikaans daily founded in 1977 initially as a mouthpiece of the RP and later the DTA.
    • *The Windhoek Observer.* This paper was established in 1978.
    • *The Namibian*. From its inception in 1985 until independence in 1990, this paper was in the forefront of chronicling detentions and other human rights violations by the colonial authorities in Namibia. It is because of its critical stance that government instituted a ban on the paper in 2001, which continue to evoke heated debate even among Cabinet members. In 2001, the government, under the leadership of President Nujoma, imposed a ban on *The Namibian* newspaper, prohibiting any government body from placing advertisements in the daily newspaper or from purchasing it with State funds. The government claimed this was because the newspaper was too critical of its policies. The ban was recently lifted.
    • *Insight Namibia*. This came into existence in 2004 as a monthly current affairs magazine based on the principle of investigative reporting.

5   Findings that the public have yet to get feedback on include:
    • Commission of Inquiry into the Activities, Affairs, Management and Operation of the Social Security Commission (2002)
    • Commission of Inquiry into the Activities, Affairs, Management and Operation of the Roads Authority (2002)
    • Commission of Inquiry into the Activities, Affairs, Management and Operation of the former Amalgamated Commercial Holdings (Pty) Ltd and the former Development Brigade Corporation
    • Commission of Inquiry into the Activities, Affairs, Management and Operation of the Government Institution Pension Fund (GIPF).

6   Personal communication with Graham Hopwood, 20 September 2011.

7   They are, however, severely hampered by the fact that they have to try and balance local needs with national demands.

8   In early 2010, the Namibia Labour Force Survey (NLFS) 2008 revealed that unemployment stood at 51.2%.

POLITICAL FREEDOM AND DEMOCRACY

PHIL YA NANGOLOH

Following a century of occupation, colonialism and apartheid, Namibia's Constitution emerged as a product of a protracted struggle that sought to achieve self-determination and sovereignty founded on a system of governance, and based on the principles of constitutionalism, the rule of law, and respect for the human rights of the individual (Amoo & Skeffers 2009:17). Namibia's Constitution is approbated for its progressive and rights-based framework. It contains an entrenched Bill of Fundamental Rights and Freedoms (Chapter Three), entirely consistent with the Universal Declaration of Human Rights (UDHR), and all and any other international human rights instruments deriving therefrom. According to the Preamble to the Namibian Constitution, the equal and inalienable rights of all Namibians 'are most effectively maintained ... in a democratic society, where government is responsible to freely elected representatives of the people ... operating under a sovereign constitution and a free and independent judiciary'.

The rights contained within Chapter Three of the Constitution may not be repealed or amended insofar as any repeal or amendment would detract or diminish such rights. They include protection of life; protection of liberty; respect for human dignity; abolition of slavery or forced labour; equality and freedom from discrimination, arbitrary arrest and detention; access to a fair trial; the guaranteeing of privacy and respect for family; the rights of children; the right to acquire property; the right to political activity; the right to administrative justice, culture; and the right to education.

Moreover, Namibia has ratified most of the core international and regional human rights instruments on civil and political rights: in particular, the Committee on the Elimination of Racial Discrimination (CERD); the Convention against Torture (CAT); the Committee on the Elimination of Discrimination against Women (CEDAW), which are all enforceable under Article 144 of the Constitution.

With respect to protecting the rights enshrined in Chapter Three of the Constitution, the role of the Ombudsman, as defined within the Ombudsman Act (No. 7 of 1990) and in Article 25(2) of the Constitution, is encompassed within the parameters of investigating violations of fundamental rights or freedoms and the conduct of outreach programmes and public education. However, the low level of human rights complaints received is partially due to a lack of public awareness about the Ombudsman's functions, as well as a relative lack of knowledge about constitutional rights (Ruppel & Ambunda n.d.:132).

CIVIL AND POLITICAL RIGHTS

The Namibian Constitution provides special protection for civil and political rights.[1] It obligates government to respect, protect and realise all the civil and political rights of all individuals and groups, without distinction of any kind, such as race, colour, sex, language, religion, political or other opinion, national or social origin, property, birth or other status, within its territory and subject to its jurisdiction.[2]

65. *How free are all people from intimidation and fear, physical violation against their person, arbitrary arrest and detention?* (5)

While Namibia is a signatory to CAT, and the Constitution and subsequent legislation has aimed to curtail the abuse of fundamental rights and freedoms, numerous serious human rights violations have taken place in Namibia since independence.

Large-scale and systematic extra-judicial killings have occurred in the country, both before and after independence, as substantiated by reports produced by human rights organisations, the media and others on the arbitrary deprivation of life, death threats, incitement to violence and threats of violence, as well as enforced disappearances.[3] Scores of human rights violations committed prior to independence by the People's Liberation Army of Namibia (PLAN) and the South West Africa People's Organisation (SWAPO) have yet to be acknowledged (Conway 2003; Parlevliet 2000). In total, these transgressions have resulted in the disappearance of over 4 200 Namibians (Namibian Information Technologies 2009). Despite CAT's recommendation that government promptly and impartially investigate such disappearances, in accordance with Article 12 of CAT, and that the results of such investigation be transmitted to the Committee, this has yet to occur (Office of the High Commissioner for Human Rights 1997: para. 247).

In the late 1990s and early 2000s, Namibian security forces in the northern Ohangwena and Kavango regions targeted a large number of supporters of opposition parties, as well as hundreds of suspected members of *União Nacional para a Independência Total de Angola* (UNITA).[4] These violations, which have also been denied by government, resulted in an estimated 1 600[5] deaths and 32 000[6] persons being arrested and/or detained before being transferred to the Osire refugee camp in central Namibia. A further 3 300[7] persons disappeared during the northern border conflict,[8] with similar violations occurring in the Caprivi region between 1998 and 2003.[9] Although mass graves were discovered near the Angola-Namibia border in 2005 and 2008, government has not yet taken any steps towards investigating the sites.

Referring to post-independence violations in the northern areas of the country, the Office of the High Commissioner for Human Rights (OHCHR) regretted that no extensive fact-finding initiatives had been undertaken to account for alleged acts of torture, extra-judicial killings and disappearances in those areas. The OHCHR urged government to establish an effective mechanism for the investigation of such acts, and the charging and punishment of those responsible (CCPR Human Rights Committee 2004: para. 12). To date this has not occurred.

ARBITRARY DEPRIVATION OF PERSONAL LIBERTY

Prolonged pre-trial detentions and repeated postponements of trial cases, resulting in a huge backlog of court cases, are common features of Namibia's criminal justice system (*The Namibian* 2004a,c,e,f; 2005a,b,c,f). A range of factors contribute towards this state of affairs and include: the Office of the Prosecutor General (OPG) taking too long to make decisions on whether or not to prosecute suspects; inexperienced and poorly trained police officers; a severe shortage of senior judicial officers; systematic violations of the 48-hour rule for bringing arrested and detained persons before judicial officers; awaiting-trial prisoners' inability to pay bond or the denial of bond; and long waiting periods for indigent persons seeking legal aid. Such factors have not only contributed to systematic and arbitrary deprivations of personal liberties, but have made the right to a fair and speedy trial without delay and effective remedy inaccessible to the majority of accused (Office of the Ombudsman 2006; *The Namibian* 2007b,d). During the interactive dialogue session with the 48-member UN Working Group on the Universal Periodic Review held in February 2011, Namibia stated that the unfavourable working conditions of legal officers had contributed substantially towards the large case accumulation and that government had taken measures to reduce the build-up of criminal cases through the appointment of additional judicial officers and prosecutors, as well as the provision of legal aid to indigent persons (United Nations General Assembly 2011: para. 29).

Namibia's prison conditions fall below international standards; they are often severely overcrowded and, more often than not, juveniles are held together with adult offenders. Inmates lack access to hygiene products and nutritious food. In December 2009, the Windhoek Observer stated that Namibia had a total prison population of 4 251 inmates in its 13 prisons – close to the country's overall capacity of 4 475 prisoners (US Department of State 2010). By December 2010, there were close to 5 000 inmates in Namibian prisons, of which 136 were women (*The Namibian Sun* n.d.). In February 2011, the 48-member UN Working Group on the Universal Periodic Review expressed concern about prison overcrowding and torture, and urged government to institute measures to prevent ill-treatment in detention, to improve prison conditions, and to ensure that detainees were brought to trial within a reasonable time frame (United Nations General Assembly 2011: para. 75).

On several occasions, the United Nations (UN) has expressed concern about the country's criminal justice system. For example, in 1997, CAT urged Namibia to introduce measures to reduce the accumulation of criminal cases resulting in long and illegal pre-trial detention, in violation of the right of defendants to be tried within a reasonable time (Office of the High Commissioner for Human Rights 1997: paras. 227-252). In 2004, the OHCHR observed that Namibia was not fully compliant with its obligation, inter alia, to ensure the right to be tried without undue delay, as consecrated in Article 14 (3)(c) of the International Covenant on Civil and Political Rights (ICCPR). Referring specifically to the backlog of cases, the OHCHR expressed concern that prolonged pre-trial detention continued to occur in Namibia and urged government to ensure strict observance of the 48-hour rule for bringing a suspect before a trial judge (CCPR Human Rights Committee 2004: para. 13). The organisation also urged Namibia to undertake urgent steps to guarantee that trials take place within a reasonable period and to address the backlog of cases, in particular through a necessary increase in the number of judges (Ibid.: para. 17).

Arbitrary deprivation of personal liberty has also manifested itself through the controversial Caprivi High Treason Trial, which began in 1999 and is hitherto the largest and longest criminal trial in Namibia's history. While it remains in progress, the UN

Working Group on Arbitrary Detention has classified the detention of 13 of the alleged Caprivi secessionists as a Category III detention, constituting a 'total or partial non-observance of the international norms relating to the right to a fair trial which is of such gravity as to give the deprivation of liberty an arbitrary character' (NSHR 2006d:130).

Since independence, refugees and asylum seekers in the country have been deprived of personal liberties on numerous occasions. In this regard, it is noteworthy that Namibia has filed a reservation to the 1951 Convention relating to the Status of Refugees on the right to freedom of movement. Moreover, Namibia's refugee law, the Namibia Refugees (Recognition and Control) Act (No. 2 of 1999) states that '[A]ny person who, without the prior permission of the authorised officer or any other person in charge of the Osire Refugee Camp, leaves or attempts to leave [Osire Refugee Camp] shall be guilty of an offence and on conviction be liable to imprisonment for a period not exceeding 90 days" (International Refugee Rights Initiative 2009). Refugees are required to obtain an exit permit to leave the facility, and only certain refugees with valid study or work permits are permitted to remain outside the camp.

In its 2010 submission under the UN's Universal Periodic Review, the United Nations High Commissioner for Refugees (UNHCR) expressed concern that Namibia continued to maintain its reservations to Article 26 of the 1951 UN Convention relating to the Status of Refugees. It posited that restrictions on the freedom of movement of refugees and asylum seekers in the country 'has had and continues to have particularly inhibiting consequences for the social as well as the economic endeavours of the refugees'.[10] Hence, the UNHCR recommended that Namibia remove its reservation and grant freedom of movement and residence to the refugees and asylum-seekers hosted in Namibia. On 2 February 2011, the 48-Member UN Working Group on the Universal Periodic Review also urged Namibia to review its reservation, with a view to authorising the free movement and residence of persons with recognised refugee status and to extend this right to asylum seekers (United Nations General Assembly 2011).

TORTURE

Prior to Namibia's independence, the use of torture was widespread under South African administration and the South African Defence Force, the South West African Police Force, as well as Namibian liberation movements, SWAPO, which used inhumane forms of punishment against their enemies, real or perceived, during the liberation struggle (Conway 2003; Parlevliet 2000). After independence, government's policy of reconciliation allowed and encouraged the members of these previously opposed forces to take up employment within the Namibian Defence Force and the Namibian Police Force (Chomba n.d.). Article 8 of the Constitution states that no person shall be subject to torture or to cruel, inhuman or degrading treatment or punishment. In 1991, in a landmark Supreme Court case, *Ex parte Attorney-General, Namibia: in re Corporal Punishment by organs of the state*, the Supreme Court declared corporal punishment imposed and inflicted by or on the authority of a State organ to be illegal. Since Namibia's domestic penal law does not define torture, and in the absence of a strict legal definition of torture in the State's penal code, including the enumeration and prohibition of explicit techniques and methods that may be used to violate the protections guaranteed within CAT, Namibian courts are unable to adhere to the principle of *nullum crimen, nulla poena sine lege previa* or to Article 4 of the CAT (Office of the High Commissioner for Human Rights 1997: para. 235).

The Criminal Procedure Act (No. 51 of 1977), as amended, regards torture as a common law offence to be charged as assault to do grievous bodily harm or *crimen injuria*. CAT has urged Namibia to integrate the specific definition of the crime of torture into its penal legislation, in terms that are legally consistent with the definition contained in Article 1 (United Nations Convention Against Torture 1997: 293 and 294/Add. 1). Furthermore, the committee stated that Namibia must address:

- the need to define torture as a specific offence committed by or at the instigation of or with the consent of a public official, with the special intent to extract a confession or other information, to arbitrarily punish, to intimidate, to coerce or to discriminate against;
- the need to legislate for complicity in torture and attempts to commit torture as equally punishable;
- the need to exclude the legal applicability of all justification in cases of torture;
- the need to procedurally exclude all evidence obtained through torture in criminal and other proceedings, except in proceedings against the perpetrator of torture himself; and
- the need to legislate for and enforce prompt and impartial investigation into any substantiated allegations of torture (Ruppel & Ambunda n.d.:134).

Numerous allegations of torture were levelled against government during its campaign against perceived enemies of the State during the armed conflicts along Namibia's northern borders between 1994 and 2003.[11] The Namibian defence and police forces were accused of participating in torture and other degrading acts against citizens. Many of the Namibians detained following the uprising in Caprivi were subjected to inhumane and degrading treatment during interrogations and pre-trial detention as a means of obtaining information and eliciting confessions.[12] In the 2010 case of *State vs. Malumo and 24 Others*, the Supreme Court declared all the statements allegedly made by 25 defendants to be inadmissible as they had been obtained through 'coercive' means.[13]

66. To what extent are people able to protect themselves against discriminatory treatment by the State? *(4)*

Under colonial rule and the South African administration, discrimination was a core tenet of government policy. Articles 1, 10, 14, 23, and Chapter 9 of the Constitution (Republic of Namibia 1990), guarantee the right to equality and non-discrimination, as well as other forms of socio-political justice for all Namibians, without distinction of any kind based on race, colour, sex, language, religion, political or other opinion, national or social origin, property, birth or other status. The Constitution also guarantees the right to a fair and public trial before competent, independent and impartial courts and tribunals established by law.[14] Furthermore, the Office of the Ombudsman has a constitutional and statutory responsibility to call up public and private institutions if racial discrimination is suspected.

The Racial Discrimination Prohibition Act (No. 26 of 1991) prohibits hate speech against all racial groups. However, this Act, as amended in 1998, abrogated citizen's abilities to seek legal action against hate speech. In 2008, the CERD, taking government to task, stated that hate speech continued to be 'practised mostly by politicians ... at an unacceptable rate' and that the Committee had not yet witnessed government taking any tangible measures to sanction verbal attacks on minority groups (*The Namibian* 2008b). The CERD has urged Namibia to review its laws and provide equal protection and treatment to all persons in the country (United Nations/CERD 2008: para. 11). It further recommended that Namibia take into account the relevant parts of the Durban Declaration and Programme of Action, adopted by the 2001 World Conference against Racism, Racial Discrimination, Xenophobia and Related Intolerance, when implementing anti-racism measures (Ibid.: para. 27). As recently as February 2011, the UN Working Group on the Universal Periodic Review urged Namibia to combat racial segregation and discrimination in various fields and to continue the adoption of special measures in the context of the Durban Declaration and Programme of Action (Office of the High Commissioner for Human Rights 2010: para. 96.23).

Instances of hate speech directed at the lesbian, gay, bisexual and transgender (LGBT) community by politicians have decreased, while Out-Right Namibia, a civil society organisation that advocates for LGBT rights, reported that the police generally did not take complaints of violence against LGBT persons seriously (US Department of State 2010:26). Section 39(e) of the Immigration Control Act (No. 7 of 1993) may be used to discriminate against people living with HIV/Aids, as it states that any person who enters, has entered, or is in Namibia, shall be a prohibited immigrant if 'such person is infected or afflicted with contagious disease or is a carrier of such a virus or disease as may be prescribed' (UNHCR/Refworld 1994).

67. To what extent are people able to use the legal system to protect their person and property against the State? (6)

The majority of Namibians are unable to access the State's legal system to protect their person and property because Namibia's legal system is unaffordable to the majority of the citizens who live in poverty. According to government reports, 13.8% of Namibia's population is classified as extremely poor, while an additional 27.6% of the population is classified as poor (Central Bureau of Statistics 2008). Although the World Bank has ranked Namibia as an upper-middle income country, it has simultaneously been described as one of the most economically unequal in the world,[15] with a Gini-coefficient ranging between 0.6 and 0.7.

While the independence of the judiciary is generally respected in Namibia, verbal attacks on its members by the political elite following unfavourable rulings are not uncommon.[16] Moreover, judicial independence has also been jeopardised by a lack of security of tenure for acting judges and a severe shortage of judges, as well as inordinate delays in the delivery of judgements.

Although lower courts have been established in terms of the Magistrates' Courts Amendment Act (No 6 of 2009) and the Community Courts Act (No. 10 of 2003) foresees the establishment of magistrates' courts and traditional courts, respectively, the Community Courts Act has not yet been implemented.

Judicial misconduct and corruption, particularly within the magistrates' courts and among prosecutors, has compromised the capacity of citizens to use the legal system to protect their person and/or property. For example, in February 2007, the Magis-trates' Commission chairperson, a High Court judge, accused some of the magistrates of being 'embarrassing and tarnishing the reputation of the judiciary' when he revealed that cases of misconduct, ranging from incompetence, theft, untruthfulness, and drunkenness on duty, to absenteeism, arrogance, impatience and insubordination were being investigated against certain magistrates (*The Namibian* 2007a).

While the Ministry of Justice, in an attempt to improve services offered by the courts has embarked on a five-year Strategic Plan (2009-2014) focusing on improving acces-sibility, timeliness, quality and integrity, it is plagued by insufficient political will, logistical challenges, and poor communication of redefined responsibilities and goals (Nakuta & Chipepera n.d.:5).

Article 16(2) of the Constitution provides for the State, or a competent body autho-rised by law, to expropriate property in the public interest, subject to payment of just compensation and in accordance with requirements and procedures to be determined by an Act of Parliament. The Namibian Constitution does not, however, define 'public interest' (Treeger 2004). The Agricultural (Commercial) Land Reform Act (No. 6 of

1995) allows for the compulsory acquisition of agricultural land classified as under-utilised, excessive or acquired by a foreign national, or of land where the application of the willing-seller, willing-buyer principal has failed (Ibid.).

Despite government's 'willing-buyer, willing-seller' policy, there have been a number of instances where white commercial farmers have either been threatened with instant expropriation of their farms or their property has, in fact, been seized without the just compensation referred to under Article 16 of the Namibian Constitution (Skadi Forum n.d.). For example, in September 2005, the government expropriated the farm 'Ongombo West' after its white owners had been accused of unfair labour practices and former Namibian President Sam Nujoma branded them as 'criminal'. Although the owners of the farm had demanded to be paid N$9 million for their property, they received only N$3.7 million from government (*The Namibian* 2005d,e; *Namibian Economist* 2005).

68. How effective is the protection of the freedoms of expression, information and assembly for all persons irrespective of their social grouping? *(4)*

While freedom of expression is guaranteed by the Constitution, no other legislation, including a freedom of information act, exist to protect this right and to ensure an independent media. However, two cases in particular, *Kauesa v Minister of Home Affairs and Others* (1995)[17] and *Group International Ltd and Others v Shikongo* (2010)[18] are viewed as landmark Supreme Court decisions (case laws) guaranteeing freedom of expression in the country. In the Kauesa case, a police officer challenged a particular section of a Namibian police regulation that prohibited members of the force from publicly criticising its top leadership. The officer argued that the regulation infringed on his fundamental right to freedom of speech and expression as guaranteed in Article 21(1)(a) of the Constitution. The court ruled in favour of the protection of the fundamental right. The Shikongo case is significant in that it rejects strict liability of the media in defamation proceedings, and strikes a fair and just balance between reasonable publication, on the one hand, and the right to dignity on the other.

Namibian law prohibits any propaganda in support of war and any advocacy of national, racial or religious hatred that constitutes incitement to discrimination, hostility or violence. In the opinion of United Nations Human Rights Council, this required prohibition is fully compatible with the right of freedom of expression as contained in Article 19 of the International Covenant on Civil and Political Rights (ICCPR), the exercise of which carries special duties and responsibilities.

Hate expression and other forms of political intolerance have, more often than not, intensified during election campaigns. For example, during the 1999 and 2009 general and presidential electoral campaigns, unprecedented acts of political intolerance and intimidation were directed against both civil society organisations and opposition political parties.[19] In 1999, the Congress of Democrats (CoD) was forced to cancel election rallies in the former Ovamboland following widespread intimidation and physical attacks against its supporters by SWAPO activists (NSHR 1999b; *The Namibian* 2008c; *Informanté* 2009). Furthermore, during the 2008 and 2009 electoral campaigns, opposition parties faced widespread verbal and physical attacks by SWAPO activists, directed specifically at members of the Rally for Democracy and Progress (RDP), especially in several parts of the former Ovamboland (*The Namibian* 1999). While it is difficult to ascertain whether some of these altercations had been organised by SWAPO, it seems that there was tacit support for these actions as the majority of members of the ruling party declined to condemn the violence.

Incidents of intimidation, hate speech, propaganda in support of war and/or advocacy of national, racial or religious hatred constituting incitement to discrimination, hostility or violence and other forms of political intolerance, have been most pronounced in the densely populated northern parts of the country, from which government derives its staunchest support. It is in these areas that political differences are, more often than not, easily construed as a threat to, or a rejection of, hard-won peace and stability.[20]

Freedom of association and participation

69. How secure is the freedom for all to practice their own religion, language and culture?   (6)

Namibia is party to ICCPR, Article 27 of which provides that 'in those States in which ethnic, religious or linguistic minorities exist, persons belonging to these minorities shall not be denied the right, in community with the other members of their group, to enjoy their own culture, profess and practice their own religion, or use their own language'. In addition, Article 18 of ICCPR, read in conjunction with Human Rights Council General Comment no. 22 of 30 July 1993 on Article 18 of ICCPR, guarantees, *inter alia*, the right to freedom of thought, conscience and religion (which includes the freedom to hold beliefs). This encompasses freedom of thought on all matters, personal conviction and the commitment to religion or belief, whether manifested individually or in community with others.

The Namibian Constitution stipulates that every person, irrespective of race, colour, sex, language, religion, political or other opinion, national or social origin, property, birth or other status 'shall be entitled to enjoy, practice, profess, maintain and promote any culture, language, tradition or religion. The enjoyment of these rights is, however, subject to the other terms of the Constitution and further subject to the condition that the rights protected by this Article do not impinge upon the rights of others or the national interest' (NSHR 1998, 1999c:24-25; *The Namibian* 2000).

Ethnic, linguistic and tribal identities are a prominent feature of Namibian society. Any such cultural bonds of affiliation were exacerbated and exploited through the South African administration's apartheid policy, in terms of which the separate development of racial, ethnic and tribal groups was used to divide and rule Namibia. Current differentiations have continued to engender perceptions of ethnic favouritism among government. Some politicians have alleged that government has withheld recognition of certain traditional and cultural leaders for political reasons.[21]

Concern has been expressed about growing incidents of tribalism and ethnicity, as well as other forms of racism in the country,[22] based on widespread views that government favours the Ovambo, Namibia's largest dominant ethnic group, over all other ethnic groups.

While the majority of politicians execute their duties in line with Namibia's legal and constitutional framework, there have been several occasions where politicians, including the former Namibian president, Sam Nujoma, have publicly attacked religious denominations and groups. For example, in June 2009, while on an electoral campaign trail for his ruling SWAPO party, Nujoma launched a vitriolic attack against the country's German-led Evangelical Lutheran Church (DELK), which he accused of, inter alia, 'having collaborated with the enemy prior to Namibian independence and possibly still remained an enemy'.[23]

70. *To what extent do people feel free to associate with others in order to influence government? To what extent does government action encourage or discourage people to associate with others in order to influence government?* (5)

Prior to independence, the objectives of most civil society groups were primarily bound together with the aims of the liberation struggle (NSHR 2009). Article 95(k) of the Constitution encourages public participation through organisations that seek to influence government policies and programmes, and Vision 2030 promotes a collaborative relationship between government and civil society. There are numerous professional and commercial associations, chambers, federations and other community-based organisations and civic groups that freely and regularly advocate on behalf of their members' interests.

Apart from this, there are approximately 230 000 wage-dependent members of 15 trade unions aligned to two federations within Namibia (Hopwood 2007:93). The National Union of Namibian Workers (NUNW) is closely affiliated to SWAPO, while the

Trade Union Congress of Namibia (TUCNA) rejects political party linkages. Trade unions not affiliated to SWAPO are often marginalised. For example, only representatives of the NUNW are allowed to serve as members of the board of directors of the Social Security Commission and the Government Institution Pension Fund (GIPF) (Kaapama, Blaauw, Zaaruka & Kaakunga 2007:44). This state of affairs has prompted the Brussels-based International Trade Union Confederation (ITUC), the world's largest trade union federation, to posit that Namibian trade unions, other than those politically affiliated to SWAPO, are faced with discrimination and marginalisation.[24]
Moreover, in its 2010 annual survey, ITUC stated that representatives of NUNW were favoured ahead of those from rival trade bodies in the country (*New Era* 2010). The right of workers to withhold their labour is limited in Namibia and strike action can only take place in cases of disputes involving specific workers' interests, such as pay rises. Moreover, strikes are also subject to a long conciliation procedure, while disputes over workers' rights, including dismissals, are referred to the Labour Court for arbitration. Dispute-solving mechanisms are generally time-consuming and cumbersome.

71. To what extent do people organise themselves into associations in order to influence government and to what extent are the associations of civil society independent of government? (5)

The Namibian Constitution guarantees the right of citizens to form or join associations in order to influence government (Ibid.). While a considerable number of civil society organisations (CSOs) operate in Namibia, many are involved in the social sectors, such as health and support services, and are regarded by government as co-operative partners in the national development agenda. Organisations involved in governance-related and rights-based issues are viewed less favourably, as they are likely to question, challenge and criticise government policies and practices. Independent associations, such as non-SWAPO affiliated trade unions and non-partisan CSOs, as well as independent private media houses and human rights organisations are, on occasion, verbally attacked, denounced in public and labelled, inter alia, as agents of Western imperialism. Although CSOs are free to solicit and receive funding from local and foreign sources, donors operating in Namibia are at times reluctant to provide funding to CSOs that are regarded as 'anti-government' and treated accordingly, apparently out of concern for being attacked by government and or SWAPO (*The Namibian* 2009; *Pambazuka News* 2009). This has been the case especially with regard to CSOs that are active in the field of democracy, human rights and good governance. While a number of organisations in this sector, such as the Legal Assistance Centre (LAC), the Namibia Institute for Democracy (NID), the Institute for Public Policy Research (IPPR) and trade unions have had some success at feeding into the policy-making process and attracting financial support, government generally perceives CSOs as 'anti-government', particularly those that deal with sensitive issues such as NamRights and Forum for the Future (FFF).

In December 2005, government introduced the Civic Organisations Partnership Policy. It recognised a need for collective responses to development challenges and opportunities. The policy proposed that non-governmental organisations (NGOs) and community-based organisations (CBOs) formally register with government, and called for an improved environment for public-private partnerships, closing the gap between government and the people and strengthening civic capacity.[25] However, this policy was rejected by Namibian CSOs under the leadership of the umbrella organisation Namibia Non-Governmental Organisations Forum (NANGOF). In 2009, NANGOF's chairperson stated that government should not view NGOs and CSOs 'as agents of imperialism or of the political opposition or only serving donor interests'. Referring to the proposed Partnership Act, based on NGO policy, he criticised the Bill, saying, '... it will only succeed in damaging the relatively good working relationship between government and the civil society organisations in Namibia'. While the Pohamba administration has denied that neither the Partnership Policy nor the proposed Partnership Act were intended to control activities of CSOs in Namibia (Republic of Namibia 2005), the Bill denies recognition to those organisations that may choose not to register (at the National Planning Commission) (*The Namibian* 2009).

Another possible factor hampering the formation and operation of independent associations capable of influencing government and/or being independent of government, is that white Namibians, who still control significant parts of the private sector, have no culture of financially supporting black CSO groups that are active in the field of democracy, human rights and good governance. This might be due to the fact that white Namibians, in general, have retreated from the political domain, have little taste for being seen to support any perceived 'anti-government' activities and/or organisations, and see little connection between the aspirations of the black majority, on the one hand, and their own minority interests on the other. Possibly those white Namibians who lived comfortably under a repressive apartheid regime before Namibian independence are also hardly likely to be concerned by the approach and actions of a post-independence autocratic 'SWAPO government'.

72. How far do women participate in political and public life at all levels?
(7)

While the Namibian Constitution guarantees the equal treatment of women, it also recognises both common and customary law. This means that discriminating legislation continues to exist *de facto*, with women in rural areas being the most vulnerable as they have limited control over property, or access to estates or small loans (Ibid.).

Although women currently make up more than 50% of Namibia's population,[26] they are often un- or under-represented in decision-making bodies and processes. Following the 2009 legislative elections, women's representation declined from 30% in the 2004

National Assembly elections to 22%. Currently, women hold 18 seats in the 78-seat National Assembly, including six appointed seats (Trading Economics 2011). There are five female ministers and four female deputy ministers among the 41 ministerial and deputy ministerial incumbents. Furthermore, there are three female judges among the 11 permanent judges of the High Court.

Despite the Constitution and several progressive pieces of legislation, including the Combating of Domestic Violence Act (No. 4 of 2003) and the Combating of Rape Act (No. 8 of 2000), discrimination against women in Namibia is pervasive within all levels of society. Violence against women accounts for the largest proportion of domestic violence in Namibia (AfricaNews.com 2009). Some 36% of Namibian women have experienced gender-based violence at the hands of an intimate partner, 31% physical violence, and 17% sexual violence. The 2006-7 National Demographic and Health Survey revealed that 41% of Namibian men believe it is justifiable for a man to beat up a woman, while 32% of women also support this notion.

73. How free from harassment and intimidation are individuals and groups working to protect human rights? *(4)*

Government has regularly targeted human rights defenders and CSOs viewed as 'anti-government' with harassment, intimidation, hate expression and other forms of intolerance (NSHR 2007b, 2008e). In 2009, the SWAPO-controlled National Council called on the judiciary and law enforcement agencies to take unspecified action against the executive director of NamRights. This came barely a week after the latter had issued a statement accusing former Namibian president, Sam Nujoma, of engaging in hate expression and inciting violence (Amnesty International 2011). The activist also received death threats (*The Namibian* 2011). Similarly, on 20 August 2007, SWAPO's chief whip in the National Council tabled a motion seeking to 'review and regulate' the status of NamRights, the weekly *Windhoek Observer* and the daily *The Namibian* newspapers in the country. The politician accused the two media houses of giving NamRights and other government critics a platform for writings 'that are uncalled for and unwarranted' (Amnesty International 2011).

On 17 January 2009, senior government and SWAPO officials threatened to expel the German-funded Konrad Adenauer Stiftung (KAS) Foundation from the country. These threats came after KAS had reported that the 2009 elections had been relatively free but not fair, and for organising meetings that were attended by Namibian opposition political parties. The KAS country representative was declared 'a threat to the country's stability' (NSHR 2007a).

Furthermore, in April 2011, the NUNW secretary general received several death threats over the more than N$600 million that had gone missing from GIPF coffers.

SWAPO's labour secretary and lands minister told the trade unionist that 'the SWAPO party is worried about the GIPF issue" and warned him to 'drop the GIPF issue unless you have a death wish!' (NSHR 2010c:126). Prior to the death threat, the labour leader had insisted the money be repaid and that those responsible be brought to book.

POLITICAL PARTIES

74. *How freely are political parties able to form, recruit members and engage with the public?* (4)

The right of all citizens to participate in peaceful political activity and, to that effect, form or join the political parties of their choice, recruit members or engage with the public, is restricted, directly and indirectly, through government actions and by cumbersome and confusing electoral legislation. For example, on 4 September 2006, the United Democratic Party (UDP) was banned on the basis that the party's 'secessionist activities ... rendered it an illegal organisation'. The ban turned the UDP into the first political party to be outlawed in the country since independence on 21 March 1990 (*Informanté* 2011).

Apart from this, opposition parties are discouraged from entering certain areas of the country to address political rallies and/or recruit new members. This state of affairs increased considerably after the formation of the CoD in 1999 and the RDP between 2007 and 2009, as both these parties were able to challenge the ruling party (NSHR 2006c). Examples of such actions include numerous incidents of political intimidation and violence, which prompted the CoD to cancel some of their election rallies in the former Ovamboland. According to human rights and other reports in the four Ovambo regions, several acts of political intimidation, some more serious than others, occurred between 15 and 23 November 1999 (NSHR 2010a). Similarly, since its foundation in November 2007 and up to the 2009 national election, the RDP has, at times, been subjected to equally discriminatory and severe treatment (*The Namibian* 1999).

In general, Namibia's electoral legislation does not create a favourable environment for opposition parties to form, recruit and/or engage with the public. While S4(1) of the Electoral Act (No. 24 of 1992), as amended, provides for the establishment of an independent Electoral Commission of Namibia (ECN) as the exclusive authority to direct, supervise and control the conduct of elections in the country in a fair, credible and impartial manner, it is perceived by many as biased in favour of SWAPO. While suitable persons are invited to apply to become ECN commissioners and those shortlisted are publicly interviewed and then recommended for final appointment by the president, with the approval of the National Assembly, recent practise has indicated a lack of clarity and transparency around the key criteria used and the reasons for the inclusion of particular candidates regarded as party-affiliated in the list of recommended commissioners.

The ECN's summary dismissal of the previous Director of Elections is one of the most blatant examples of the lack of impartiality, independence and credibility of the electoral body; he was fired amid accusations that he had failed to inform the SWAPO leadership about the registration of a breakaway faction, the RDP. This action followed closely on calls from the SWAPO Party Youth League (SPYL) that the electoral official resign with immediate effect or be summarily axed.[27]

Several observers of repute have expressed concern about the prevailing restrictive political environment in Namibia. Most recently, a prominent local academic concluded that the political space for opposition parties in Namibia was inherently limited for various reasons, including the fact that Namibia was a one-party-dominated system that lacked a credible opposition to act as a counterweight to SWAPO (NSHR 2008b).

Similarly, in October 2009, ahead of the general and presidential elections, a South African Institute for Security Studies (ISS) researcher noted that 'the absence of undemocratic behaviour and or undesirable (violent) political culture ... in the form of harassment of the opposition, acts of political intolerance and violence, monopolisation of the democratic space by actors closely linked to power and State machinery, abuse of State resources by the ruling party or uneven distribution of such resources to gain greater advantage over other political parties during election campaigns' (Du Pisani 2010).

75. How free are opposition or non-governing parties to organise within the legislature and outside of it?   (5)

Owing mainly to Namibia's proportional representation electoral system, smaller opposition parties are represented in the country's parliament, which consists of the National Assembly and the National Council. As such, they are fully entitled to participate actively in all parliamentary debates, including those relating to the national budget, and the introduction of bills, resolutions and motions. This presence includes opposition participation in the seven parliamentary standing committees, including the Standing Committee on Public Accounts, which is often chaired by an opposition lawmaker and leader of one of the smaller opposition parties in parliament.

However, the extent to which these opposition parties are able to organise both within and outside the legislature is considerably restricted. Apart from the fact that, due to the overwhelming majority of the ruling party and the numerical weakness of the opposition, their lack of technical and administrative capacity and resources, high levels of political polarisation and acrimony driven by partisan agendas, personality differences and debates that lack substance and focus, often, if not always, characterise Namibian parliamentary discussions (Institute for Security Studies 2009). Although opposition parties have the right to introduce the so-called Private Members' Bill in terms of Article 60(2) of the Constitution, this has never happened with any success since Namibian independence. Any bills, resolutions or motions introduced by members of the opposition are routinely rejected, without regard for merit, by their ruling SWAPO counterparts who make up a two-thirds majority of parliament. Moreover, SWAPO lawmakers shout down their opposition party counterparts, even before they rise to speak on contentious issues.

While opposition party lawmakers are also entitled to put questions to the president during the annual State of the Nation address, responses and outcomes have usually been the same as those for any other parliamentary sessions or budget debates where SWAPO MPs and Cabinet members predominate. In terms of Article 67 of the Namibian Constitution, a simple majority vote is sufficient for a Bill to pass the National Assembly, but SWAPO's two-thirds majority stifles attempts by opposition legislators to make alterations to legislation or to pass any of their own acts into law. Moreover, for reasons referred to or discussed under Questions 71, 73 and 74, *supra*, as well as Question 77, *infra*, Namibian CSOs have little or no effective influence on either government or any of the political parties, ruling or otherwise.

76. How fair and effective are the rules governing party discipline in the legislature and within the party? *(5)*

In Namibia, the internal functioning of political parties is governed by their own constitutions. SWAPO is guided by the party's constitution, operational guide and political programme. The Congress is SWAPO's highest body, with delegates selecting members of the Central Committee and the party's president through a simple majority by secret ballot. The party is guided by the Central Committee, a national executive body, that includes the party leader, party MPs, members of regional and local branches, and auxiliary groups (Koep 2009). Additionally, the Central Committee members elect members of the politburo, which is responsible for implementing its decisions, including policy formulation (Tonchi & Shifotoka 2005:22). Internal democracy within SWAPO is stifled by the party's top-down bureaucratic structure. The party has been known to dismiss elected officials who are accused of not towing the party line – for example, the removal of democratically elected SWAPO members in Ongwediva, Oshana Region in 2004 and again in Windhoek East in 2007.

The National Assembly has the authority to make rules of procedure for the conduct of its business and to ensure compliance from each party discipline (Ibid.). At times, however, these rules have been rendered inoperative as a result of one–party dominance.

Occasionally, SWAPO MPs act with impunity and the rules of procedure in parliament are not always respected or are accepted selectively.

77. How far are parties effective membership organisations, and how far are members able to influence party policy? Are all individual members privy to sufficient information about their party, including details of private donors? (4)

Namibian political parties have the right to determine their own organisational structures insofar as these are not in conflict with the overriding terms and conditions consecrated in the Namibian Constitution. These structures include party constitutions, manifestos and other political programmes, in terms of which the rights and obligations of all party members are stipulated.

However, in practice, parties are not effective membership organisations; several factors have severely undermined the extent to which rank-and-file party members are able to influence the policies of their respective parties. This is due to the fact that they hardly have the right to obtain sufficient information about their parties, including details about sources of funding, private donors and the amounts involved. Lack of inner-party democracy, coupled with an unquestioning acceptance of political hierarchies and a culture of intolerance towards dissenting voices, is probably the key factor undermining the extent to which ordinary party members can shape the policies and/or composition of their respective parties.

Another factor severely undermining inner-party democracy is the party-list system. Although, theoretically, lower-level party structures, such as sections, branches, district committees and regional conferences should play a significant role in the election of party leaders in a bottom-up fashion, these decisions are often overridden at the higher levels, where decisions are made in a top-down fashion (Republic of Namibia 2009). Accordingly, in terms of the choice of 'appropriate' candidates to be included on the final party lists submitted to the ECN for national election purposes, party superstructures trump substructures.

78. To what extent are political parties able to aggregate the interests of all social groups? (4)

Namibia is a multicultural and multi-ethnic country. Colonialism and apartheid accentuated ethnic cleavages that contributed to a political system in which the boundaries between political parties and ethnic groups are very thin. Virtually all of the political parties in Namibia largely contain members of a particular ethnic group or are perceived as such. For example, SWAPO and the RDP primarily comprise Oshiwambo speakers, while the United Democratic Front (UDF), the National Unity Democratic Organisation (NUDO), the Monitor Action Group (MAG) and the newly formed Democratic Party of Namibia (DPN) predominantly consist of members of the Damara, Herero, Afrikaner and Nama communities, respectively. SWAPO relies heavily on the support of Oshiwambo speakers (NSHR 1999a; Hopwood 2008). Political divisions along ethnic lines can also be attributed to policy failures that have yet to achieve genuine national reconciliation, foster loyalty to a single State, and secure justice, liberty, equality and fraternity among themselves. This includes the lack of enthusiasm and commitment from politicians and government officials to encourage the formation of integrationist and multiracial organisations and movements by removing barriers between racial and ethnic groups.

The regulation of traditional authorities in Namibia is guided by two pieces of legislation: the Traditional Authorities Act (No 25 of 2000) and the Council of Traditional Leaders Act (No. 13 of 1997). While traditional leadership offers Namibians in rural and marginalised areas a form of representation, in practise, many have played a mixed role in ensuring the protection of rights and advancement of interests of minorities. Too often they have been co-opted into Namibia's political process and become extensions of political parties, particularly by SWAPO. Allegations that government has withheld recognition from traditional leaders for political reasons continue. In this regard, the plight of the San people is of particular note. While SWAPO committed itself to addressing the intransigent problems they face, the government has refused to recognise the existence of traditional San communities and leaders, including the Khwe San in western Caprivi, and has largely omitted the San from land reform and redistribution processes (UNHCR/Refworld 1994).

As Namibia's most dominant party, SWAPO has an obligation to be inclusive. While the party is composed of sections representing women, elders, youths and workers, all of them strictly adhere to party policy (Suzman n.d.). Continued issues around the abuse of political power through selective implementation of laws and regulations, unaccountable State institutions and the administration of public resources have not been adequately addressed by the ruling party. It seems that cronyism, favouritism, patronage and a culture of entitlement have been institutionalised at the expense of advancing the interests and needs of all Namibians in a non-discriminatory manner.

MEDIA RIGHTS

79. *To what extent does the legal system ensure that print and electronic media are free to print or say what they want about those in power in both government and the private sector?*   *(6)*

80. *To what extent are people and organisations able to disseminate their views via print or electronic media?*   (6)

81. *To what extent are the print and electronic media independent from government? How pluralistic is the ownership of print and electronic media?*   (6)

Although freedom of expression is guaranteed under Article 21(1) of the Constitution, Namibia has several restrictive media laws, including the Official Secrets Act 1963, the National Key Points Act 1980 and the Criminal Procedure Act 1977, each conceived under South African administration. S205 of the Criminal Procedures Act 1977 permits a magistrate to order a journalist to reveal his or her source during a criminal trial or to imprison a journalist should he or she refuse to comply, and these laws have been applied in a few cases (Tötemeyer 2007:5). The Protection of Information Act 1982 restricts the information civil servants can release to the public and the absence of an Information Bill makes it difficult for the public, and particularly the media, to gain access to public information held by the State.

According to the African Media Barometer (2011:14), the level of free expression in Namibia varies among media, with broadcast media more likely to exhibit self-censorship. The Namibian Broadcasting Act (No. 9 of 1991) mandates the government to appoint the board of directors, thereby impinging upon the organisation's impartiality, with the result that the Namibian Broadcasting Corporation (NBC) is largely perceived to be a SWAPO mouthpiece. However, while the NBC has a monopoly on free-to-air television, the 2008 launch of privately-owned One Africa Television is viewed as a positive step towards diversifying the range of media opinions available on television.

Media organisations and journalists critical of government and members of SWAPO are, at times, subjected to harassment by the authorities and their supporters. There are two notable examples. First, for a period of over 10 years, government banned advertisements by State-affiliated bodies and parastatals in *The Namibian* because of its critical views and opinions of government and SWAPO (African Media Barometer 2011:13). This ban was lifted in August 2011 (Amnesty International 2011). Secondly, in January 2010, a well-known freelance journalist was attacked by four male SWAPO activists for writing an article published in *The Namibian* (2011b), in which he had pointed out the lack of transparency in a business deal involving prominent members of SWAPO.

During its interactive dialogue on Namibia in February 2011, the 48-Member United Nations Working Group on the Universal Periodic Review expressed concern about the 'reported harassment of journalists, media organisations, human rights defenders and non-governmental organisations' in Namibia (Amnesty International 2011). For example, addressing a SWAPO elections rally in the Ohangwena Region in 2009, the SWAPO secretary general and justice minister branded *The Namibian*'s then editor a 'big snake in the country', and accused the country's leading independent daily of publishing false news aimed at tarnishing the country's image, as well as 'desiring to bring war' (United Nations General Assembly 2011: para. 64). The politician report-edly also labelled *The Namibian* newspaper as 'a bad newspaper, reporting only on nega-tive things like crimes, baby dumping and court cases, and never on positive things that are happening in the country' (Ibid.). While only one example is cited, this kind of vitriolic attack on the media engenders a hostile atmosphere that undercuts the media's ability to perform vital watchdog duties.

Namibia boasts a broad cross-section of media, with five daily papers, six weekly news-papers, several periodicals, two commercial television stations, one religious television station and at least 12 commercial radio stations (Ibid.). NBC Radio, which is heard by more than 90% of the country's population, is accessible, although not all of its various language services transmit to all parts of the country. Local NBC TV covers less than 70% of the country, while the prohibitive cost of television license fees and a lack of electricity in rural areas further limit accessibility. Radio is more affordable, but various languages services are limited because government cannot afford to install more trans-mitters throughout the country (African Media Barometer 2011). Although there are positive indications that young people are increasingly accessing the Internet via mobile phones or Internet cafés, the cost of Internet access is still prohibitively expensive. In 2010, only 6.5% of Namibians accessed the Internet (Ibid.).

The ownership of print and electronic media in the country is relatively pluralistic, and the press reflects a wide range of political views. Namibia's media can be divided into two main categories in terms of ownership: public and private. Public media, specifically NBC television and radio, as well as print media, such as *New Era* and the Namibia Press Agency, is accessible to approximately 90% of the population (Freedom House 2011). However, they are directly controlled by government and indirectly by SWAPO. The director general of NBC TV is appointed by a board of directors that, in turn, is appointed by the Minister of Information and Communication Technology and subject to approval of the Cabinet. Hence, the minister and, by extension, the Cabinet, maintain a direct hand over the activities of NBC TV, at times subjecting the broadcaster to political interference. For example, on 3 March 2009, the popular chat shows on NBC Radio were banned, after the SWAPO Party Elders' Council had expressed their unhappiness about the content of the shows, as they were perceived as criticising the party's leaders and government.

Owing to a combination of historical and cultural factors, issues that affect margin-alised and poor Namibians are not always given sufficient prominence in the local press. The extent to which citizens and CSOs are able to disseminate their views via print and electronic media is dependent on ownership and editorial policy. While the SMS and letter pages of *The Namibian* newspaper (which until very recently had a white female editor) are among the most widely used outlets for popular (and often highly critical) participation, the fact that private media in Namibia is still concentrated in the hands of white Namibians, with only two of the seven privately owned independent newspapers, the *Windhoek Observer* and *Confidénte*, being owned by black Namibians, remains a challenge. While some white-controlled newspapers have difficulties shaking off perceptions around pre- and post-independence political alliances, in general, black-owned independent newspapers are regarded as not being as inherently vulnerable to association with the apartheid past or perceived as fronting a Western imperialist agenda.

82. *To what extent do citizens have equal access to adequate information, including news and other media?* (5)

Although the county boasts a broad cross-section of media and circulation figures for newspapers are relatively high (with penetration into the rural areas), owing largely to the size of the country and low population density, all Namibian citizens generally do not have equal and adequate access to comprehensive and accurate information. While television and newspaper coverage is of necessity higher in urban areas, the various radio services are usually more accessible to the majority of Namibians, especially in the outlying parts. Additionally, unhealthy rivalries among Namibia's private media organisations lead to the suppression of news and other newsworthy events, simply because such items have been covered first by rival media. This state of affairs affects the extent to which Namibian citizens have equal and sufficient access to information, including news and other media.

CONCLUSION

The Namibian Constitution gives special protection to civil and political rights. The Constitution obligates government to respect, protect and realise all the civil and political rights of all individuals and groups, without distinction of any kind, such as race, colour, sex, language, religion, political or other opinion, national or social origin, property, birth or other status, within its territory and subject to its jurisdiction. The ratification of numerous international and regional human rights instruments on civil and political rights has, overall, strengthened the Constitution and, thereby, Namibians.

However, as this chapter has demonstrated, Namibian democracy faces significant challenges in terms of political freedom. The lack of credible opposition parties and the centralisation of power in the hands of one political party threaten to erode the rights that were fought for during the liberation struggle. All political parties, but particularly SWAPO, must respect the democratic choices of the people, overcome partisan divisions and work together for all Namibians.

An overburdened and under-capacitated judiciary continues to undermine the rights of citizens as they are unable to seek and attain justice as the Constitution intends. The prolonging of the Caprivi trial is a grievous injustice that continues to defy the defendant's right to a fair trial. Finally, while Namibia has a relatively diverse media, it is not consistently and sufficiently independent from political interference to be able to adequately represent the situation and reflect the aspirations of the majority of Namibians.

SECTION SCORE: 5

REFERENCES

AFRICA NEWS.COM. 2009. *Namibia: Women MPs to reduce to 25* [online]. Available: http://bit.ly/4nxLrl

AFRICAN MEDIA BAROMETER. 2011. *African Media Barometer Report*. Windhoek: MISA

ALLAFRICA.COM [online]. 2008. 'Namibia: Mass graves found in Angola – NSHR'. 10 September 2008.

___ 2011a. 'Namibia: Tribalism irks Govt'. 30 April 2011. Available: http://allafrica.com/namibia/

___ 2011b. 'Namibia: Tribalism closes school'. 8 June 2011. Available: http://allafrica.com/namibia/

AMNESTY INTERNATIONAL. 2000. *Angola/Namibia: Human rights abuses in the border area*. 22 March 2000. Available: http://bit.ly/xR7Ytf

___ 2003. 'Namibia: Justice delayed is justice denied: The Caprivi treason trial'. AI Index: AFR 42/001/2003.

___ 2011. 'Human Rights in Republic of Namibia' (Annual Report 2011).

AMOO, S.K. & SKEFFERS, I. 2009. 'The rule of law in Namibia' in Horn, N. & Bösel, A (eds). *Human rights and the rule of law in Namibia*. Windhoek: Konrad Adenauer Foundation.

ARASA. 2010. *Namibian Immigration Control Act discriminatory to people living with HIV* [online]. Available: http://bit.ly/AmITtO.

BBC NEWS ONLINE. 2008. 'Namibian "mass graves" discovered'. 9 September 2008.

CCPR HUMAN RIGHTS COMMITTEE (81st Session). 2004. *Concluding observations of the Human Rights Committee: Namibia*. 30 July 2004.

CENTRAL BUREAU OF STATISTICS. 2008. *A review of poverty and inequality in Namibia*.Windhoek: The Government of Namibia. Available: http://on.undp.org/zGYwwF.

CHOMBA, S.M. n.d. *The universality of human rights: Challenges for Namibia* [online]. http://bit.ly/wjYTqn.

CONWAY, P. 2000. *Truth Commissions in Africa: The non-case of Namibia and the emerging case of Sierra Leone*. International Law Forum du Droit International.

___ 2003. 'Truth and reconciliation: The road not taken in Namibia' in *The Online Journal of Peace and Conflict Resolution*. 5.1 Summer:66–76.

DIPLOMACY NAMIBIA. 2011. *Namibia now ranks as 'upper-middle income'* [online]. Available: http://bit.ly/zDs5UB.

DU PISANI, A. 2010 *The political arena: The Regional Council and Local Authority elections 2010* [online]. Available: http://bit.ly/yIW2Ds

FREEDOM HOUSE. 2011. *Freedom of the Press 2011, Namibia* [online]. Available: http://bit.ly/rnoJe1

FRONTLINE FELLOWSHIP. n.d. 'Namibia's "Shoot on Sight" Policy' [online]. Available: http://www.frontline.org.za.

HOPWOOD, G. 2007. *Guide to Namibian Politics*. Windhoek: Namibia Institute for Democracy.

___ 2008. *Strengthening political parties*. Windhoek: NID/USAID.

HUMAN RIGHTS WATCH. 1992. *Accountability in Namibia: Human rights and the transition to democracy* [online]. Available: http://bit.ly/zBrG7I

INDEX MUNDI. 2011. *Namibia demographics profile 2012* [online]. Available: http://bit.ly/xATII5.

INFORMANTÉ. 2009. 'Political intolerance unconstitutional'. 28 January 2009.

___ 2011. 'Kaaronda gets 2nd death threat over GIPF'. 28 May 2011.

INSTITUTE FOR SECURITY STUDIES. 2009. *The myth of democratic consolidation in Namibia*. Available: http://bit.ly/zprOK6.

INTERNATIONAL REFUGEE RIGHTS INITIATIVE. 2009. *Congolese in danger of being deported from Botswana*. Available: http://bit.ly/zqNsST

IRINNEWS ONLINE. 1999. 'Namibia: The Caprivi secessionist crisis'. 9 August 1999.

___ 2000. 'Angola-Namibia: IRIN focus on Kavango insecurity'. 1 September 2000.

___ 2002. 'Namibia: Focus on Caprivi killings'. 13 November 2002.

ITUC. 2011. *Annual survey of violations of trade union rights* [online]. Available: http://bit.ly/ytRCLF

KAAPAMA, P., BLAAUW, L., ZAARUKA, B. & KAAKUNGA, E. 2007. *Consolidating democratic governance in southern Africa: Namibia*. Johannesburg: EISA.

KOEP, M. 2009. 'Current Parliamentary Environment' in *Namibia Country Report 2009*. Cape Town: Centre for Social Science Research, University of Cape Town

MINORITY RIGHTS GROUP. 2003. *Minorities in Independent Namibia* [online]. http://bit.ly/yTai0Q.

NAKUTA, J. & CHIPEPERA, F. n.d. *The justice sector and the rule of law in Namibia: Management, personnel and access*. Windhoek: Namibia Institute for Democracy and the Human Rights and Documentation Centre.

NAMIBIAN ECONOMIST [online]. 2005. 'What criteria were used for Ongombo West expropriation?' 23 September 2005.

NAMIBIAN INFORMATION TECHNOLOGIES. 2009. *International day on missing persons* [online]. Available: http://bit.ly/zkC41e.

NAMRIGHTS. n.d. 'Freedom from torture' in *Namibia Human Rights Report*. Windhoek: NSHR.

___ 2009. *Why SWAPO party is violently against NSHR* (press release). 28 September 2009. Available: http://bit.ly/y3fSPv

NEW ERA [online]. 2010. 'Namibia: Trade union claims discrimination'. 10 June 2010.

___ 2011. 'Geingob launches counter attack'. 1 July 2011.

___ 2011. 'Poverty in a sea of riches'. 14 October 2011.

NEWS24 ONLINE. 2008. 'Mass graves found in Namibia'. 10 September 2008.

NSHR. 1998. 'Fundamental freedoms: Freedom of opinion and expression' in *Namibia: Human Rights Report 1998*. Windhoek: NSHR.

___ 1999a. *Choose your own representatives*. Windhoek: NSHR.

___ 1999b. 'Comprehensive report: Political intimidation on the increase' (press conference). Windhoek, 17 November 1999.

___ 1999c. *Namibia: Human Rights Report 1999*. Windhoek: NSHR.

___ 2001. *Special report: War crimes and other atrocities*. 15 May 2001.

___ 2004. 'Human rights violations' in *Namibia Human Rights Report 1995-2004*. Windhoek: NSHR.

___ 2006a. 'Help end Namibian impunity relating to enforced disappearances, torture & other grave breaches'. NSHR submission to ICC, 30 November 2006.

___ 2006b. 'Opinion: The Caprivi case and absolute prohibition of torture'. 11 January 2006.

___ 2006c. 'Peaceful activities are constitutional' (press release). 7 September 2006.

___ 2006d. 'UN Working Group Charges GoN' in *Namibia Human Rights Report 2006*. Windhoek: NSHR.

___ 2007a 'Attacks on freedom of expression and opinion' in *Namibia Human Rights Report 2007*. Windhoek: NSHR.

___ 2007b. 'Discrimination against women' in *Namibia Human Rights Report 2007*. Windhoek: NSHR.

___ 2008a. 'Deportations or forcible transfer of population' in *Namibia enforced disappearances: Discovery of 'No Name' gravesites*. Windhoek: NSHR.

___ 2008b. 'Kanime's dismissal an assault on democracy' (press release). 9 March 2008.

___ 2008c. 'Massive forced displacement' in *Namibia enforced disappearances: Discovery of 'No Name' gravesites*. Windhoek: NSHR.

___ 2008d. 'Objective of this report' in *Namibia enforced disappearances: Discovery of 'No Name' gravesites*. Windhoek: NSHR.

___ 2008e. 'Right to personal security' in *Namibia Human Rights Report 2008*. Windhoek: NSHR.

___ 2008f. 'Summary executions' in *Namibia enforced disappearances: Discovery of 'No Name' gravesites*. Windhoek: NSHR.

___ 2009. 'Nujoma issues threats of violence' (press release). 16 June 2009.

___ 2010a. 'Freedom of association' in *Namibia Human Rights Report 1999-2010*. Windhoek: NSHR.

___ 2010b. 'Fundamental freedoms' in *Namibia Human Rights Report 2009*. Windhoek: NSHR.

___ 2010c. 'GoN declares KAS director as threat to stability' in *Namibia Human Rights Report 2010*. Windhoek: NSHR.

___ 2010d. 'Right to community security' in *Namibia Human Rights Report 2008-2010*. Windhoek: NSHR.

___ 2010e. 'Summary executions' in *Namibia Human Rights Report 1994-2010*. Windhoek: NSHR.

OFFICE OF THE HIGH COMMISSIONER FOR HUMAN RIGHTS. 1997. *Concluding observations of the Committee against Torture: Namibia* [online]. Available: http://bit.ly/zZsSLz

___ 2010. *14th Session of the Human Rights Council*. UN Document A/HRC/14.

___ 2011. *17th Session of the Human Rights Council*. UN DOCUMENT A/HRC/17/14.

OFFICE OF THE OMBUDSMAN. 2006. *Special report on conditions prevailing at police cells throughout Namibia*. November 2006. Windhoek: Office of the Ombudsman.

PAMBAZUKA NEWS. 2009. *Namibian politics: The pathology of power and paranoia* [online]. Available: http://www.pambazuka.org/en/category/features/60518

PARLEVLIET, M. 2000. *Truth Commissions in Africa: The non-case of Namibia and the emerging case of Sierra Leone* [online]. Available: http://bit.ly/ylODFd.

REPUBLIC OF NAMIBIA. 1990. *The Constitution of Namibia*. Windhoek: The Government of Namibia.

___ 2005. *National Planning Commission: Policy on civic organisations partnership policy*. Windhoek: Government of Namibia.

REPUBLIKEIN [online]. 2009. 'RDP on pre-election violence'. 23 November 2009.

RUPPEL, O.C. & AMBUNDA, L.N. (n.d.) *The justice sector & the rule of law in Namibia: Framework, selected legal aspects and cases*. Windhoek: Namibia Institute for Democracy and the Human Rights and Documentation Centre.

SKADI FORUM [online]. n.d. 'The expropriation of white farms in Namibia'. Available: http://bit.ly/xza0jS

SOCIETY OF ADVOCATES. 2011. Press release: 8 August 2011. Available: http://bit.ly/AxHr9L

SUZMAN, J. *Minorities in independent Namibia*. Minority Rights Group International. Available: http://bit.ly/yTai0Q.

THE NAMIBIAN [online]. 1999. 'CoD is the main target of intimidation – NSHR'. 30 November 1999. Available: http://allafrica.com/stories/199911300090.html

___ 2000. 'Govt intolerance of civil society on rise – US report'. 29 February 2000.

___ 2004a. 'Delayed justice gets armed robbery suspects off the hook'. 6 April 2004.

___ 2004b. 'Tribalism in Namibia is real, not imagined'. 13 April 2004.

___ 2004c. 'Ipula case delayed for the 15th time'. 7 July 2004.

___ 2004d. 'DTA slams Govt over recognition of Herero chiefs'. 20 August 2004.

___ 2004e. 'Justice system needs some serious work, says PG'. 31 August 2004.

___ 2004f. 'Three-year-old robbery case deferred for trial'. 8 December 2004.

___ 2005a. 'Investigate the lawyers'. 18 January 2005.

___ 2005b. 'Fatal car crash delivers treason trial's latest jinx'. 25 January 2005.

___ 2005c. 'Peeping Tom case postponed again'. 28 January 2005.

___ 2005d. 'Ongombo West to be expropriated'. 22 July 2005.

___ 2005e. 'Ongombo West: How it played out'. 11 November 2005.

___ 2005f. 'Nujoma blames lawyers for backlogs in courts'. 22 November 2005.

___ 2005g. 'Non-recognition a non-issue: councilor'. 16 December 2005.

___ 2007a. 'Magistrates taken to task'. 21 February 2007.

___ 2007b. 'PG is working through case backlog'. 26 April 2007.

___ 2007c. 'Poverty rate down says new survey'. 28 February 2007. Available: http://bit.ly/x1k8nQ

___ 2007d. 'Criminal delays mar case'. 26 July 2007.

___ 2007e. 'Tribalism and ethnicity'. 9 November 2007.

___ 2008a. 'Swapo blames media for election violence'. 29 February 2008.

___ 2008b. 'UN report lambastes Nam for hate speech'. 21 August 2008. Available: http://bit.ly/wO8slj

___ 2008c. 'Make 2009 a year of political tolerance'. 19 December 2008.

___ 2009. 'Government conveniently rediscovers civil society'. 3 September 2009.

___ 2010. 'Namibia: National Council wants action against Ya Nangoloh'. 29 October 2010. Available: http://allafrica.com/stories/201011010587.html

___ 2011a. 'The referee and the race card'. 16 June 2011.

___ 2011b. 'The Namibian unbanned'. 31 August 2011.

THE NAMIBIAN SUN [online]. n.d. 'Prisons overcrowding hits crisis level'. Available: http://bit.ly/w8yurn

THE ZIMBABWEAN. 2009. 'Namibia: Violence rocks Outapi'. 9 November 2009.

TONCHI, V.L. & SHIFOTOKA, A.N. 2005. *Parties and political development in Namibia*. Johannesburg: The Electoral Institute for Sustainable Democracy in Africa.

TÖTEMEYER, G. 2007. 'The management of a dominant political party system with particular reference to Namibia'. Contribution to an international seminar held in Maputo, Mozambique, 10–12 December 2007.

TRADING ECONOMICS. 2011. *Population: Female (% of total) in Namibia* [online]. Available: http://bit.ly/wu3cNO.

TREEGER, C. 2004. *Legal analysis of farmland expropriation in Namibia*. Windhoek: Namibian Institute for Democracy. Available: http://bit.ly/yLJ4vs.

UNDP. n.d. *Understanding poverty and inequality in Namibia* [online]. Available: http://on.undp.org/zX4JuK

UNHCR | REFWORLD. 1994. *Immigration Control Act, 1993*. Available: http://bit.ly/x9NsOh

UNICEF. 2010. 'Namibia is the most unequal society in the world' in *Children and adolescents in Namibia 2010: A situation analysis*. Windhoek: National Planning Commission.

UNITED NATIONS | CERD. 2008. *Consideration of Reports submitted by States Parties under Article 9 of the Convention: Concluding observations of the Committee on the Elimination of Racial Discrimination.* CERD/C/NAM/CO/12. 19 August 2008.

UNITED NATIONS CONVENTION AGAINST TORTURE. 1997. *CAT/C/SR.293 and 294/ Add.1* [online]. Available: http://bit.ly/z7Zxtt

UNITED NATIONS GENERAL ASSEMBLY. 2011. *Report of the Working Group on the Universal Periodic Review: Namibia*. 24 March 2011 [online]. Available: http://bit.ly/ybfw8c

US DEPARTMENT OF STATE. 2010. *2010 Human Rights Report: Namibia* [online]. Available: http://1.usa.gov/Au6yJd.

USAID AFRICA. n.d. *Namibia* [online]. Available: http://1.usa.gov/zbgDUD.

WIKILEAKS. 2008. *Political violence in Northern Namibia foreshadows contentious election* [online]. Available: http://bit.ly/zSgZNe

WINDHOEK OBSERVER [online]. 2011. 'Geingob rejects judiciary as a holy cow'. 22 August 2011.

ENDNOTES

1   Republic of Namibia (1990) Chapter 3 and Articles 95(d), 96(d), 143 and 144

2   Ibid. Articles 5 and 18

3   NSHR (2004); Frontline Fellowship (n.d.); IRIN News Online (2000); Amnesty International (2000); NSHR (2001); News24 Online (2008); BBC News Online (2008); AllAfrica.com (2008)

4   NSHR (2004); Frontline Fellowship (n.d.); IRINNews Online (2000); Amnesty International (2000); NSHR (2001); News24 Online (2008); BBC News Online (2008); AllAfrica.com (2008)

5   NSHR (2008d:8) para. 11; NSHR (2008f:19) para. 40.

6   NSHR (2008c:40) para. 102.

7   NSHR (2008f:20) para. 42; NSHR (2008a:41) para. 105.

8   NSHR (2008f); Amnesty International (2000); NSHR (2006a); NSHR (2008c)

9   NSHR (2004); IRIN News Online (1999); IRIN News Online(2002); Amnesty International (2003)

10   Submission by the United Nations High Commissioner for Refugees for the Office of the High Commissioner for Human Rights' Compilation Report - Universal Periodic Review: Namibia

11   NSHR (2004); Frontline Fellowship (n.d.); IRINNews Online (2000); Amnesty International (2000); NSHR (2001); News24 Online (2008); BBC News Online (2008); AllAfrica.com (2008)

12   NamRights (n.d.); NSHR (2006b); Amnesty International (2003); Amnesty International (2000)

13   *S v Malumo* (P 4/2010) [2010] NASC 10 (14 September 2010). Available: http://bit.ly/xk0OCz.

14   Republic of Namibia (1990) Articles 12, 18, 25(2) & Chapter 9

15   Central Bureau of Statistics (2008); Diplomacy Namibia (2011); UNICEF (2010:26); *New Era* (2011b); UNDP (n.d.); USAID Africa (n.d.)

16   *The Namibian* (2011a); *Windhoek Observer* (2011); Society of Advocates (2011); *New Era* (2011a)

17   http://www.saflii.org/na/cases/NASC/1995/3.pdf

18   http://www.saflii.org/na/cases/NASC/2010/6.pdf

19   Ibid.

20   NSHR (1998:203-222); *Republikein* (2009); *The Namibian* (2008a); Wikileaks (2008); *The Zimbabwean* (2009); NSHR (2010b:139-160)

21   Republic of Namibia (1990) Article 19, read in conjunction with Article 66 (1)

22   Minority Rights Group (2003); *The Namibian* (2005g); *The Namibian* (2004d); NSHR (2010d)

23   NSHR (2010d); *The Namibian* (2004b); *The Namibian* (2007e); AllAfrica.com (2011a, b)

24   http://survey10.ituc-csi.org/+-Namibia-+.html

25   http://bit.ly/Ahrhuc; NamRights (2009)

26   http://www.kas.de/upload/auslandshomepages/namibia/Women_Custom/boesl.pdf

27   NSHR (1998:203-222); *Republikein* (2009); *The Namibian* (2008a); Wikileaks (2008); *The Zimbabwean* (2009); NSHR (2010b:139-160)

SECTION 5

HUMAN DIGNITY AND DEMOCRACY

TONY HANCOX AND RICARDO MUKONDA[1]

In its Preamble, the Namibian Constitution states:

> *Whereas recognition of the inherent dignity and of the equal and inalienable rights of all members of the human family is indispensable for freedom, justice and peace;*
>
> *Whereas the said rights are most effectively maintained and protected in a democratic society, where the Government is responsible to freely elected representatives of the people, operating under a sovereign constitution and a free and independent judiciary.*

Conde (1999:57) defines human dignity as 'the innate value or worthiness of a human being'. He proclaims that 'human dignity is preserved and enhanced by the setting of international human rights standards that limit the State from committing acts or failing to act in such a way as to violate human dignity'. As such, the link between democracy and socio-economic development – on which the very premise of human dignity is upheld and sustained – must, therefore, be critically examined. The needs of citizens must be advanced by the State, as failure to do so may result in a loss of faith in democracy. Although the Namibian Constitution does not recognise the majority of socio-economic rights as justiciable, no dignified life can be led without access to those most basic needs.

Human rights are indivisible and are essential for the true enjoyment of other rights. All persons must be afforded the ability to acquire adequate clean water, food, housing, health care, education and employment, in order to enjoy their right to dignity. While the needs of citizens determine the emphasis to be placed on the primacy of various rights, a democratic government that fails to ensure adequate protection of socio-economic and cultural rights will fail to provide a level of human development that is sufficient and essential to sustaining a democracy.

To guide this process of democratic nation-building, the government has formulated a plan of action in conjunction with civil society and the private sector. This plan of action was introduced by the former President, Sam Nujoma, in June 2004 and is called Vision 2030. It sets out a number of desired results which are to be achieved by the year 2030. The overall aim of Vision 2030 is to attain 'a prosperous and industrialised Namibia, developed by her human resources, enjoying peace, harmony and political stability'.

There are eight identified major objectives that arise from this vision. For the purposes of this chapter, the most important of these are:

(1) Ensure that Namibia is a fair, gender-responsive, caring and committed nation in which all citizens are able to realise their full potential in a safe and decent living environment. – This objective can be aligned with social welfare and equality; and

(5) Ensure a healthy, food-secure and breastfeeding nation in which all preventable, infectious and parasitic diseases are under secure control; and in which people enjoy a high standard of living, with access to quality education, health and other vital services, in an atmosphere of sustainable population growth and development. – This objective can be aligned with socio-economic rights and quality of life.

Vision 2030 is a fundamental tool to guide the five yearly National Development Plans (NDPs) of which the first related to the period 1995–2000. The NDPs provide direction to government ministries, non-governmental organisations (NGOs) and the private sector by clarifying strategies for achieving developmental goals.

The plan of action also contains milestones meant to guide and alert stakeholders as to whether they are on track to achieve what is required by 2030. Some of these milestones will be referred to in this chapter.

SOCIO-ECONOMIC AND CIVIL RIGHTS' PROTECTION

83. *How far are economic and social rights, including equal access to work, guaranteed and enforced for all? Are civil rights of the marginalised and post vulnerable protected in civil and criminal procedure law?* (5)

84. *How effectively are the basic necessities of life guaranteed, including (a) Clean, adequate and reasonably accessible water, (b) Adequate food, (c) Adequate housing and shelter, and (d) Adequate and unimpeded access to land?* (4)

Under South African–imposed apartheid, there were varying rules for different races in the then South West Africa. The minority white population had access to better quality education and health care, as well as to improved housing and public services, than the majority black, Coloured and Indian people. The result of this unequal treatment formed the basis of the current systemic inequalities in Namibia. This state of affairs has been exacerbated by government's lack of effective policies to address the educational and skills deficits of the past and the resultant diminished access to employment opportunities. The latest statistics indicate that formal unemployment currently stands at 51.2% (Ministry of Labour & Social Welfare 2008:39). This figure has been the focus of some dispute, since the formula used to classify gainful employment is controversial and the statistics gathered have been queried both from outside and within government. In the Namibian context, the term 'unemployed' is used for any person who has not been employed gainfully for one hour in the preceding week. If the current statistics are accurate, therefore, this would mean that there is no way to gauge accurately what percentage of the employed is actually self-sufficient and able to live a dignified existence. The effect of over 50% unemployment in a nation of marginally over two million inhabitants has serious repercussions for the economy and potential growth of Namibia.

With the exception of the right to free basic education and the right to culture, the Constitution does not enshrine socio-economic rights within its entrenched Bill of Rights (Republic of Namibia 1990, Articles 19 & 20). Instead, in Chapter 11, socio-economic rights are constitutionally protected to a lesser degree under 'Principles of State Policy' (Republic of Namibia 1990: Article 95). The principles do not have the force of law in the same way as those contained in the Bill of Rights, and are only meant to guide government in the making of laws while simultaneously enjoining the courts to take note of such principles when called on to interpret legislation. The Principles of State Policy are not entrenched and may be amended.

While socio-economic rights may be promoted for all on paper, legal enforcement is problematic, since innovative ways may be required to reframe them within the ambit of the Bill of Rights, should legislative redress be sought.

In an attempt to increase and widen access to employment opportunities, the government has enacted affirmative action legislation.[2] This legislation requires employers to have an affirmative action policy in place, as well as to periodically report to the Employment Equity Commission (EEC) on how such policy is being implemented. The legislation is meant to empower the previously disadvantaged, women and disabled persons. However, affirmative action legislation has not led to widespread equity in the labour sphere, in part due to the lack of qualifications and skills of potential candidates, as well as the lack of consistent oversight by the Commission. Responding to the most recent unemployment figures, government has embarked on an employment creation scheme entitled the Targeted Intervention Programme for Employment and Economic Growth (TIPEEG) (Ministry of Finance n.d.). This programme is highly ambitious and has led to a number of local economists being doubtful about the projected impact of the initiative (*The Namibian* 2011b; *New Era* 2011). It is, however, indicative of government's acknowledgment that unemployment is a major concern for the healthy growth of Namibia and must be urgently addressed. Government has released tenders for a number of projects under TIPEEG, which shows that this initiative is moving forward, but results are not yet apparent and instances of alleged corruption and lack of transparency around the relevant procurement procedures are already being raised.

Criminal law and procedure applies equally to all. However, serious problems relating to the conduct of a trial within a reasonable period, a right which is constitutionally entrenched, are cause for much concern (Republic of Namibia 1990, Article 12(1)(b)). The Judge-President of the High Court of Namibia published a report titled *Promoting access to justice in the High Court of Namibia: The case for judicial case management* in 2010, in which he cited statistics obtained from the Registrar of the High Court indicating that, as of March 2010, a backlog of approximately 62% was created on number alone in the case of criminal appeals. In addition, during 2010, there was an average of only five to seven permanent judges allocated to criminal trials, limiting the number of trials that can be heard, as every additional criminal case added means a corresponding decrease of judges for the civil roll. It is, therefore, apparent that the capacity and congestion within the higher and lower courts inhibit the speedy movement of trials, with further delays being attributed to the investigating and prosecuting authorities, as well as legal practitioners (The Namibian 2008a). Legal Aid granted by the State is insufficient to cater for the needs of indigent accused,[3] and there is currently no public protector system within Namibia, in terms of which junior legal practitioners might be utilised to defend accused in the lower courts, with the result that a majority of criminal matters take place without the presence of legal counsel, contributing to delays in resolution and compromising the quality of justice provided by the State. The Caprivi treason trial has been widely cited as a miscarriage of justice, due to the length of time it has been ongoing (the event occurred in 1999). In Namibia's defence, however, it should be said that an event of this magnitude posed a huge challenge to the prosecuting authorities of such a young democracy and initial mistakes with regard to the number and formulation of the actual charges have contributed towards the delays in the entire criminal process. Apart from this, many of the procrastinations in the trial have been at the behest of the accused and their legal counsel.

While an independent judiciary, as well as sufficient legislation, is in place to ensure protection of the civil rights guaranteed to all Namibians, legal aid is limited and the assistance rendered by civil society is unable to cater for the needs of all potential litigants seeking redress. Therefore, full enjoyment of these rights is dependent primarily on litigants being able to afford the cost of litigation.

ACCESS TO WATER

Attaining adequate access to clean water often determines a person's ability to attain access to a number of other basic and essential needs, such as the right to health care and adequate sanitation. Linkages to education and dignity can also be drawn.

In an arid country like Namibia, access to water is an ongoing developmental challenge. A survey conducted by the Ministry of Health and Social Services[4] in 2006/07 determined that 88.1% of households in Namibia have access to improved sources of drinking water, although urban households are more likely than rural households to have access to such sources. This is well within the targets of Vision 2030 and, if the trend continues, it is quite possible that 100% coverage will be attained by 2030. Namibia has, therefore, made substantial strides in this area with the support of donor aid. The 2008 Water Supply and Sanitation Sector Policy[5] published by the Ministry of Agriculture, Water and Forestry sets clear sectoral objectives that prioritise water for domestic use over water for economic activities. Vision 2030 identified a need for desalination processes to promote future water security, but this directive initially favoured the needs of the uranium industry over citizens.[6] The construction of a desalination plant was finally started in early 2008 and was expected to be operational by mid-2011, although this has not yet materialised.

There is no free basic water policy in Namibia. Government created the State-owned enterprise NamWater by legislation[7] in 1997 with the mandate that it not make profits, but that it charge the full cost of supplying bulk water to consumers through its pricing policies. NamWater, therefore, operates on a cost-recovery basis, with government being able to subsidise water through transfers to NamWater from the national budget. Rural water supply has remained the mandate of the Ministry of Agriculture, Water and Forestry. In addition, the abovementioned water and sanitation policy states that 'In all instances it will be essential to recover the full financial cost or, in low income rural and urban areas, at least the operational and maintenance costs with support from government subsidies or cross-subsidies amongst consumers.'[8] Many informal settlements operate on a system of *ad hoc* payment for access to a certain amount of water from taps. This is not ideal in a country with high unemployment rates, where choices must then be made with regard to the basic need priorities.

The Water Resources Management Act (No. 24 of 2004) is an ambitious attempt by government to regulate the management, development, protection, conservation and use of water resources. It is, however, not yet implemented and remains under review by the Ministry of Agriculture, Water and Forestry and by Cabinet. While the fundamental principles underlying the Act are based on international norms and confirm access to safe drinking water as a basic human right,[9] a major weakness of the Act is rooted in a lack of capacity regarding implementation. Since the Act is so comprehensive, it requires a number of experts to monitor resources on a localised level, as government does not itself have the capacity to undertake the proper actions and oversight needed to enforce the Act. Furthermore, as the Act is currently under review, it is not known whether it will be amended or an alternative approach will be taken.

ACCESS TO FOOD

For a country with high levels of unemployment and wide income disparities, access to adequate food remains a serious challenge.

Selected indicators	Official census 2001[10]	Official census 1991
Population	1.83 million[11]	1.4 million
Population growth rate %	2.6	3.1
Population destiny/sq. km	2.1	1.7
Literacy rate (+15 years old) %	81	76
Urban/rural settlement %	33 / 67	28 / 72

Approximately 67% of the population lives in rural settlements. These settlements depend on subsistence crops for survival. Furthermore, north-central and north-eastern Namibia is prone to annual flooding that directly impacts the region's annual harvest. In March 2009, these regions experienced flooding of great magnitude due to torrential rains. This was surpassed only by the flooding experienced in the same areas in 2011. After the 2009 floods, and with the assistance of the international community, a comprehensive post-disaster needs assessment (PDNA) was conducted by government. In addition, government solicited international assistance to deal with the immediate effects of the floods. Approximately US$36 million was raised in these efforts. In both 2009 and 2011 a State of Emergency was declared and relocation camps catered for those who were displaced. In 2011, according to the United Nations World Food Programme (WFP), government allocated approximately US$4.4 million in response to the flood emergency. With the assistance of the WFP, food was delivered by way of helicopters and boats when necessary.

It is recognised that the findings of the PDNA need to be consolidated with the NDPs and Vision 2030. In addition, in October 2009, with the financial and technical assistance of the United Nations Development Programme (UNDP), Namibia prepared a proposed Climate Change Strategy and Action Plan which was preceded by the 2008 Climate Change Vulnerability and Adaptation Assessment. Government is, therefore, aware and responding to the impacts of climate change.

According to the latest Namibia Household Income and Expenditure Survey of 2003/2004, 28% of households are poor, an improvement on the 38% from the previous survey of 1993/1994. This survey quantifies a household as 'poor' if 60% or more of its total consumption is spent on food. The government has enacted social programmes designed to enhance food security for the poor. These include old age pensions, child grants and disability grants, as well as a food-for-work programme (*The Namibian Sun* 2011). Access to social grants requires identification of the recipients. This is hampered by the considerable backlog at the Ministry of Home Affairs and Immigration insofar as the issuing of identity documents is concerned. One food programme that has had mixed results is the National School Feeding Programme. In 2008, approximately 83 000 children benefited from this programme which provides one meal per day to needy children (National Planning Commission 2010). According to the Minister of Education at the National Education Conference held in Windhoek in June 2011, this figure had risen to more than 200 000 children by 2011. Although the increase may be regarded as positive, since it accommodates a larger number of needy children, it may also be construed negatively because it indicates a rising number of children that require such assistance.

The Basic Income Grant (BIG) scheme, propagated by a number of NGOs, has sought to provide needy Namibians with an amount of N$100 per month per person and has shown some indications of success.[12] For example, childhood malnourishment in Omitara, where the project was initially piloted from January 2008 to December 2009, decreased by 10%, unemployment decreased by 15% and non-attendance at schools dropped by 42%.[13] Despite these achievements, government has not shown any willingness to introduce the scheme on a national level. In early 2011, President Hifikepunye Pohamba went as far as to state publicly that he believes the programme would encourage Namibians to be 'lazy' (*The Namibian* 2010b).

ACCESS TO HOUSING[14]

Development priorities during the immediate post-independence period included a focus on inequitable access to adequate housing. The National Housing Policy adopted in 1991, and reviewed in 2009, outlines a number of strategies to address housing challenges, which include viewing housing as an agent of economic growth; providing investment and infrastructure for the acceleration of land delivery; providing subsidies and grants to support social housing; and creating an environment where affordable credit is available to finance housing. The use of appropriate and alternative technologies, methods and services to provide affordable housing solutions is strongly promoted.

Vision 2030 envisages that, by 2030, Namibians will have access to adequate housing, with water and sanitation facilities for all. In effect, this means that 3 000 houses would need to be built each year in order to deal with the backlog of some 80 000 houses.

While the relevant policy framework exists, problems arise in practice. Currently, government expenditure on housing is a mere 0.3% of national expenditure, one of its lowest percentages since independence. There is no integrated and cohesive plan to supply housing, with the 2009 updated National Housing Policy and Vision 2030 providing different targets, and there being no clear policy guidelines to address the question of relief to categories of people in desperate need of shelter. It is suggested that government review the South African Constitutional Court case, *Government of the Republic of South Africa & Others v Grootboom & Others* (2001(1) SA 46(CC)), where the court required the South African government to reasonably implement a programme that, at minimum, provides shelter for those living in intolerable or crisis situations.

Statistics on the provision of low-cost housing by the National Housing Enterprise (NHE), a State-owned enterprise of the Ministry of Regional and Local Government, Housing and Rural Development, show that only 576 houses were built in 2009, above the 492 average number of houses delivered by the NHE per annum since 1990, but far from its target of 1 200 houses per year.

The NHE is further impeded by the need to finance the servicing of land even before building houses on the land,[15] a task that is not strictly within their mandate and means that fewer resources are available to build houses (*The Namibian* 2010d). The NHE caters primarily for those who can afford its products and have an income of between N\$5 000 and N\$20 000 per month, or a maximum of N\$30 000 per month in joint income, and are able to furnish a deposit or some form of collateral, thus creating a growing black middle-income class. Currently the backlog in housing is estimated at 80 000, with 30 000 of those in need earning between N$1 501 and N$4 600 per month, which means they do not fall within the parameters of the NHE housing policy.

The Build Together Programme, catering for those households earning a maximum of N$3 000 per month, is also subsidised by government, but statistics on its efficiency are unavailable. Government's main responses to the housing crisis, therefore, do not focus on the neediest in a country with 51% unemployment, as the backlog includes 45 000 who earn less than N$1 501 per month. However, while the jobless and low earners are insufficiently catered for, a number of self-help societies that receive some support from government, are attempting to fill the gap. The Shack Dwellers Federation is one such self-help society and is assisted by government matching every Namibian dollar saved by the Federation.[16] Compared to both the NHE and the Build Together Programme, the Federation has statistically been the most efficient at providing housing.

Access to adequate housing is also impeded by the inability of local authorities to provide the infrastructure necessary in addressing the increased pressures due to accelerating urbanisation. Government has failed to actively implement innovative ideas around the use of solar power and energy-saving devices proposed by the government-subsidised Habitat Research and Development Centre, the use of locally produced materials, or the installation of alternatives to water-based toilets. Lastly, there is no requirement that compels developers to concentrate a percentage of their development on low-cost housing, a measure utilised successfully by other countries such as Malaysia and the United Kingdom.

In conclusion, if the current trend continues, government will not meet the targets set out in Vision 2030 by a considerable margin.

ADEQUATE AND UNIMPEDED ACCESS TO LAND

Pre-independence apartheid land policies deprived the majority of black Namibians of unimpeded ownership of land. In 1991, a year after gaining independence, Namibia's total land mass of approximately 824 000 km² could be divided into four categories: national parks, consisting of 114 500 km² of Namibia's total land mass; 21 600 km² of restricted diamond areas; 469 000 km² set aside for title deed or freehold land; and 218 000 km² of non-title deed/communal land, which, for all practical purposes, was occupied by blacks. At the same time, 34 362 764 hectares out of a total of 36 164 880 hectares of commercial land was owned by individuals, with the rest being in the hands of the State, local government and the churches. Furthermore, 6 123 of Namibia's 6 292 commercial farms were white-owned, of which 382 belonged to foreign absentee landlords. Only 181 farms belonged to blacks. Since then, and by the beginning of 2011, 279 farms, totalling some 1 745 000 hectares, have been purchased under the national resettlement programme. Together with some 400 000 hectares donated by the Ministry of Agriculture, Water and Forestry, these are being utilised for the resettlement of previously disadvantaged Namibians. Apart from this, a total of 3 236 289 hectares has been transferred to black owners in commercial market-related transactions since the inception of the Affirmative Action Loan Scheme in 1992.[17] This initiative has mainly advantaged the group of newly emerging middle- and upper-class blacks, including several members of Cabinet and parliamentarians.

In terms of constitutional requirements for just compensation, the government operates its land acquisition process on a 'willing seller – willing buyer' policy. However, this policy has not achieved the anticipated results, as the land offered for sale is often located in agriculturally marginal areas, is not arable and/or is ill-suited for resettlement. Furthermore, inadequate levels of support in the form of agricultural training, extension support services and access to finance are provided to the recipients of resettlement land and, therefore, more often than not, the land is not used to its full potential (Werner & Odendaal 2010).

The Ministry of Lands and Resettlement is of the opinion that recipients should make a contribution towards infrastructural development on resettlement farms, something the very poor obviously cannot easily afford. Thus, despite the intention to address the needs of poor and landless blacks, the land-reform programme in its present form is perceived by many to be mainly benefiting a rising black urban-based political and business elite.

In February 2004, in a renewed effort to fast-track land reform, government decided that the expropriation principle, an option in terms of the Namibian Constitution (Article 16(2)) and the Agricultural (Commercial) Act (No. 6 of 1995), would be applied parallel to that of the 'willing seller – willing buyer' approach. Expropriation has proved to be not unproblematic and has, at times, been tainted by political motives, when labour issues with farm owners seem to have been the primary reason for its application. In one often-cited case, the owners of a well-developed and profitable farm exporting flowers to the European market on a daily basis became involved in a petty dispute with workers. After nasty allegations, physical threats and dismissals, the affected workers turned to the Ministry of Labour for assistance and reinstatement was ordered by the Labour Court. When the owners refused, expropriation proceedings followed, with the owners accepting less than half the amount initially requested from government. After resettlement, no expertise remained to continue the lucrative farming enterprise. While the present occupants – seven workers and their families, including two government employees who commute daily to work in the capital city Windhoek – keep a few cattle and small stock, the farm is underutilised and the workers rely mostly on their pension incomes. They have received no government support for either subsistence or operating the farm. This incident was widely reported in the European press and created much concern in the white farming community around the possibility that expropriation would be used as a means of retaliation in similar social disputes in the future (Harring & Odendaal 2007:4). Since then, a number of other landowners faced with notices of expropriation have challenged the process in the High Court and, when administrative procedures have been found to have been applied wrongly, such expropriation notices have been set aside.[18]

In an attempt to improve the system of communal land tenure, Communal Land Boards, which control the allocation and cancellation of customary land rights by chiefs or traditional authorities within a particular communal area, have been created under the Communal Land Reform Act (No. 5 of 2002). Importantly, the Act not only grants women equal rights to communal lands, but also protects the surviving spouse of a deceased holder of the customary land right, by giving the surviving spouse the right to apply to the chief or traditional authority for the re-allocation of the customary land right in his or her name.

While the Communal Land Reform Act outlaws arbitrary land enclosures, its provisions are seldom implemented as the Act lacks an appropriate framework to deal with such actions and to defend the rights of small-scale customary land holders. As a result, the communal land policy has been marred by illegal fencing and disputes between traditional leaders over access to such land. In addition, since independence, a number of land enclosures by politically and economically well-connected persons have taken place in communal areas. A largely successful enterprise has been the utilisation of conservancies to allow the people living within such designated areas to benefit from the land and the tourism opportunities so provided.[19] Conservancies have become increasingly sophisticated in running their own affairs with the assistance of development partners.

The table below illustrates land distribution according to the most recent data from 2004 (LEAD 2005).

Owned by	% Title deed land	% Agricultural land	% Namibia's land surface
White individuals	40	24.7	20.6
Companies	14.9	9.2	7.7
Black individuals	4.7	2.9	2.4
Government[20]	23	14.2	11.9
Non-Namibians	1.1	0.7	0.6
Municipalities, organisations and trusts	1.4	0.9	0.7
Unclear	14.9	9.2	7.7

It is clear that the distribution of land does not reflect the racial demographics of the population.

HEALTH CARE

85. *To what extent is the right to adequate health care protected in all spheres and states of life? Is treatment available for illnesses such as HIV/Aids? Is access to this treatment equitable and is the health service of reasonable quality?* (5)

Equity in access to health care is compromised by two major factors: accessibility and affordability. The distances to health facilities, particularly in rural areas, continues to negatively impact individual citizen's abilities to access services (The HIV/AIDS Treatment Survey 2005). For example, 30% of the participants in a qualitative study in the northern part of the country mentioned being more than 20 km away from a health centre, equivalent to four walking hours (BEN Namibia 2008). In the southern part of Namibia, in order to seek improved treatment at a health centre, one has to travel for more than 50 km. This lack of physical access is further exacerbated by the economic means of an individual, as a 2008 study clearly established a link between transport costs, medical fees and its effect on the accessibility of health services (Ibid.). The same study has highlighted the challenges around access to health facilities as a result of cost factors. Access to emergency medical treatment in the northern part of the country (Ruacana) translates into payment of up to the equivalent of U$58.00. The same is true in the southern part of the country where one has to pay the equivalent of U$43.00 (Ibid.:12). These figures should be considered in light of the high unemployment rate and the fact that subsistence farming accounts for a high percentage of household income in rural areas.

Namibia's sparsely populated areas, combined with a high Gini-coefficient of 0.6 and an unemployment rate of more than 50% means that access to health care is highly compromised (Republic of Namibia 2008:4). Based on these statistics alone, it is apparent why the abovementioned figures of U$58.00 and U$43.00 respectively for emergency health care heavily taxes the majority of Namibians (UNDAF Namibia n.d.:15).

In Namibia there are serious shortcomings and gaps when it comes to equity in health care, reflected in significant disparities in terms of access to services, as well as the nature of the interventions. In rural areas, only 74% of births are attended to by skilled health personnel, compared to 94% in urban areas. Only 60% of births among the poorest 20% are attended to by skilled health personnel, while the wealthiest 20% are attended to in 98% of cases (World Health Organisation 2011). Inequities are also reflected in terms of infant mortality, with an incidence of 7.6% infant mortality in rural areas, compared to 6% in urban areas. The poorest 20% have a 9.2% incidence of infant mortality compared to a 3% incidence among the wealthiest 20% (Ibid.).

While the right to health care is covered in Article 95 of the Namibian Constitution, which deals with the promotion of the welfare of the people, it is not protected under the Bill of Rights and is, therefore, not justiciable. There are various provisions that may be construed as promoting the right to health, as the following sub-sections under Article 95 of the Constitution state that:

> *The State shall actively promote and maintain the welfare of the people by adopting,* inter alia, *policies aimed at the following:*
>
> *(e) ensurance that every citizen has a right to fair and reasonable access to public facilities and services in accordance with the law,*
>
> *(g) enactment of legislation to ensure that the unemployed, the incapacitated, the indigent and the disadvantaged are accorded such social benefits and amenities as are determined by Parliament to be just and affordable with due regard to the resources of the State,*
>
> *(j) consistent planning to raise and maintain an acceptable level of nutrition and standard of living of the Namibian people and to improve public health.*

As such, the Constitution places an obligation on the State to ensure widespread access to public facilities and services, including clinics and other public health facilities. Legislation and the development of a policy framework are both envisaged by the Constitution as a means to ensuring access to affordable public health facilities.

In turn, the Namibian government has been responsive to the need for health care provisions through the establishment of treatment centres. Government has consistently provided free childhood immunisations on a country-wide basis, with about 70% of all children having received all their vaccinations by 2006 (Republic of Namibia 2008:21). Furthermore, government has made a concerted effort to address the incidence of malaria, which has been reduced from 207 cases for every 1 000 persons in 1996 to 62.2 cases per 1 000 in 2008 (Republic of Namibia 2010a:6). In 2010, the government spent on average U$280 per capita on health, which compares favourably with the regional average of less than U$100 per capita (World Health Organisation 2011). Yet, the ratio of nurses to patients is currently 27 nurses for every 10 000 patients, while there are 3.7 physicians for every 10 000 patients.

Regarding HIV/Aids, a 2010 Sentinel Survey posits that Namibia has a prevalence rate of 18.8%, with the most economically active group, 15-49 year olds, accounting for the highest rate of infection. It has been established that 16 new infections occur each day (25% among infants aged less than one year, 31% among youth aged 15-24, and 37% in persons aged 25 or older) (Ministry of Health & Social Services 2010:7).

The availability of treatment for HIV/Aids-related illnesses in Namibia has made significant progress, specifically seen in greater provision of antiretroviral therapy (ART) since its introduction in 2003 when coverage was only 3%. To date, the State, with substantial inputs from the Global Health Fund and the US President's Emergency Plan for Aids Relief (PEPFAR), provides ART to 75 681 people (approximately 90% of those in need) through 141 health facilities and clinics (Ibid.:16). Government uses the CD4 count to determine the eligibility of a person in need of ART, with any person who has a CD4 count of below 350 qualifying for treatment.

In an effort to reduce the risk of HIV transmission from mother to child, government also provides treatment to pregnant mothers. By 2008/2009, around 6 744 (58% of those in need) HIV-positive pregnant women were receiving antiretroviral prophylaxis. Since the system is, in fact, able to provide for all pregnant women who test positive, this is a relatively low percentage and is due to women not being offered or accepting voluntary counselling and testing, or not returning to the clinic to collect the prophylaxis.

Greater progress on the provision of adequate health services is also stymied by a lack of adequate sanitation (United Nations Human Rights 2011). Serious outbreaks, such as that of polio in 2006, were caused and facilitated not only by the lack of immunisations during certain periods, but also by the lack of proper sanitation and clean water.

EDUCATION[21]

86. *How extensive and inclusive is the right to education and training, including education in the rights and responsibilities of citizenship? (4)*

Article 20 of the Namibian Constitution, contained in the Bill of Rights, makes the right to education justiciable in certain circumstances. Education is compulsory and free for children up to the age of 16 or until they have completed their primary education, whichever is sooner. In addition, adult literacy classes are provided free of charge. Article 20(2) states:

> *The State shall provide reasonable facilities to render effective this right for every resident within Namibia, by establishing and maintaining State schools at which primary education will be provided free of charge.*

Private schools and centres of higher learning are afforded constitutional protection, provided there are no race, colour or creed-based restrictions concerning the entry of pupils or recruitment of staff, and provided that a certain acceptable standard of education is maintained. It is apparent that government takes this fundamental right seriously, since it is incorporated in the justiciable Bill of Rights and 20–25% of the national budget is allocated to education.

In response to development objectives contained in Vision 2030, which aim to set a path for Namibia to achieve higher levels of industrialisation and earnings, thereby promoting greater social equity, the Namibian education sector has devised a 15-year strategic plan (2006–2020) entitled Education and Training Sector Improvement Programme (ETSIP). It specifically seeks to improve the quality of education in all spheres, as well as the relevance of tertiary education, and promotes a culture of life-long learning.[22] A mid-term technical review of ETSIP in May 2011 presented a mixed bag of progress and bottlenecks. Education experts cited, among others things, a lack of priority choices and sufficiently skilled staff, as well as financial constraints. Regardless of these opinions, the permanent secretary of the Ministry of Education rated the implementation positively (Sasman 2011). However, the National Education Conference of 2011, referred to below, attested that satisfactory progress had not been made.

Real access to primary education and the quality of such education remains a concern. Numerous factors contribute to this situation:

The influx of people to urban areas in the search of improved livelihood has left some urban centres with insufficient schools to cater for all the children, especially at school entry level (*The Namibian* 2011f).

While the Education Act (No. 16 of 2001) allows for a school development fund to be set up by individual school boards and, while it is technically possible to have such a fee waived upon application, the reality is that many parents are not aware of this procedure and many are not able to make the necessary application that is required. Parents are also expected to cover the costs of items such as stationery, relief teachers and school building maintenance. At times, the consequences of non-compliance may be harsh: a child might not be allowed to take part in any extra-curricular activities, report cards might be withheld, parents and children might be named publicly, or children might possibly not be allowed to register at all. A related point of concern is that the Public Expenditure Review of the Education Sector in 2010/11 found that school development funds made up 2% of all funds available for education, and had grown from N$67 million in 2007, to N$80 million in 2008 and N$115 in 2009. Despite the increasing reliance on school development funds, the report stated that there was no procedure for reimbursing the schools for those learners whose school development funds had been waived.

Apart from this, the cost of compulsory school uniforms is also a barrier to access, as is the vastness of Namibia with its relatively small number of inhabitants. Currently, teaching in mother tongue is advocated for grades 1 to 3, but teachers are trained in English and they then have to translate the information into their mother tongue, which leads to unequal standards.[23]

Upon independence, teachers were expected to be able to immediately begin teaching in English, the official language of Namibia, with little assistance in the transition. This has resulted in many teachers being unable to properly impart knowledge in English and, at the same time, learners are expected to master the content and write examinations in the language. This problem was highlighted at the National Education Conference and all teachers were subsequently required to take an English proficiency test. It was established that 98% of teachers would require continuing professional development in this regard (*The Namibian* 2011h). While the figures were not denied, these results were downplayed by the Minister of Education who stated that the test was not meant to indicate a pass or failure.

School dropout and repetition rates are high, and are another cause for worry. Failure to complete schooling is predominately caused by pregnancy, demands from parents, distance to school, poverty and hunger. Apart from this, as a result of HIV/Aids, approximately 121 000 orphans are enrolled in school, accounting for 21.2% of the total number of learners (Republic of Namibia 2008:12).

School facilities differ widely from region to region, with rural schools in general being more poorly equipped. This is due to the fact that employment opportunities are more favourable in urban areas, with schools being more likely to be able to raise the deficit required to buy school books through the school development fund. Rural learners are also faced with the lack of proximity to schools and the resultant higher transport costs. While about 78% of schools have toilet facilities, 81% have access to water and 56% to electricity, the availability of equipment and basic goods and services, or lack thereof, affects the quality of education (Ibid.).

In 2009, in an effort to improve the prevention and management of learner pregnancies, Cabinet approved a new Learner Pregnancy Policy. However, it has not been finalised and rolled-out, despite the problem being regarded as a priority issue, following the 2011 National Education Conference. This Conference took place in Windhoek in June/July 2011 and was attended by over 1 000 delegates under the theme of 'Collective delivery on the education promise: Improving the education system for quality learning outcomes and quality of life'. During the proceedings, the speaker of the Children's Parliament stated: Namibian children are 'confronted with various challenges in almost every sphere of our existence' (*The Namibian* 2011d). He also lamented obstacles ranging from unqualified teachers, lack of textbooks, school's proximity to shebeens and low standards in the education system.

The conference recommendations, approved by Cabinet, highlighted a number of priorities, including learner pregnancies, proximity of shebeens to schools, the practice of automatic promotion, the need to expand the school feeding programme, the building of hostels in flood-prone areas to minimise the disruption caused by annual

floods, and the need to increase the development portion of the education budget from
the 8% to 20%. Cabinet tasked the Ministry of Education to establish two committees
to implement the decisions made and to monitor and evaluate the implementation
process. The committees were to be made up of officials from the Ministry of Education and institutions of higher learning, as well as representatives from NGOs.[24]

Civic education, including the rights and obligations of citizens, are part of the formal
school curriculum, and are incorporated informally through learner representative
bodies at secondary level. Voter education is largely undertaken by a small number of
NGOs, with the Electoral Commission of Namibia (ECN) providing inputs during
voter registration and election times.

POVERTY

87. Are vulnerable and marginalised groups such as children, the disabled
and women adequately protected from poverty?   (5)

Namibia is among the most unequal countries globally, with a Gini-coefficient of 0.6.
Among the goals identified by Vision 2030, aimed at achieving a reduction in poverty
levels, are income redistribution and a Gini-coefficient of 0.3. However, this figure
appears to be rising, as the richest 10% of Namibians earns 128 times more than the
poorest 10% of the population (Human Rights Council 2011:6). According to the
most recent Namibia Household Income and Expenditure Survey 2003/04 (NHIES),
28% of Namibian households live below the poverty line compared to 38% in the
1993/1994 survey. This improvement might be due to the fact that Namibia is one of
only a few Southern African Development Community (SADC) countries to provide
non-contributory social grants to pensioners, people with disabilities, war veterans and
orphans. These payouts have certainly had some impact on poverty rates, reducing
poverty by 4.2% and, more significantly, closing the poverty gap from 16.8% to 12.9%
(Levine, Van der Berg & Yu 2009). In addition, Namibia has developed a poverty
reduction strategy, with its implementation currently being guided by the National
Poverty Reduction Action Programme.

Poverty is more concentrated in some parts of the country, with 48.7% of people in
rural areas being poor, compared to 17% of the urban population. Certain regions are
also more adversely affected, with the majority of the poor being Oshivambo speakers
(the ethnic group constituting 60% of the population). While the San and the Ruka-
vango are the most likely to be poor, with poverty rates of 71.6% and 63.5% respectively, only 8.1% of the population in the central Khomas region – which includes
Windhoek – qualifies as poor (UNDAF Namibia n.d.:20). The disparities among

Namibians have an exclusionary effect on the marginalised and vulnerable, who are particularly disadvantaged when it comes to access to public goods and services.

Women-headed households are more likely to be poor than male-headed households (40.3% compared to 35.9%). Furthermore, poverty rates are very high for individuals in households whose main source of income is pensions (66%) and subsistence farming (48.3%), compared to 19.5% of people in households whose main source of income is based on salaries and wages (National Planning Commission 2008).

Children are more susceptible to poverty than adults. According to the NHIES 2003/04, 43.5% of Namibian children live in poor households, compared to 37% of the general population. Child poverty rates stand at 20.1% in urban areas, compared to 52.3% in rural areas, but do not differ on the basis of age or gender. With statistics showing that only 17.7% of children do not experience any poverty or deprivation, it becomes clear that poverty is a major problem in Namibia affecting most population groups.

Government has employed a number of strategies to address poverty, ranging from social grants to food-for-work programmes. However, the unemployment rate is jeopardising the successes of such strategies and is the single most pressing problem that has to be addressed.

88. *How much impact on political participation does poverty have? How far are poor people able to participate in the wider Namibian society? To what extent are they excluded?* (5)

According to Article 17 of the Namibian Constitution, every 'citizen shall have the right to participate in peaceful political activity intended to influence the composition and policies of government'. All citizens over 18 years have the right to vote and those 21 years or older are eligible for public office. However, the costs associated with standing for election inhibits most Namibians from seeking office.

Voting polling stations are sufficiently represented in the regions to ensure that those that cannot afford to travel have the chance to vote.

With the increasing unemployment rate, Namibians have been more vocal in their demands for services and there are indications that the voter mentality is shifting from voting along party lines to voting for actual change. Namibians are realising that the actions of government are meant to improve their lives and there is less tolerance of self-serving politicians, although 33% of respondents in the 2008 Afrobarometer survey felt that more respect should be shown to authority figures *vis-à-vis* the 26% who felt that citizens should be more active in questioning their leaders. The same study indicates that 59% of Namibians are collectively somewhat or very interested in public affairs, and that 19% of respondents frequently discuss political matters with friends and family.

It is still difficult for poor Namibians to access central government figures and to be able to advocate for reforms. Visits are made to the regions by government officials, but these are infrequent and seem to increase only before elections – apart from the fact that there is usually no follow-up or feedback after these visits.

89. To what extent is the state 'progressively realising' the social, cultural and economic rights in accordance with its Constitutional obligations?
(4)

Namibia has ratified the International Covenant on Economic, Social and Cultural Rights (ICESCR). Article 2(1) of the ICESCR, in conjunction with Article 144 of the Namibian Constitution, obligates the State to progressively realise the economic, social and cultural rights of all Namibians. However, save for the rights to culture and education, all the economic, social and cultural rights are listed in Chapter 11 of the Constitution, under articles 95 and 101, termed 'Principles of State Policy', which promote but do not guarantee such rights.

Although these so-called second-generation rights are not justiciable in terms of the Namibian Constitution, government is required to show that they are moving forward in providing these rights as per their international obligations. While government efforts have been acknowledged throughout the text, it is cause for concern that the budget for secondary education was halved from 5.9% in 2000/01 to 2.5% in 2011/12. In recent years, health expenditure has declined to 9.3% of total expenditure in 2011/12. This is far below the commitments made in terms of the Abuja Declaration that mandates the committal of 14% of government budget on health (UNDAF Namibia n.d.). However, comparatively speaking, Namibia is fulfilling the right to health more adequately than most other SADC countries and Africa in general. Namibia has established a non-discriminatory, human rights-based response to HIV/Aids, both in law and policy, and ART is available to all those who qualify for the treatment. While there is a minimal fee of N$10 per consultation payable by some people living with HIV/Aids, no one can be denied treatment for failure to pay this fee (Ibid.).

Government has made efforts to fulfil the right to food by implementing safety-net interventions, including school feeding programmes, cash for work, and food for work for drought and flood-affected populations, as well as emergency food distributions for populations affected by natural disasters (Ibid.). The Comprehensive Food Distribution Scheme (CFDS) has provided food assistance to vulnerable communities to mitigate the impact of such occurrences on household vulnerability (Ibid.).

Currently, old age pension and disability grants run to N$500 per month, while war veterans are paid N$2 000 per month, subject to an income means test of N$36 000 *per annum*. In December 2008, around 130 000 people were receiving old age pensions and 20 000 were receiving disability grants. Child welfare and child foster grants are currently N$200 per month, with special maintenance grants of the same amount being paid to disabled children under the age of 16. The 'Place of Safety Allowance' is a grant of N$10 per day for children placed in short-term institutional care. By 2010, a total of about 114 000 children were benefiting from the various forms of support targeting children (Ibid.).

While the Namibian Constitution (1990, Article 89) provides for the establishment of the Office of the Ombudsman, tasked with promoting and advancing the protection of human rights in Namibia, this entity is insufficiently funded, relying largely on external donor support to fulfil this particular mandate, as government's allocation to this office is largely geared towards the more conventional role of investigating maladministration.

In response to high unemployment figures, government established the TIPEEG to run from 2011/12 to 2014/15, with the aim of creating 105 000 jobs by supporting agriculture, transport, housing, sanitation, tourism and public works (National Planning Commission 2011; Ministry of Finance 2011). The success of the TIPEEG initiative remains to be seen as numerous concerns are being raised in the local media around the perceived lack of coordination, non-transparent procurement procedures and nepotism.

While it is evident that there has been some progress in the realisation of social, economic and cultural rights, it is submitted that, in a country with just over two million inhabitants and adequate mineral resources, Namibians should not be suffering from this level of poverty; the country has achieved remarkable economic growth and is regarded as politically and socially stable. The writers would argue that the slow rate of progress is not necessarily attributable to a lack of resources, but rather to the inadequate and inappropriate use of such resources.

JOBS, AND RIGHTS IN THE WORKPLACE

90. Is there equal opportunity for all in the workplace? (5)

In its Bill of Rights, the Namibian Constitution (1990, Article 23) enshrines the principle of affirmative action. Parliament is permitted to enact legislation to advance the needs of citizens disadvantaged by colonial apartheid policies enacted prior to independence, in order to achieve a more racially balanced structuring of the public service, police force, defence force and prison service, with recognition of the special discrimination suffered by women. The Affirmative Action (Employment) Act (No. 29 of 1998) was enacted to satisfy Article 23(2) of the Namibian Constitution, which requires the advancement of persons who have been 'socially, economically or educationally disadvantaged'. While the legislation is clear, the implementation thereof has been a cause for concern as perceptions exist that this corrective intervention, at times, disregards the importance of suitable qualifications. While female representation in parliament was previously on the increase, there has been a regression in the progress made in terms of gender representation (*The Namibian* 2011a).

While findings contained in the Employment Equity Commission's 2004/05 Annual Report had stated that 'blacks were mostly in middle and lower level positions in the majority of companies visited' and 'males still predominantly occupied top and senior management positions', the following figures from the 2009/10 Annual Report provide information on the cumulative workforce profile with regard to executive directors, showing some improvement.

Whites	Blacks	Women	Black women
58.8%	27.5%	18.1%	8.2%

However, the 2009/10 Annual Report also indicated that 50% of new recruits at executive director's level were white and almost all of them men, which is a significant increase compared to the figure of the previous year, namely 34.6%. Only 13.1% of women and no persons with disabilities had been recruited at this level. While there had been an overall marked increase of black Namibians in positions of top management, the percentages are still skewed, given that the Namibia Demographics Profile of 2011 places the percentage of black people at over 87% of the population, raising concerns around the latest trend in recruitment percentages.[25] Underlying causes might include the poor standard of education in general and shortcomings in tertiary education, including vocational training, in particular, leading to low levels of appropriate knowledge and skills, especially among the youth.

The Namibia Labour Force Survey 2008 reveals the following statistical percentages regarding unemployment:[26]

Men	Women	Youth (15-19)	Rural	Urban	Total 2008	Total 2004
40%	58.4%	83%	65%	36%	51.2%	36%

The official unemployment rate stands at 51% and is skewed to the detriment of black Namibians, with youths and women disproportionately affected. The situation is compounded by an unbalanced national education system in which the rural poor remain marginalised and the presently advantaged and privileged urban elite is able to access better-resourced urban public and private schools.

91. How far are workers' rights to fair rates of pay, just and safe working conditions and effective representation guaranteed in law and practice?
(6)

Labour rights have been the subject of extensive legislation in Namibia, with labour laws revised on numerous occasions. While the current Labour Act (No. 11 of 2007) has introduced the use of conciliation and arbitration to encourage speedy conflict resolution, the lack of capacity hinders its full and efficient implementation. Arbitrators are very often under-qualified, an excessive amount of disputes are lodged with the office of the under-resourced Labour Commissioner, and there is no working mechanism to investigate allegations.

Collective agreements in the construction, security and agricultural sectors have been gazetted by the Ministry of Labour and Social Welfare, detailing minimum wages and a number of ancillary issues agreed upon between the relevant employers' and employees' representatives. In the last year, the National Union of Namibian Workers (NUNW) has sought to protect its members by calling on government to investigate monies that have gone missing from the Government Institution Pension Fund (GIPF) and to support the Basic Income Grant (BIG) scheme. At the same time, NUNW has been characterised by infighting and has steadily seen its ability to shape labour disputes and relations diminish. Most recently, Namdeb, a diamond mining company, was involved in a month-long dispute over the benefits of certain workers who were being transferred. Despite the intervention of government mediators, the Mineworkers Union of Namibia (MUN), a member of NUNW, continued with the strike that led the mine to take the matter to court, asserting that the strike was illegal. This application was ultimately removed from the roll and an agreement was made an order of court which read that Namdeb and the MUN 'shall dedicate themselves in good faith to rebuilding their relationship and restoring good labour relations at Namdeb'. The company further undertook to redeploy the affected employees to its other operations, 'provided it makes business sense'. According to the mine, millions of dollars were lost every day during the one-month strike. The Namdeb situation has shown that the union can wield considerable power if it unifies its structures and acts with one voice, something which has not always been apparent in the past.

As employment in the formal employment sector had decreased, the informal sector has grown considerably. In recognition of this development, municipalities have designated specific areas from which this sector can operate. Innovation is being encouraged by the Polytechnic of Namibia, an institution established by government to provide post-secondary career education, with its Business Innovation Centre providing support ranging from business plans to basic financial administration courses to entrepreneurs. In addition, small and medium enterprises are afforded certain tax benefits by government in an attempt to encourage the growth of such enterprises. However, while the sector is unregulated, workers are vulnerable to poor working conditions and low wages.

92. How far are wage levels and social security or other welfare benefits sufficient for people's needs, without discrimination/equally?   (5)

Social security contributions, based on the relevant scales of remuneration, must be paid into a designated social security fund on behalf of all employees registered by an employer (Social Security Act (No. 34 of 1994)). This fund provides a certain level of income for those on maternity or sick leave, with some benefits paid out upon retirement, death or disability. Maternity benefits increased in 2011 by just over 11%, with the maximum monthly payout now standing at N$10 000.[27]

While there were no increases to State pension payouts in the 2011 budget (they remain at a very modest N$500 per month for all Namibians who have reached the retirement age of 60), Namibia is one of only three countries in the region that provides non-contributory old age support. Those who were previously gainfully employed and who contributed to private or work-based pension funds may also obtain additional benefits from such pension fund. This is largely not the case for those who were previously disadvantaged, since they would have been least likely to contribute to private pension funds.

As stated above (see Q89), old age pension and disability grants are N$500 per month. Child welfare and child foster grants are currently N$200 per month for the first child and N$100 per month for each additional child up to a maximum of six children, with special maintenance grants of the same amount being paid to disabled children under the age of 16. The 'Place of Safety Allowance' is a grant of N$10 per day for children placed in short-term institutional care. By 2010, a total of about 114 000 children were benefiting from the various grants targeting children.[28]

As previously mentioned in this chapter, a coalition of civil society organisations and church organisations have advocated the BIG scheme of N$100 per month for all Namibians.[29] Pilot projects have shown the programme to have achieved some successes that could be replicated if the initiative were to be rolled out. BIG advocates for an additional amount to be levied on those who have sufficient income, with the added revenue being utilised to provide the proposed grant to those who have no other income and are not taxed at all. In extended families, which are now a reality of Namibian life in the wake of the HIV/Aids pandemic, a sum of N$100 per person in a household might well make the difference between feeding a family and going without.

For a family of five, which corresponds to the average household size according to the 1991 and 2001 censuses, this would mean an income of N$500 in addition to any other grants or pensions. However, government does not support the BIG initiative as the programme is not seen as being sustainable.

In terms of the Veterans Act (No. 2 of 2008), people classified as war veterans and the dependents of deceased veterans receive additional government grants. This grant is currently N$2 000 per month and is subject to an income means test of N$36 000 per annum, as well as other disqualifications such as a child reaching 18 years of age in normal circumstances and a spouse remarrying. In order to qualify for assistance as a veteran, one must have been a member of the liberation forces; participated or engaged in any political, diplomatic or underground activity in furtherance of the liberation struggle; or been convicted, whether in Namibia or elsewhere, of any offence closely connected to the struggle and sentenced to imprisonment. Any person who deserted the liberation struggle is disqualified, unless that person subsequently rejoined the struggle.[30] The Act does not address the challenges faced by children of deceased veterans who are unable to present proof of the documentation required to justify their claims.

While it is acknowledged that great strides have been made in terms of providing social grants, the sums provided are not able to sustain the requirements of a dignified existence that includes access to housing, education and adequate food. The high unemployment rate means that a large number of Namibians have no access to any other form of income. At the same time, they are exposed to reported excesses of government spending, ranging from an opulent state house to N$15 million being spent on a new government fleet of Mercedes Benz vehicles for senior politicians (*The Namibian* 2011g).

DELIVERY OF SOCIAL AND ECONOMIC RIGHTS

93. Are public goods, for example water provision or local services such as waste collection, equally available to citizens and communities at similar levels of efficiency and competence? (5)

Equitable access to water and sanitation remain major development challenges, especially as Namibia faces increasing demands for clean water. While problems concerning the provision of water are being comprehensively addressed by government, access to sanitation facilities lag behind, with only 58% of urban and 14% of rural households having access to such services (Ibid.). Moreover, only three-quarters of health facilities in Namibia have access to running water in all service areas and only 78% of learners have access to toilets at school (Ministry of Health & Social Services 2009; *The Namibian* 2011e).

The main sources of drinking water for the majority of households are piped water (75%) and water from boreholes or protected wells (12.2%). In terms of water provision by region, there is considerable disparity. While all households in Omaheke get their water from piped or boreholes/protected wells, a significant proportion of households in Kavango (39.2%), Omusati (28.4%), Oshikoto (21.8%), Ohangwena (19.1%) and Caprivi (18%) draw their drinking water from flowing streams/rivers or stagnant sources (National Planning Commission n.d.:16). With regard to the provision of piped water, the differences are equally stark, with 99.3% of all the households in urban areas, compared to 58.4% of those in rural parts, having access to piped water (Ibid.).

Waste collection is usually linked to the provision of piped water, particularly in towns where these services are efficiently provided by municipal councils.

94. To what extent has privatisation had an impact on the adequate provision of public goods and services? (6)

Namibia has no privatisation policy and, therefore, no rating has been provided. For background purposes, it may be informative to note that the majority of public goods and services are provided by the government line ministries, State-owned enterprises and municipalities. A considerable number of State-owned enterprises provide basic services in the telecommunication, transport, water and power supply markets. A number of these, such as Air Namibia, the Namibia Airports Authority, the Social Security Commission and TransNamib, are regularly accused of mismanagement and of providing a breeding ground for corrupt activities (BTI 2010/Namibia 2010:20). Bail-outs by government, and by implication from taxpayers' money, are not uncommon, which has a negative impact on the costs of public services. According to Robin Sherbourne (2010:319) in his Guide to the Namibian Economy 2010: 'In the final analysis, it is hard to see Namibian SOEs [State-owned enterprises] raise the massive amounts of finance needed to invest in the country's infrastructure without involving private capital.'

95. To what extent do public-private partnerships facilitate or impede access to socio-economic rights particularly for the poor? (3)

While liberalisation of the Namibian economy has encouraged external investment in the country, it is difficult to assess to what extent this has had a direct impact on poverty, given that the overall unemployment rate in 2010 stood at 51.2% and that Namibia is rated among the most unequal societies in the world (UNDAF Namibia n.d.).

Although the average per capita income is comparatively high, with the World Bank classifying Namibia as an upper-middle income country with a per capita income of approximately U$4 310 *per annum*,[32] this categorisation conceals the enormous inequalities in income distribution and masks other social factors such as poverty and unemployment. This inequality, though created mainly by the historical legacy, is sustained by an economy that disproportionately benefits those previously advantaged prior to independence, and emerging black political and business elites. According to the most recent Bertelsmann Transformation Index, Namibia's situation is not expected to change fundamentally in the immediate future; neither are the living conditions of the rural poor and high unemployment figures likely to improve soon (BTI 2010/Namibia 2010). This may be due to the aspirations of Vision 2030 being perhaps overly ambitious in a country only emerging relatively recently from huge disparities in terms of opportunities and service, but is arguably also due to the mismanagement of available funds, insufficient accountability in terms of government spending, insufficient follow-through on practical reforms, and lack of skills and expertise in government (Human Rights Council).

The government is preparing a Public Private Partnerships (PPP) Framework, as required by NDP 3, to facilitate investment in service provision and improve Namibia's infrastructure (Republic of Namibia 2010b). Current PPPs, such as the Walvis Bay Corridor Group and Tungeni Africa, have no particular focus on advancing socio-economic rights to the poor. The PPP Framework envisions enabling government to embark on the commercialisation and privatisation of State-owned enterprises, in order to facilitate private financing options for national development priorities.[33] However, it would seem that even if PPPs take proper root in Namibia, it is unlikely that this would address the historical inequalities significantly, or the economic, social and cultural rights of especially poor Namibians. While privatisation and PPPs are based on sound business principles and the maximisation of profit, their responsibilities for the provision of public services and goods, although it may promote access, will in all probability not make same affordable to the most needy unless subsidised by government.

96. *To what extent are private companies accountable for the delivery of socio-economic rights as a result of public-private partnerships? To what extent is this accountability overseen by citizens or their representatives?* (4)

There is presently no legally enforceable duty that companies owe to citizens in terms of the direct delivery of economic, social and cultural rights. Although this duty is not the primary focus of private companies *per se*, there is a worldwide trend towards increased accountability to the society in which a company operates. In Namibia, this has not translated into any onus on private companies for the delivery of socio-economic rights, and a framework for PPPs has not yet been finalised. The Companies Act (No. 28 of 2004 538(1)) posits that a company registered in Namibia has the capacity and powers of a natural person of full capacity, insofar as a juristic person is capable of having that capacity or of exercising those powers. Article 5 of the Namibian Constitution states that the Bill of Rights shall be upheld not only by government, but also by all natural and legal persons, and shall be enforceable by the courts. The right to education is contained in the Bill of Rights, therefore, at the very least, the actions of private companies should in no way impair access to such right.

Namibia has enacted laws and adopted policies, strategies and principles to advance sustainable development and economic, social and cultural rights. Among these are the Environmental Management and Assessment Act of 2007, the Disaster Risk Management Bill, the National Policy on Climate Change of 2011, the National Drought Policy, the National Urbanisation Strategy, the National Sanitation Strategy, and the White Paper on Energy (UNDAF Namibia n.d.:37). Private companies are expected to conduct their businesses in accordance with the laws and policies of Namibia, and may be taken to task by the relevant line Ministry within government or by aggrieved parties. In the final analysis, apart from extracting taxes and levies for the Treasury, such compliance is all that can be required from private companies at this point.

97. To what extent do citizens feel they are receiving equal access to public resources regardless of their social grouping?   (5)

All those entitled to old age pensions, as well as child and disability grants, have access thereto, irrespective of their social grouping, although this is dependent on their ability to obtain the required identification documents. Access to health and education (particularly primary education) is equally open to all Namibians, regardless of their ethnic, language or cultural identity, although the quality of these services may differ from region to region.

Government has, for the most part, successfully integrated the various societal interests and demands of the majority of the people, and dissociated itself from ethnic biases (BTI 2010/Namibia 2010:12). There are minority groups such as the San and the Himba, however, which still lack the same levels of access as other groups. Although the Office of the Prime Minister has a separate desk dealing with developmental issues pertaining to the San, there appears to be a general lack of understanding in terms of facilitating access to public resources with regard to the particular circumstances and needs of different cultural and ethnic groups. Despite claims regarding equitable access by all, this is not necessarily borne out in practice. According to the 2008 Afrobarometer survey, 66% of the respondents felt either 'strongly' or 'very strongly' that the government's economic policies had hurt most people and only benefited a few. In addition, a combined 81% felt that their ethnic group is 'sometimes', 'often' or 'always' treated unfairly by government.

Although the effects of historically entrenched inequalities have contributed to the lack of equal access among Namibians, according to the findings of the 2008 Afroba-rometer survey, it may be argued that government has contributed to the widely-held perception that certain ethnic groups have been privileged since independence, with the 13 sub-national regions not being treated equally in terms of infrastructure and public services.

CORPORATE GOVERNANCE

98. How rigorous and transparent are the rules on corporate governance; and how effectively are corporations regulated in the public interest?

(4)

Namibia's economy is primarily based on the extraction of raw materials, agriculture and tourism. The rules and regulations governing competition and the money and capital markets in Namibia are closely tied to those of South Africa, although they are governed by separate Namibian laws. South African banks (foreign shareholding in the local banking sector was 65% in 2010) and companies still dominate the Namibian market, although Namibian participation in ownership of the banking and financial sector has increased (*The Namibian* 2010c; BTI 2010/Namibia 2010:12).

According to the 2009 King Report on corporate governance, the manner in which a company conducts its business (internal and external) should conform to ethical busi-ness practice. Any company should align its conduct with the values that drive its busi-ness. Company directors are responsible for considering the legitimate interests and expectations of shareholders on behalf of the company, should weigh and promote the interests of all stakeholders and be able to justify their decisions to them. To ensure transparency, directors need to disclose information in a way that enables stakeholders to make informed decisions about the company, its performance and its sustainability. However, even if stakeholders are aggrieved by the actions of the company, there is no legal route for them to follow in order to enforce a change in policy.

Save for corporate governance, which is self-regulatory, companies in Namibia are regulated by government in the public interest. To this end, government enacted the Competition Act (No. 2 of 2003) 'to safeguard and promote competition in the Namibian market', with the relevant Commission becoming operational in 2008. In addition, while legislation on consumer protection, labour, tax, monetary control, companies and disclosure of information has been put in place, it has yet to be fully implemented. The Bank of Namibia, for example, regulates the entire banking sector in the public interest. However, although the Namibian banking system seems to have served large companies and the business community well, a June 2005 research paper by the Namibian Economic Policy Research Unit concluded that the banking sector had created market imperfections with social costs in the form of 'wider interest spreads and higher bank charges' than those present in South Africa (BTI 2010/Namibia 2010:17). This remains so in practice.

Although State-owned enterprises, too, are formally required to comply with the State Owned Enterprises Governance Act (No. 2 of 2006) – an Act that seeks to enhance corporate governance and encourage sustainable business practises – not a year goes by without government bail-outs being necessary, and mismanagement appears to draw little censure or have noticeable consequences for those responsible. In addition, State-owned enterprises have not been consistent in their reporting, both financially and regarding their activities, with some of them not having produced publicly available annual reports for a number of years. There is a lack of transparency and disclosure to the public. Thus far, the State Owned Enterprises Governance Council, created under the Act, has not insisted on standard reporting and public disclosure (Sherbourne 2010:331-332).

99. To what extent are companies duty-bound to play a role in the realisation of socio-economic rights? And to what extent do they prioritise responsible social investment? (5)

Companies are legally obliged to the extent that they are required to be accountable for the impact of their activities on society and, more particularly, the environment that can affect access to socio-economic rights. Despite their not being duty-bound to play a role in the delivery of socio-economic rights, and it can be argued in their defence that this is not their primary function, many companies operating in Namibia take an ethical point of view on this matter. While laws and regulations such as the Companies Act regulate companies, but do not necessarily impose obligations on them to ensure corporate investment, a number of larger companies (especially in the mining and banking sectors) have established corporate social responsibility policies and created funds to implement programmes and projects that impact positively on communities in the areas in which they are located, or more widely across the country in key sectors such as health and education.

100. Is the private sector meeting its new obligations, such as in relation to equity and empowerment responsibilities? (5)

In comparison to other countries in the region and Africa in general, Namibia is relatively well-developed and has the status, whether justified or not, of an upper-middle income country in terms of purchasing power parity. However, huge income and social disparities still exist between urban and rural areas, between blacks and whites, and between the new upper class and the majority of the population, between the regions, between males and females, and children and adults (Ibid.:15). By 2010, over half of the workforce was unemployed and the distribution of income and access to development was among the most unequal in the world. Despite the efforts of government to influence and change social disparities through legal regulations, to attract investment and provide developmental incentives and measures, this gap has scarcely narrowed, primarily because low efficiency and productivity hampers growth (Ibid.). Affirmative action legislation[34] requires the private sector to shoulder empowerment responsibilities through employment creation and training, especially of previously disadvantaged persons, women and persons with disabilities. These laws also require that each non–Namibian employee must be supported by a Namibian understudy who will be groomed to ultimately fill that position. According to the 2009/10 Annual Report of the Employment Equity Commission, 89.2% of all persons trained during that period were from previously racially disadvantaged groups. At the higher levels of employment, 57% of executive directors and 41.6% of senior managers trained were from previously racially disadvantaged groups. The percentage of women trained was 42. In addition, the private sector contributes towards creating an environment of empowerment by paying taxes and royalties meant to be utilised by government in an appropriate manner to the benefit of those most in need of empowerment.

CONCLUSION

Judging by the positive strides made in the provision of social and economic rights in Namibia, it is clear that government is cognisant of the link between human dignity and democracy. However, such efforts are undermined by the high percentage of unemployed and exacerbated by the poor state of education. One important substantive shortcoming with regard to the enforcement of such rights lies within Article 95, the 'Principles of State Policy', as it does not protect socio–economic rights to the same extent that first generational rights are covered. Socio–economic rights are not justiciable to the extent that they may be definitively claimed by law. The only obligation on government with regard to the provisions of Article 95 is that it should promulgate policies or develop programmes that advance or promote the welfare of the Namibian people.

Read together with the ICESCR, to which Namibia is a signatory, it can be concluded that the promotion of such principles of State policy is dependent on the availability of sufficient State resources. It has been argued that sufficient financial means do indeed exist, but that they are mismanaged and focus on the wrong priorities, such as the construction of a new State house and the purchase of expensive vehicles for government officials. This perception is further substantiated by the World's Banks estimates of per capita income and the resultant categorisation of Namibia as an upper–middle income country.

The troubled education sector is, however, covered under the Bill of Rights and this right is therefore justifiable. While there has been no significant litigation surrounding this issue, this is an area where NGOs could make a positive intervention on behalf of the Namibian people.

Although there is no direct remedy for enforcing the other rights under discussion, should government fail to adequately promote the economic and social welfare of the Namibian people, the only possible route to be considered finds its basis in the indivisibility of all human rights and the argument that human dignity is served by access to basic socio-economic rights. The focus on dignity would then place the context within the justiciable Bill of Rights. To reinforce this argument, international instruments such as, *inter alia*, the ICESCR and the Convention on the Rights of the Child could be brought into Namibian jurisprudence by way of Article 144 of the Namibian Constitution, which provides that international agreements binding upon Namibia shall form part of the law of Namibia.

However, one issue that is hampering the realisation of rights as promoted in the international instruments is government's lack of commitment to reporting requirements. Insufficient resources are made available to encourage timely reporting and there is no transparency with regard to the recommendations made by the committees that oversee compliance. Lack of transparency, in turn, translates into ignorance among the general public in relation to areas in which government is falling behind in its obligations. A consequence of this is a lack of civic activity and insufficient pressure being placed on government to deliver and perform.

Although government reports indicate that various Millennium Development Goals (MDG) targets relating to education, gender equality and combating HIV/Aids and other diseases have already been reached, it can be argued that the levels reached do not reflect the necessary depth and quality, especially in relation to education and gender equality. In addition, it does not seem possible at this juncture that the targets in respect of MDG's 1, 4, 5, 7 and 8 will be reached by 2015.

While Namibia certainly has many appropriate policies and legislation in place to promote the requirements for human dignity, the problem lies with policy cohesion, lack of capacity, insufficient political will and ineffective implementation. In a country with a relatively small population of just over two million and sufficient natural resources, it should be possible to adequately meet the basic needs of a far greater proportion of the Namibian population.

SECTION SCORE: 6

REFERENCES

BEN NAMIBIA. 2008. *Impact of transport on access to health services for PLWHA in Namibia*. Windhoek: Yelula-Ukhai.

BTI 2010 | Namibia. 2010. *Namibia country report*.

CHUNG, D. 2010. *Basic income grants alleviate poverty in Namibia* [online]. Available: http://bit.ly/cajFFH.

CONDE, H.V. 1999. *A handbook of international human rights technology*. Lincoln: University of Nebraska Press.

EMPLOYMENT EQUITY COMMISSION (n.d.) *Annual Report – 2009/10*.

HARRING, S. & ODENDAAL, W. 2007. *No resettlement available: An assessment of the expropriation principle and its impact on land reform in Namibia*. Windhoek: Land, Environment and Development Project, Legal Assistance Centre.

HARTMANN, A. 1999. *Biotechnology and biosafety in Namibia: A country study*. Windhoek: Namibian Biotechnology Alliance.

HUMAN RIGHTS COUNCIL. 2011. *Universal Periodic Review*, 10th session.

KING REPORT ON GOVERNANCE FOR SOUTH AFRICA – 2009 [online]. Available: http://www.library.up.ac.za/law/docs/king111report.pdf.

LEAD. 2005. *Our land we farm: An analysis of the Namibian commercial agricultural land reform process*. Windhoek: Land, Environment and Development Project, Legal Assistance Centre. Available: http://www.lac.org.na/projects/lead/Pdf/landwefarm.pdf.

LEVINE, S., VAN DER BERG, S. & YU, D. 2009. *Measuring the impact of social cash transfers on poverty and inequality in Namibia*. Stellenbosch Economic Working Papers 25/09. Stellenbosch: Stellenbosch University.

MINISTRY OF AGRICULTURE, WATER & RURAL DEVELOPMENT. 1991. *Current land tenure system in the commercial districts of Namibia* (position paper). National Conference on Land Reform.

MINISTRY OF FINANCE. n.d. *The Namibian Budget 2011/2012* [online]. Available: http://www.mof.gov.na/budget.htm.

___ 2011. *Midterm expenditure framework 2011/12 to 2014/15*.

MINISTRY OF HEALTH & SOCIAL SERVICES. 2009. *Namibia Health Facility Census, 2009*. Windhoek: The Government of Namibia.

___ 2010. *Review of universal access progress in Namibia*, July 2010. Windhoek: The Government of Namibia.

MINISTRY OF LABOUR & SOCIAL WELFARE. n.d. *Employment Equity Commission, Annual Report 2009/10*. Windhoek: The Government of Namibia.

___ 2008. *Namibian Labour Force Survey*. Windhoek: The Government of Namibia.

NAMIBIA DEMOGRAPHIC AND HEALTH SURVEY, 2006-07 [online]. Available: http://www.measuredhs.com/pubs/pdf/PB4/PB4.pdf.

NATIONAL PLANNING COMMISSION. n.d. *Namibia household income & expenditure survey 2003/2004*.

___ 2008. *Review of poverty and inequality in Namibia*.

___ 2010. *Children and adolescents in Namibia 2010: A situation analysis*.

___ 2011. *Targeted intervention programme for employment and economic growth*.

REPUBLIC OF NAMIBIA. 1990. *The Constitution of Namibia*. Windhoek: The Government of Namibia.

___ 2008. *Namibia Millennium Development Goals, 2nd Report*. Windhoek: The Government of Namibia.

___ 2010a. *Namibia Millennium Development Goals, 3rd Report*. Windhoek: The Government of Namibia.

___ 2010b. *Assessing the performance of State owned enterprises in Namibia –Financial regulation point of view* [online]. Available: http://bit.ly/AlkgwM.

SASMAN, C. 2011. *Namibia: ETSIP gets mixed progress review* [online]. Available: http://bit.ly/kUfMbR.

SHERBOURNE, R. 2010. *Guide to the Namibian Economy*. Windhoek: IPPR.

THE HIV/AIDS TREATMENT SURVEY. 2005. IBIS Namibia, Lironga Eparu and the Rainbow Project.

THE NAMIBIAN. 2008a. 'Justice delays 'criminal''. 18 January 2008.

___ 2008b. 'Legal Aid battling 'cash-flow' problems'. 21 October 2008.

___ 2010a. 'Half of all Namibians unemployed'. 4 January 2010.

___ 2010b. 'President rejects 'money for nothing''. 28 April 2010.

___ 2010c. 'Pohamba wants banks in local hands'. 19 July 2010.

___ 2010d. 'NHE gears tackles housing backlog'. 22 October 2010.

___ 2011a. 'Numbers of women in government declining'. 4 January 2011.

___ 2011b. 'Economists shocked by drastic budget'. 10 March 2011.

___ 2011c. 'Slow changes in employment equity'. 4 April 2011.

___ 2011d. 'Iyambo gets it from babe's mouth'. 29 June 2011.

___ 2011e. 'Toilets for all schools by 2039'. 29 June 2011.

___ 2011f. 'Grade One applicants compete for space in Swakop'. 4 July 2011.

___ 2011g. 'N$15m for new Govt. Fleet'. 30 September 2011.

___ 2011h. '98% of teachers not fluent in English'. 9 November 2011.

THE NAMIBIAN SUN. 2011. 'City/Govt getting to grips with dumpsite scavenging'. 2 September 2011.

NEW ERA. 2011. 'Experts slam budget'. 11 March 2011.

UNDAF NAMIBIA. n.d. 'Country Situation Analysis 2013/17 – Achieving the MDGs with equity' (discussion document)

UNITED NATIONS HUMAN RIGHTS. 2011. Special Rapporteur on the human right to safe drinking water and sanitation [online]. Available: http://bit.ly/iPV3X5

WERNER, W. & ODENDAAL, W. 2010. *Livelihoods after land reform: Namibia country report*. Windhoek: Land, Environment and Development Project, Legal Assistance Centre.

WORLD HEALTH ORGANISATION. 2011. *Namibia Health: Profile*. Last updated 14 April 2011.

Acts

Affirmative Action (Employment) Act (No. 29 of 1998)

Agriculture (Commercial) Act (No. 6 of 1995)

Communal Land Reform Act (No. 5 of 2002)

Companies Act (No. 28 of 2004)

Competition Act (No. 2 of 2003)

Education Act (No. 16 of 2001)

Labour Act (No. 11 of 2007)

Namibia Water Corporation Act (No. 12 of 1997)

Social Security Act (No. 34 of 1994)

State Owned Enterprises Governance Act (No. 2 of 2006)

Veterans Act (No. 2 of 2008)

Water Resources Management Act (No. 24 of 2004)

WEBSITES

http://featured.matternetwork.com/2011/5/an-african-success-namibia-people.cfm

http://oxforddictionaries.com/definition/democracy

http://www.bignam.org

http://www.etsip.na

http://www.mawf.gov.na/Documents/wsaspolicy.pdf

http://www.namwater.com.na/data/Projects_Desalination.htm

http://www.ssc.org.na/

http://www.worldbank.org

ENDNOTES

1   Toni Hancox (director) and Ricardo Mukonda (legal practitioner) are both employed by the Legal Assistance Centre, Windhoek, Namibia, the only public interest law firm in Namibia working in human rights and constitutional matters.

2   Affirmative Action (Employment) Act (No. 29 of 1998).

3   *The Namibian* (2008b). The situation has not improved since then, with the delays in finalising legal aid applications also being a catalyst for lengthy delays in especially criminal matters.

4   Namibia Demographic and Health Survey, 2006-07 (p. 17).

5   http://www.mawf.gov.na/Documents/wsaspolicy.pdf

6   Namwater, the State-owned water supplier lists desalination as one of its projects. See http://www.namwater.com.na/data/Projects_Desalination.htm.

7   Namibia Water Corporation Act (No. 12 of 1997)

8   See http://www.namwater.com.na/data/Projects_Desalination.htm (p.10)

9   Water Resources Management Act (No. 24 of 2004), S3(c).

10   The next census is due to take place in the latter part of 2011.

11   The latest figure estimated by the NPC is 2.1 million.

12   According to BIG, all Namibians would qualify for the grant, which would be subsidised by increased taxation of the gainfully employed. See http://www.bignam.org/BIG_pilot.html for details of the research undertaken and findings.

13 http://www.policyinnovations.org/ideas/briefings/data/000163.

14 The writers wish to acknowledge the assistance of the IPPR in providing most of the statistics referred to in this section.

15 This is compounded by the absence of legislation providing for cheaper land servicing options to informal communities.

16 Unpublished speech by a representative of the Shack Dwellers Federation at a Conference of Economic, Social and Cultural Rights hosted by the University of Namibia, 18 July 2011.

17 Hartmann (1999); Ministry of Agriculture, Water & Rural Development (1991); Information on National Resettlement Programme obtained from the Ministry of Lands and Resettlement on 23 February 2011; Information on Affirmative Action Loans Scheme obtained from Agribank of Namibia on 18 February 2011.

18 Kessl v Ministry of Lands and Resettlement and Two Others and two similar cases 2008 (1) NR 167 (HC)

19 http://featured.matternetwork.com/2011/5/an-african-success-namibia-people.cfm

20 This includes the so-called Odendaal Farms, which were bought out from white farmers in the 1960s to form part of the 'homelands'. The black families resettled there have a right of occupation only.

21 The writers thank Mr Justin Ellis for his assistance in preparing this chapter.

22 http://www.etsip.na

23 A participant at the National Education Conference held in Windhoek, 27 June 2011 to 1 July 2011.

24 Press release by the Minister of Education on the decisions by Cabinet on the outcome of the National Conference on Education, 31 August 2011, Windhoek.

25 Ministry of Labour & Social Welfare (n.d.); The Namibian (2011c) for a summary of the findings.

26 *The Namibian* (2010a) for further statistics as reported.

27 http://www.ssc.org.na/

28 Ibid.

29 http://www.bignam.org

30 Ibid, S1

31 Klaus Schade from the IPPR is thanked for his input.

32 http://www.worldbank.org

33 Report on the public meetings on the National Development Plan 3 (NDP3) held 26-30 September 2007.

34 Affirmative Action (Employment) Act (No. 29 of 1998)

BIOGRAPHICAL INFORMATION

Lesley Blaauw obtained his PhD in International Studies from Rhodes University in 2007. He is a senior lecturer and head of the Department of Political and Administrative Studies at the University of Namibia. Blaauw lectures on International Relations and Political Economy. His most recent publications include 'A Note on the Namibian Elections of 2009' in the Journal of African Elections (2010:9(1)) and, with Sydney Lestholo, 'Namibia' in Compendium of Elections in Southern Africa 1989–2009: 20 years of multiparty democracy (2009).

Toni Hancox holds a BProc from the University of South Africa (UNISA) and is currently studying for an LLM, Fundamental Rights Litigation at UNISA. In addition to her experience as a legal practitioner and conveyancer, Toni is a councillor of the Commonwealth Lawyers Association and currently serves as the director of the Legal Assistance Centre, a public interest law centre advocating human rights in Namibia by making the law accessible to those with the least access. She previously worked in private practice and as a legal officer at the Office of the Government Attorney of Namibia.

Theunis Keulder is one of the founding members of the Namibia Institute for Democracy (NID) and currently serves as the Institute's executive director. He has extensive experience in the conceptualisation, design, overall coordination and implementation of projects funded by a variety of donors in Namibia, in areas such as civic education, integrity promotion, anti-corruption, organisational management skills and elections. He has managed voter education programmes for every election since Namibia's independence and has vast experience in the coordination of civil society election observation programmes. He is currently managing an electoral law reform programme in partnership with the Law Reform and Development Commission in Namibia. Keulder holds a Masters Degree in Business Leadership from the University of South Africa Business School and a Masters Degree in Communications.

Monica Koep currently practises as a democracy and governance consultant, having previously worked as a senior advisor to the Director General of the National Planning Commission in the President's Office; senior technical advisor for democracy and governance for the United States Agency for International Development (USAID) in Namibia; lead researcher for Namibia under the African Legislatures Project (ALP); and as a consultant for USAID Southern Africa. Koep has been a board member of the Institute for Public Policy Research (IPPR) since 2000, and its chairperson since 2007. She currently serves as a public member of the Media Complaints Committee, and has been on the board of the Namibia Chapter of the Media Institute of Southern Africa (MISA) Trust Fund since 1999. She had previously been a board member of the Namibian Broadcasting Corporation (NBC) from 1990 to 1994, and an elected member of the Media Council in the early 1990s. From 1988 until 1994, Koep was an executive committee member of Namibia Peace Plan 435 (NPP 435), which campaigned for Namibian independence under the terms of UNSCR 435. She holds Bachelor's and Honours degrees from the University of Cape Town, and an MPhil in Policy Studies from Stellenbosch University.

William Lindeke is a former Professor of Political Studies at the University of Namibia in Windhoek and Professor (retired) University of Massachusetts Lowell. He is a senior research associate at the IPPR in Windhoek, Namibia, and served as co-national investigator for the fourth (and upcoming fifth) round of the Afrobarometer opinion survey in Namibia. Lindeke has published widely on Namibian and southern African politics, among other issues. His PhD is from Claremont Graduate School in California, while his BA and MA degrees are from San Diego State University.

Ricardo Mukonda holds a BA in Social Work from the University of Namibia, and an LLB from UNISA. He is currently studying for an LLM in International Human Rights Law and HIV/Aids in Africa at the University of Pretoria. Mukonda has been a legal practitioner at the Legal Assistance Centre and was previously employed by the United Nations Children's Fund (UNICEF) in Mozambique, Tanzania and Angola where he served as a child protection specialist.

Bryan M. Sims is an analyst with the States in Transition Observatory (SITO) unit at Idasa. He previously worked for the National Endowment for Democracy (NED) in Washington, DC. Sims is a founding member of the South Africa-Washington International Program (SAWIP), and has served on its board of directors since 2006. He holds an MA, with honours, in International Conflict Analysis from the University of Kent in the United Kingdom, and a BA in both International Relations and Political Science from Northeastern University in Boston, Massachusetts. Currently, he is pursuing a PhD at Stellenbosch University in South Africa.

Phil ya Nangoloh is a Namibian human rights defender and activist, with more than 26 years of experience in the field of human rights monitoring and advocacy. As a human rights activist, Ya Nangoloh has received formal training in international human rights, customary and humanitarian law, and has received numerous certificates from, inter alia, the University of Strasbourg, France, and the University of Prince Edward Island and the University of Montreal, both in Canada. A researcher and political commentator since 1982, Ya Nangoloh has authored numerous newspaper and magazine articles, as well as reports on human rights, history, law and politics. He is the founder and executive director of NamRights, formerly known as the National Society for Human Rights (NSHR), which is a human rights monitoring and advocacy organisation in Namibia.

FOR FURTHER READING

African Media Barometer. 2011. *Namibia 2011*. Windhoek: Friedrich-Ebert-Stiftung.

Bertelsmann Stiftung. 2009. *BTI 2010 – Namibia Country Report*. Gütersloh: Bertelsmann Stiftung. Available at: http://bit.ly/zwrP4F

Bösl, A, Horn, N and du Pisani, A. 2010. *Constitutional Democracy in Namibia: a critical analysis after two decades*. Windhoek: Konrad Adenauer Foundation. Available at: http://bit.ly/xIBaz4

Du Pisani, A. 2009. The Impact of Democracy in Namibia: assessing political, social and economic developments since the dawn of democracy. Johannesburg: Center for Policy Studies. Available at: http://bit.ly/yYR66m

Du Pisani, A. 2010. The Political Arena in Namibia: the Regional Council and Local Authority Elections 2010.

Du Pisani, A. and Lindeke W. 2009. Stuck in the Sand: Political Party Opposition in Namibia.

Hopwood, G. 2007. *Guide to Namibian Politics*. Windhoek: Namibia Institute for Democracy.

Human Rights Watch. 2011. *World Report 2011*. New York: Human Rights Watch. Available at: http://bit.ly/fzMaFS

International Budget Partnership. 2010. *The Open Budget Survey 2010*. Washington, D.C.: International Budget Partnership. Available at: http://bit.ly/Aey6sf

International Food Policy Research Institute. 2011. *Global Hunger Index*. Washington, D.C.: International Food Policy Research Institute. Available at: http://bit.ly/ogWlEo

Keulder, C (ed.). 2010. State, Society and Democracy: a reader in Namibian politics. Windhoek: Konrad Adenauer Stiftung. Available at: http://bit.ly/wus4xV

Mo Ibrahim Foundation. 2011. *2011 Ibrahim Index of African Governance: summary*. Swindon: Mo Ibrahim Foundation. Available at: http://bit.ly/p7ofXo

National Planning Commission. 2008. 2nd Millennium Development Goals Report: Namibia 2008. Windhoek: Government of Namibia. Available at: http://bit.ly/yy7HT2

Sherbourne, R. 2010. *Guide to the Namibian Economy 2010*. Windhoek: Institute for Public Policy Research.

Swedish Trade Council. 2009. *Namibia 2020*. Available at: http://bit.ly/yPJjpZ

Transparency International Zimbabwe. 2010. *NURU Promoting Transparency and Accountability in Political Finance in the SADC Region*. Harare: Transparency International Zimbabwe.

Wallace, M. 2011. *A History of Namibia: from the beginning to 1990*. Auckland Park: Jacana Media (Pty) Ltd.

World Bank. 2010. *World Development Indicators 2010*. Washington, D.C.: World Bank. Available at: http://bit.ly/blY9gu

World Economic Forum. 2011. *The Global Competitiveness Report 2011-2012*. Geneva: World Economic Forum. Available at: http://bit.ly/mU68zg

USEFUL NAMIBIA-RELATED WEBSITES

Afrobarometer: www.afrobarometer.org

Corruption Watch Namibia: www.corruption–watch–namibia.com

Election Watch: www.electionwatch.org.na

Electoral Institute for the Sustainability of Democracy in Africa: www.eisa.org.za

Forum for the Future: www.forfuture.org.na

Friedrich Ebert Stiftung: http://fesnam.org

Idasa: An African Democracy Institute: www.idasa.org

Institute for Public Policy Research: www.ippr.org.na

Konrad–Adenauer–Stiftung: www.kas.de/namibia/en/

Legal Assistance Centre: www.lac.org.na

Legal Assistance Centre – Namibian Legislation Index: www.lac.org.na/laws/lawsindex.html

NamRights: www.nshr.org.za

The Namibia Institute for Democracy: www.nid.org.na

The National Planning Commission: www.npc.gov.na

www.ingramcontent.com/pod-product-compliance
Lightning Source LLC
Chambersburg PA
CBHW081740270326
41932CB00020B/3340